Climate Anxiety and Spiritual Resilience

Climate Anxiety and Spiritual Resilience

A Guide to Kinship, Justice, and Hope

Suzanne Crawford O'Brien

BLOOMSBURY ACADEMIC
NEW YORK • LONDON • OXFORD • NEW DELHI • SYDNEY

BLOOMSBURY ACADEMIC
Bloomsbury Publishing Inc, 1359 Broadway, New York, NY 10018, USA
Bloomsbury Publishing Plc, 50 Bedford Square, London, WC1B 3DP, UK
Bloomsbury Publishing Ireland, 29 Earlsfort Terrace, Dublin 2, D02 AY28, Ireland

BLOOMSBURY, BLOOMSBURY ACADEMIC and the Diana logo are trademarks of Bloomsbury Publishing Plc

First published in the United States of America 2026

Cover design by Jen Huppert
Cover image: Kelp Forest by Preston Singletary, 2025

A catalog record for this book is available from the Library of Congress.

ISBN: HB: 979-8-216-27883-2
ePDF: 979-8-216-27881-8
eBook: 979-8-216-27882-5

Typeset by Integra Software Services Pvt. Ltd.
Printed and bound in the United States of America

For product safety related questions contact productsafety@bloomsbury.com.

Online resources to accompany this book are available at https://bloomsbury.pub/climate-spirit. If you experience any problems, please contact Bloomsbury at: onlineresources@bloomsbury.com

Contents

Preface

November 6, 2024

I've got to get to class.

But I am heartsick. Disappointed. Scared. Furious.

It's the day after the presidential election, and I am at a loss. How can I possibly carry on with business as usual? The answer is simple: I can't. That lecture on comparative contemplative practices will just have to wait. Breathing deep, I draw strength from the towering Doug Firs outside my office window. I think of my students, and my heart hurts. Ours is a very diverse university campus, a place that welcomes immigrants and the children of immigrants, an intentionally safe place for everyone, however they identify. And this semester I'm teaching a class on climate anxiety and spiritual resilience, to a group of students already distraught—even before the outcome of this election.

Later, perched on the edge of a desk at the front of the room, I will blink back mutinous tears. "We don't all have the same political views," I begin, then swallow hard.

> Some of us are devastated this morning. And some of us may be happy. If that's you, that's okay. But I ask that you hang in there with us today. Because I also know this to be true: *I know you care about*

> *each other.* I know you don't want your fellow students to be afraid, or in pain. And many of your friends are terrified this morning. Many of them are hurting and frustrated and disappointed. So we need to take some time to care for each other.

We spend the hour talking. Some students share their fears, others ask questions. I'm pleased to see real curiosity when they disagree. They are *models* of respectful listening, and I am so damn proud of them. But I am struggling—there's just so much fear and sorrow and anger swirling in the air, and I'm not sure how to hold it all.

Then, one student leans forward, actually picking up his class reader, holding it aloft like a talisman. "You guys! It's just hitting me! This is exactly what this class has been about! How to handle times like this! *This is exactly what we've been training for!*"

My jaw actually drops. In the midst of my own barely contained overwhelm I'd managed to forget. But he was right. This is what our class is for—to understand how human beings build spiritual resilience—*collective, transformative* resilience—even when the world is coming apart.

1978

In one of my earliest memories, I'm trying to get my balance.

Water, splashes, sparkling, below my feet. Arms outstretched, I'm a gymnast on a beam, the gentle sway of the fallen log nodding in time to my steps. Reaching the center, I lower myself down, eventually finding a perch over a perfect alpine stream. Secure that it will hold my four-year-old weight, I settle in, rough bark against skinny legs, my finger following the whorls of insect trails etched into its surface: secret traceries of an arcane language. I kick my feet, loose and easy in the morning air.

The sun is slanting steeply through the trees, hitting the creek so it glints and sparkles, dazzling my eyes. I don't know what time it is, and, deliciously, it doesn't matter. Clocks are irrelevant in the high country. The streambanks are a tumble of washed-clean stones, tall grasses, alpine flowers, but I am mesmerized by the water: flaming crystal. It's chilly and my bare skin greedy for its refracted heat.

Just up the trail is our campsite, where my parents and sister are making breakfast. Mom says I can help best by staying out of the way. Later today we'll gather our gear and hike up the mountain, deeper into the wilderness. There's no great plan—just be in the woods, eat when we're hungry, wander on a whim, or toy with the danger of balancing on a log in midstream.

It is Sunday morning so I am doubly glad to be here, instead of fidgeting with boredom on a wooden pew. I've managed to sneak off with some dry sugar cereal, a rare treat and one my all-natural mama only allows on camping trips. I savor every crunch: ambrosia sugar crystals melting on my tongue. Inspired, I drop a piece, then another and another, one for each year of my life, caught up in the stream, carried away. They are my offering to the spirit of the creek, and I am warmed by my own beneficence, imagining grateful fish and tadpoles, delighted to share in this highly refined, sugary goodness.

I don't remember which of our many camping trips this is, just the creek, the water, the fallen tree. Cascade babbling, sun like a blessing. The smell of growing things and crisp high mountain air. The feeling of utter safety, even though I am very small, and even though we are in the wild.

When I return to camp, mom and dad will pull out the Bible, and my sister and I will tuck in beside them. They'll read a Jesus story to us.

It might be the loaves and fishes. Or the good Samaritan. Or the woman at the well. Or how Jesus overturned the money tables, chasing those greedy people out of the temple. This counts as church,

Back country Bible study with (left to right) me, my mother Jeanne, and my sister Michelle.

because we are together, because we have these stories. I understand that this is what it means to be a Jesus person. It means hemlock trees and alpine meadows. It means multiplying loaves and fishes, because everyone knows it's easier for a camel to pass through the eye of a needle than for a rich man to enter heaven. It means standing up for the powerless, loving the unloved, caring for a neighbor—and that your neighbor might just be a marmot, or a mountain stream.

1990

Jesus camp!

At 16, I've opted out of my parents' sedate congregation for something more exciting. A church of my own! There is a band! The crowd is young and sexy! Each week the pastor announces another couples' engagement, who stand while the congregation applauds. ("A religious meat-market," my older and wiser sister once called it.)

I'm drawn to this place because it's an interracial congregation, and I long for a community where faith and racial justice come together. I've been joining protests against apartheid in South Africa and become increasingly irate about the casual racism my school friends experience on a daily basis. The Jesus I know is all about justice, and I hope to find that here. But I've started to wonder if I got it wrong. Not long before, a visiting pastor had delivered a sermon about racism as America's original sin. I nodded along, but soon became aware of the discomfort of those around me. "She should talk about getting people saved, not politics," the guy next to me muttered, shifting in his seat. "I'm pretty sure women shouldn't be preaching anyway."

My misgivings are growing, but I don't want to leave. The joyful music and spirit-filled spaces are a balm for my teenage depression and anxiety, a safe place when I really need one. I don't know what others think about when they sing beside me (finding a spouse? getting married?) but when I close my eyes I think about the lilies in the field, about Desmond Tutu and the brave activists in Soweto, about mountain glaciers, and the stories my parents read to me, when fallen logs were our pews.

So it made sense when I volunteered for Jesus Camp—surely we would find that God of justice in the woods. And here I am. On this lakeshore, bagging up recycling. Sticky tin cans and dusty plastic bottles fill my black trash bag. Then, one of the youth-group leaders stops me. He is annoyed. And I am confused.

"*What* are you doing?"

I gesture at my haul. "There's no recycling here, so I'm gonna drive it back to town."

"Don't you know it's all going to burn?" His tone is both aggravated and triumphant. "This whole world is going to burn, and God is going to make a new one, just for us. Don't waste your time on that stuff."

I am stunned into silence. My parents have been recycling since the 70s. Sorting and driving to the recycling center is as much an expression of their faith as reading their Bible, or planting a garden, or donating to the foodbank. Driving back to town, a hundred indignant responses churn through my mind: theological, scriptural, philosophical. I aim my 1980 powder blue Datsun (45 mpg) toward the recycling center. For me, this is another kind of collection plate. And to my mind, it's a better one. How should I honor the Creator, if not by caring for creation?

1994

I swear, the air is just *different* on Iona.

It's taken multiple research grants, months of planning, three trains, two ferries, and a nausea-inducing bus ride, but I've finally arrived on this wind-swept island on the west coast of Scotland. Iona was the site of St. Columba's sixth-century monastic community, one of the oldest continuously occupied places of worship in the British Isles, and a sacred center of Celtic Christianity.

It's the end of my junior year abroad, and I've been living with a wonderful host family in Watford, England. I make it to Iona just in time for the summer solstice. One in the morning, the sky is full of light, and I am ebullient. Proud of myself for overcoming my fears and becoming an independent traveler, for getting to this remote spot on my own.

This is a place where ecumenical prayers for peace and justice precede vegetarian meals, and while I am here, I pray and hike and giggle alongside Episcopalians, Presbyterians, Quakers, Hindus, and Neo-pagans. It is so unlike my church back home, that consigned everyone else—even other Christians—to the fires of hell.

I fall in love with Iona.

It's here I realize that belief systems without ambiguity or complexity cannot bend. Instead, they shatter on impact. Iona is a different kind of place, one where Spirit radiates from every stone, hill, and bright beach—that transcends any exclusive theology. On St. John's Eve, I will run up a hillside, buoyed by warm summer air, by midnight sun and a full moon, and pagan bonfires celebrating Christian saints.

Celtic knotwork adorns the standing stone crosses, zoomorphs fill the abbey, a sheila na gig presides over the ruined nunnery, medieval image of female fertility surviving in the stones. It's easy to imagine the *Book of Kells* being composed here. It's a place of color and magic where the same Spirit moves through human beings, animals, forces of nature. I never thought my heart would find another home outside of the Pacific Northwest. But I have ancestors in these western isles and the green hills speak to my soul.

2009

My newborn son Declan spends his first night clutching my pinky with a fist so tight I don't dare pry it loose. I lay awake until dawn, enraptured with this miracle, refusing to miss a moment of our first night together. Ours was a perilous delivery—a mad dash to the operating room, emergency surgery that saved us both. And now here we are, breathing this precious air. My husband Michael is sound asleep on the nearby hospital couch. I let him be. I am thinking about ancestors, about the countless women standing behind us, each of whom passed through this fire—suffering, grieving, surviving—for as long as there have been mothers and babies. I feel them around me, sharing my amazement. I've been awake for 48 hours. I am vibrating with wonder.

2013

I've stumbled into fairyland. The darkened trail is illuminated, lined by an other-worldly glow of votive candles. I follow them, scarcely daring to breathe. It is the eve of St. Declan's day, and we have returned once again to Ardmore in County Waterford, Ireland. It's a mid-way point between one half of my husband's family in County Cork and the other in County Waterford, and one of our sacred centers. We named our son after this place, the site of St. Declan's first hermitage and his holy well.

It was Michael who had insisted I leave the tranquility of our hotel room, sending me out into the gathering dusk. My agnostic Irish-Catholic spouse had *almost* been at a loss for words. "It's *holy*," he'd whispered, something I'm not sure I'd ever heard him say before. "You have to go."

The trail takes me to the ruins. Light clings to the western sky, but it's dark under these trees, and I'm both grateful for and delighted by candles marking the way. The well's caretakers have put them everywhere: tealights line the path, cover the stones. Tomorrow, pilgrims will come to do their rounds and pray their rosary, but tonight it lies in flickering solitude.

A chough hops alongside me, all black wings and red beak, and chattery conversation. It flies on ahead, and I follow, charmed by how it waits, lets me catch up, and then leads me farther along, drawing me down the cliff walk. I accept without question that it's talking to me—no fault of his that I don't speak the language. Clouds part, stars slipping through, and I delight in moon glow, bird song, sea, and stone.

2022

It's two in the morning, and I am doubled over in bed, holding my belly, pain like a punch to my gut. This isn't the first time I've felt the visceral impact of late-night anxiety, but I never get used to it.

Careful not to wake Michael—one of us should get some sleep tonight, after all—I feel my way to the living room, rudely rousing my cat from his feline slumbers. (Mr. Mumford is very forgiving in the late-night hours.) I stifle a cough. Even inside, and despite our constantly running box-fan air purifiers, the acrid smell of smoke is strong. Wildfires are bad this year, shrouding Seattle in an apocalyptic murk. My gut twists: the perfect Pacific Northwest summers of my childhood are gone for good, replaced by a new waiting game.

"When will it clear?"

"Will we be able to go outside tomorrow?"

We used to pray for sun. Now we pray for rain.

Curling up on the couch, I surrender to tears. These are the doubled-over, shoulders heaving, messy, open-mouthed, beyond caring, shuddering, snot-producing kind of tears. The only-when-I'm-alone kind of tears. Mumford gives me a slow blink: cat language for "relax, human."

As my sobs subside, he settles beside me, low purr like Mother Earth's comforting rumble. My sensible self knows a sleepless night of emotional overwhelm will not help anything. Quite the opposite. If I don't get to sleep, tomorrow will be a wash. Forget thinking clearly or making good choices.

But this smoky apocalypse is impossible to ignore: our climate is already changing. We've started to call summers "smoke season." Salmon runs are declining. Orca are starving in the Sound. I've spent the day researching Indigenous communities in the Arctic, who have been trying to alert us to the dangers of receding sea ice for decades.

Our spaniel joins Mumford and I on the couch, and together they hedge me in, as they always do when I'm sick or sad. In the predawn quiet, I accept this gift with gratitude. My breathing deepens, the knot in my belly easing. And in that darkness, I know only one thing: this problem is so much bigger than me. If I'm going to make it—if *we're* going to make it, we're going to need help. There's no way we humans can do this on our own.

What we need is a good ceremony

"The only cure
I know
Is a good ceremony,
That's what she said."
—*Ceremony*, by Leslie Marmon Silko[1]

Many of us have That Book in our lives. The one we can read over and over—because it never gets old, never ceases to make us pause, and go back to that one sentence, one more time. The book that meets us at every age of our lives. For me, that book is *Ceremony* by Laguna Pueblo author Leslie Marmon Silko. The novel tells the story of Tayo, a young man broken by loss and the violence of war, trying to find a way back to himself and his homelands. The novel is itself a kind of ceremony, telling the story of Tayo's own healing journey, his step-by-step movement toward remembering. But it also tells a far more epic story about the healing of the Earth herself. Through ritual and ceremony, through love, and trust, and a lot of painful struggle, this young man is restored to relationship with his sacred mountain, and comes to see that his own struggle is part of the whole, that his own soul-sickness is inseparable from his people's grieving bewilderment, and a world-destroying witchcraft unleashed in the mining of uranium, and the splitting of an atom. Silko does not shrink away from the pain and horror of it all. But she also shows the way forward—one grounded in personal transformation.

We are living in a moment when so much is coming undone. It is a time of terror. But it is also a time of possibility. Because this generation has a chance to write a new story, a new way of being in the world, one that is just and sustainable. And that is no small thing. "I will tell you something about stories," Silko reminds us, "they aren't just entertainment. Don't be fooled. They are all we have, you see, all we have to fight off illness and death." And in Silko's novel, it is through ceremony that her characters embody the stories that (re) make the world.

I'm not a particularly optimistic person. I'm not at all certain that things are going to be okay. No matter what we do, there will be loss and sorrow in the years to come. And that breaks my heart every day. But I am nonetheless determined to be hopeful. Before you dismiss me, please understand my definition of hope. For me, hope is not a state of being. It's not an object we are *given*. We don't *have* hope, and we can't *lose* it. Instead, it's an orientation to the world, one that relies on the knowledge that we are not alone—that we are part of a family of creation, all of whom are doing their part, playing their role in this wider ceremony of world renewal. We choose hope, when we do what needs to be done—because giving up is simply not an option. Hope is taking the next step forward, even when there's no guarantee we'll succeed. I don't mean to say that hope comes through sheer force of will, through gritting-teeth and clenching-jaw. Rather, it's a way of being that needs daily tending. Hope is the story we enact, of the way we want the world to be. Hope is a ceremony.

The turning point in Tayo's story is his chantway, performed by Navajo medicine man Betonie. Like many chantways, it tells a story of a lost young man who must find his way home. Chantways often include sandpainting, graphic representations of the story behind the ceremony, and here Betonie draws paw prints in black sand beside colored hoops, each representing the four sacred mountains that define the Navajo homeland. Step by step, Tayo performs the chantway's story, his feet following those pawprints, learning the trail back home. The chantway is just the beginning: Tayo has more work to do. He must recover what has been stolen and repair what has been broken. But that ceremonial story becomes his trail guide, constellations to navigate through the days ahead.

The chapters that follow are another kind of guide, inspired by the work I do with my students, written during a time when many of us are struggling to find the emotional and spiritual resilience we need to persevere and persist. Many are overwhelmed by sorrow. Many feel caught in fierce political headwinds, buffeted about by unrelenting bad news. I certainly share those struggles. I started researching this book because I needed to find a way to manage my own sometimes debilitating climate anxiety and grief. I struggled (and sometimes still do) with sleepless nights and emotional overwhelm. A bad news report can send me to a Very Dark Place.

So I read everything I could find on the psychology of climate anxiety. And I found good, pragmatic advice. But I couldn't help but notice that these authors returned, again and again, to a similar conclusion: that climate change is, ultimately, a *spiritual* problem, and that if we really want to solve it, we need to turn to the wisdom found in religious and Indigenous traditions. As a professor who has spent three decades teaching and learning about comparative religions, Indigenous traditions, ecology, and mental health, I had to agree. This book is my contribution to that broader conversation, a trail guide for those of us who know that restoring the world is sacred work, who know that the only way forward is through, and that we must nurture our very best selves if we're going to get there.

In her beautiful book *Crisis Contemplation,* the Rev. Dr. Barbara A. Holmes offers this insight, gleaned from her own experience in the Black church and her scholarship on contemplative practice. "The truth of the matter is that if I am going to survive, I had better have a spiritual regimen that strengthens my immune system, fortifies my resolve, beckons the ancestors, and connects me to the creative spirit of all life—and if I don't do that now, later will be too late." What that spiritual regimen might be will look different for each one of us. But it's my hope that this book will provide us with resources to build the resilience we need, to metabolize our grief and anxiety into purposeful action, before it really is too late.

This book is for those of you who are feeling stuck, for those who are struggling with burnout, emotional overwhelm, or a sense of powerlessness in the face of climate change and systemic injustice. It is for anyone who cares about clean air, safe water, and healthy soil. For anyone who has lain awake at night worrying what life will look like for future generations, or sorrowing over our other-than-human relatives on the brink of extinction. It's for those of you who care about justice. And it's for those of you who are willing to respectfully listen to and learn from sacred traditions that are not your own—without resorting to cultural appropriation.

Because here's the other truth of the matter: so many things we thought we could rely on—the changing of seasons, the predictability of nature's cycles—are no longer reliable. This is a transformative moment in human history, and the decisions we make now will have profound consequences for future generations. That is frightening. But it should also be inspiring. After all, as Native American Studies professor Lawrence Gross (White Earth Band of Ojibwe) has said, "It is not very often in human history that a people have a chance to build a new world."[2]

Acknowledgments

The idea for this book was born during a late-night, fire-side conversation, in an off-the-grid cabin, on the edge of the Olympic National Park, with Tanya Barnett. It took shape on long walks, longer drives, and fog-shrouded ferry rides around Vancouver Island with Linh Vu. And it found its voice in carpool conversations with Heather Mathews. I am so thankful for these dear and beautiful friends. Before this was a book, it was a class, and so it's with deep affection that I thank my students at Pacific Lutheran University, who joined me in wrestling with these ideas, and who continue to give me reasons to be optimistic about the future of our species. That I have been able to do this work at all is a gift bestowed by my most precious of teachers: my parents, my sister, and my grandparents. What an incredible privilege to be born into so much love, and deep, abiding care. With gratitude to those educators who showed me new ways of thinking, challenging and encouraging me at pivotal moments in my life: Allan Siegel, Ellen Eisenberg, Lane McGaughey, Dave McCreery, Volney Gay, Howard Harrod, Bill Powell, Wade Clark Roof, Laury Oaks, and my doctoral mentor and dear friend, Inés Talamantez. And to four amazing teachers and healers who have helped me learn how to take care of myself so I can better take care of others: Michele Mecum, Elana Kupor, Amy Matthias, and Swansea Mo. Thanks to friends and colleagues who read drafts of this book, and offered helpful correction, critique, and questions: Evan Berry, Erik Hammerstrom, Elizabeth Hawkins, Michelle Jacob, and Kevin O'Brien. To my agent Trinity McFadden of The Bindery, and my editor at Bloomsbury, Richard Brown—thank you for sharing the vision behind this project, and helping to make it a reality. And finally, this book is for Michael O'Brien and Declan Crawford O'Brien—my home, my heart, and the ones who keep me going.

1

Climate resilience is spiritual resilience

We are already experiencing the consequences of climate change. We've all heard about or seen first-hand the impacts of heatwaves, droughts, wildfires, flooding, hurricanes, and extreme storms. Arctic communities have been alerting us to changing sea ice and permafrost for decades. Louisiana loses a square acre of land every 100 minutes. As I write this, the island nation of Tuvalu is evacuating all of its residents due to rising sea levels. In 2024, the world experienced three of its top-twenty costliest disasters in recorded history.

The National Oceanic and Atmospheric Administration (NOAA) reported in January of 2025 that, since 1980, the United States alone has experienced 403 major weather events that exceeded $1 billion in damages, the total of which exceeds $2.915 trillion. According to the United Nations High Commissioner for Refugees's (UNHCR's) Global Refugee Forum, an average of 21.5 million people have been forcibly displaced each year by weather-related events or hazards since 2008, and the number is growing. Climate change has arrived, with terrifying consequences.

Given this, it should not be surprising that the vast majority of us are concerned. National and global studies show that we agree climate change is caused by human activity, and we want those in power to do more about it. In a recent survey, researchers from the University of Bonn, Germany, found that 89 percent of people worldwide want their governments to do more to address climate change.[1] Similarly, Yale University's 2024 survey of 59,000 people around the world found that 86 percent believe that climate change poses an *existential threat* to humanity. The United States (along with the UK, Russia, and Australia) tends to have the most climate-skeptics. But even here, more than two-thirds of Americans worry "a great deal" or "considerably" about the impacts of climate change, and a growing majority feel that human health is already being harmed "a great deal" by climate-related impacts. Nearly 80 percent of Americans support research and investment in renewable energy. Seventy-five percent of Americans support regulating CO_2 as a pollutant, providing tax incentives for renewable energy and electric vehicles, and teaching about global warming in public schools, while 66 percent agree that developing renewable energy should be a government priority. Only 11 percent of Americans actually dismiss the notion of climate change. It is hard to imagine an issue on which there appears to be more collective consensus.[2]

That is why inaction on climate is so hard to understand. If all this is true, why have we not done more? How is it that we seem to be carrying on with business as usual? What's holding us back? In a word, why are we *stuck*?

I believe the answer has a lot to do with the sheer emotional overwhelm that the threat of climate change evokes. We are, after all, facing potential ecosystem collapse—the end of life as we know it—something not easy to wrap one's head around, let alone one's heart. For me, that difficulty is borne out by the finding that while 80 percent of us are worried about climate change, only 30 percent of us actually *talk* about it. And our inability to face reality has real consequences, preventing us from making an honest assessment of our situation and leaving us in a state of paralysis.

Climate change is a (mental) health catastrophe

There's no question that climate change threatens our physical health: extreme weather events like heatwaves, droughts, wildfires, floods, hurricanes, coastal storms, and severe thunderstorms pose an immediate risk of injury or death. Then there's the long-term repercussions of such events, including economic disruption and displacement, which increase poor health outcomes and elevate morbidity. Climate change is a risk multiplier, amplifying existing health threats like poverty, food and water insecurity, warfare, or diseases like malaria, cholera, and other vector-borne ailments. It makes the vulnerable far *more* vulnerable.

But climate change also impacts our mental health. Climate-fueled natural disasters trigger post-traumatic stress disorder (PTSD). They worsen physical insecurity, and food and water scarcity—all of which further undermine mental health.[3] Studies find that those at particular risk include farmers, poor and low-income communities, migrants, Indigenous and Hispanic communities, pregnant women, sexual minorities, the elderly, and the disabled. And it's getting worse. In 1990, the World Health Organization ranked depression as the fourth leading cause of disability. By 2018, it was the first.[4] In an era with more technology, lower rates of hunger, and better overall access to healthcare than ever before, it appears we are also more anxious and depressed than ever before. Many public health experts are increasingly convinced that climate change is at least partly to blame.

We also know that extreme temperatures worsen existing mental health problems, while being contraindicated for some psychiatric medications. Reports of aggression, crime, self-harm, and suicide spike during heatwaves, while periods of extreme cold lead to increased rates of depression and chronic isolation. Those who've experienced extreme weather events like floods or hurricanes are more likely to suffer from poor sleep, poor cognitive function, and increased rates of high-risk behaviors, including violence and substance abuse. Other studies point to impacts on the *social* health of disrupted and displaced communities. Forced migration fractures social cohesion, and with the loss of mutual support, comes higher unemployment, and greater resource insecurity. Among traditional societies, the cultural consequences of forced migration are particularly devastating, with loss of community identity, cultural integrity, sense of historical continuity, and belonging to place.

And, across every demographic, children are particularly vulnerable. Wildfires and wildfire smoke don't just impact respiratory health, they're also tied to higher rates of PTSD, depression, anxiety, and substance abuse—particularly among youth, who show patterns of lowered self-esteem and quality of life scores following wildfires. Extreme weather, higher temperatures, food scarcity, and financial insecurity threaten early childhood brain development, and disrupt access to education. Children who have gone through climate-related disasters report higher rates of sleep disruption, phobias, attachment disorders, and are more likely to experience mental illness as adults.

There's a good reason for this. Experiencing disasters first-hand triggers our fight, flight, or freeze response. In this state, our amygdala takes over, short-circuiting our prefrontal cortex, and making it near-impossible to think clearly, make good decisions, find creative solutions, or engage our empathy. When our system is flooded with stress hormones, we may feel paralyzed. That paralysis can take many forms: shutting down, going blank, becoming unreactive, or feeling overwhelmed and stuck. But a growing number of studies demonstrate that the slower-moving effects of climate change have real mental health impacts as well. Even if we've not personally experienced a major disaster, recent studies are shedding light on the impacts the *anticipatory anxiety* of climate change can have. These include increased rates of stress-related disorders like depression, anxiety, and the "nocebo effect," where our expectations of bad outcomes become self-fulfilling prophecies. In one global study, 45 percent of adolescents and young adults reported that concerns about climate change were impacting their well-being, with growing numbers reporting depression, anxiety, substance abuse, and suicidal ideation.

In 2003, Environmental philosopher Glenn Albrecht coined the term *solastalgia* to describe the grief and anticipatory loss caused by ecological collapse, and in 2006 Higginbotham et al. developed the Environmental Distress Scale (EDS), in order to better understand the experience of solastalgia among Australians following a series of devastating wildfires.[5] Neville Ellis and Ashlee Cunsolo opted for the term *ecological grief* to describe, "the grief felt in relation to experienced or anticipated ecological losses, including the loss of species, ecosystems, and meaningful landscapes due to acute or chronic environmental change."[6] For its part, the American Psychological Association adopted the term *climate anxiety*, referring to the "chronic fear, fatalism, anger, and exhaustion" sparked by climate change. And, in the last decade, the new subfield of ecopsychology has emerged to address the trauma of climate-related disasters and the cumulative stress experienced by anticipatory loss or industry burnout for those working in conservation and sustainability. Rather than pathologizing our emotional responses to climate catastrophe, ecopsychology aims to support personal agency and reconnection with the natural world. As Theodore Roszak, one of the founders of the field, explains, the discipline is not particularly radical. It is simply, "to define 'sanity' as if the whole world mattered."[7]

Why *religion*, though?

A central assumption I make in this book is that climate change is a spiritual problem, and that it demands a spiritual response. Thankfully, I'm not the first to make this claim. In 2023, ecologist and essayist Terry Tempest Williams put it perfectly: "Do we have the courage to understand that this is not just an ecological crisis or a political crisis or even an economic crisis? Because it is all of those things, but at its heart, it is a spiritual crisis."[8] James Gustave Speth, co-founder of the Natural Resources Defense Council, is widely reported to have said:

> I used to think the top environmental problems were biodiversity loss, ecosystem collapse and climate change. I thought with 30 years of good science we could address those problems. But I was wrong. The top environmental problems are selfishness, greed and apathy .... And to deal with these we need a spiritual and cultural transformation—and scientists don't know how to do that.

The late Pope Francis also argued for a spiritually inclusive approach to our environmental crisis, in which "no branch of the sciences and no form of wisdom can be left out."[9] The point is, if we're to solve the heart of the problem (and not just treat the symptoms) we need to fundamentally change our *ontology*—that is, how we understand our relationship to the natural world and each other. And that work goes deeper than intellect. That's the work of spirituality.

When I tell people I teach about religion and environmental justice, I often hear some variation of: "But didn't religion cause this mess to begin with?" Like most things having to do with the complexity of the human experience, the answer is both *yes* and *no*. And *maybe*. And also, *it depends*.

It's important to take care when making broad assumptions about religion or its meaning in people's lives. Traditions are highly localized, internally diverse, and they change over time. And while religious institutions—and Christianity in particular—have been tools of colonialism, extraction, and economic injustice, they also include voices that uplift the moral urgency of climate change and environmental justice. That work happens every day in local communities and global organizations such as the World Council of Churches. Every major religious denomination or organization has issued a formal statement on climate change calling for an immediate response.

But whether or not you're religious, understanding religion is essential if we're to respond effectively to the climate crisis. Why? Because the study of religion and ecology reminds us that while climate may be a global phenomenon, it is experienced and interpreted locally. As Environmental Humanities professor Evan Berry explains, "religion operates upstream from climate change," because religious worldviews shape how we understand our relationship to the land. Berry and his colleague David Haberman remind us that understanding religious diversity—particularly at the local level—is essential to tackling the climate crisis, because culture, nature, and politics shape our understanding of changing climates and our moral obligations to the natural world and to each other.[10] It matters if we understand the world to be governed by a benign protector, an angry God, an integrative Spirit, or an abstract but ultimate unity, because that understanding shapes the way we live in and on the world. Are we taught to welcome strangers, or protect ourselves from outsiders? To care for the weak, or claw our way to the top? Do we understand human history to be a story of progress, or moral decay? Is the Earth sacred, or simply a cache of resources to be utilized? While we often assume climate change solutions lie in the realm of science, politics, and international relations, the reality is that for most of the world—and particularly for those communities who will bear the brunt of climate change and whose voices are consistently left out of the debate—our relationship with the Earth is a profoundly sacred concern. These assumptions shape how and if we support extractive fossil-fuel economies or the transition to clean energy. They can inspire us to act, or placate us into docility.[11] Human beings will protect what we think is sacred—so it's important to understand what we hold dear. In short, religion matters.

Understanding religious and cultural diversity is particularly important for those of us coming from the industrialized West, where our (often unexamined) assumptions about the world have a great deal to do with our Christian heritage. Learning from other traditions can challenge those assumptions, and reveal other ways of living.

Of course, not all religious traditions are helpful. Some have made the climate crisis worse, by celebrating consumerism, refuting scientific conclusions, or coding wealth inequality as a sign of God's approval. Some (like that church camp leader of my youth) actually welcome catastrophe as a fulfillment of apocalyptic prophecy. In his seminal 1967 essay, "The Historical Roots of Our Ecological Crisis," historian Lynn White blames Christian doctrines of dualism and dominionism for the historical realities of colonialism and industrial exploitation—the systems that in turn laid the groundwork for our current climate crisis. Indigenous scholars likewise locate the origins of our ecological decline in Christian colonialism, with particular ire reserved for the Doctrine of Discovery, a late medieval papal doctrine that made of Christianity a colonial cudgel, and justified genocide, enslavement, and the ravaging of the natural world.

If you want to understand why political opponents of renewable energy refer to solar power as "un-American," or even "un-Christian," you've got to understand the history of religion. In his book *Anointed with Oil: How Christianity and Crude Made Modern America*, historian Darren Dochuk describes the rise of "petro-religious nationalism." He paints a picture of a new religious movement, one emerging from the unholy marriage of the oil industry, evangelical Christianity, and the Prosperity Gospel. Here, oil is viewed as a sacred resource and divine blessing, proof of America's call to global dominance. As the oil industry helped to fund the rise of the religious right, it promoted a Christian nationalist mythology grounded in the beliefs of manifest destiny, divine right to resource extraction, a resistance to multilateral institutions, and xenophobia.[12] Contemporary politicians who adhere to this view see the pivot toward renewable energy as a blasphemous rejection of God's blessings. In *Meeting the Enemy: The Fossil Fuel Industry and the Power of Christian Climate Resistance*, ethicist Kevin O'Brien builds on Dochuk's work to identify three false mythologies that sustain this petro-religious nationalism—human exceptionalism, radical individualism, and the myth of unlimited growth—and explores their complicated relationship with the history of Christian thought.

These false mythologies aren't just abstract ideas: they have material consequences, reflected in the statistics around climate concern. In the United States, Christians are less likely than any other religious group to be concerned about climate change. In a 2022 study by the Pew Foundation, only half of self-identified Christians reported being concerned about climate change, in contrast to 72 percent of Americans who identified with another religion (Judaism, Islam, Buddhism, Sikhism, or Indigenous traditions). But, of course, that number belies Christianity's internal diversity: 68 percent of Black Christians, 57 percent of Catholics, and 55 percent of mainline Protestants were very concerned about climate change. Among white evangelicals, 34 percent are concerned. (For some, this will seem like a small number. I'm actually encouraged to learn that more than a third of conservative, white, evangelicals are concerned about climate change! My nineteen-year-old environmentalist-evangelical self would have been delighted to find herself in such good company.) When we get more granular, we see another cause for hope: white evangelical Christians under thirty-nine are much more likely to be concerned about climate than their elders.[13]

My point is this: while religion has the power to make things worse, it can also call us to more ethical, sustainable ways of living, to care for the vulnerable, to a vision of the future that centers hope and renewal. And this is important. Because our survival depends not just on transforming our energy grid, but on transforming the stories we tell about who we are, and the kind of world we want to build. Our spiritual orientation—when guided by radical relationality, justice, and care for the vulnerable—can empower our sense of agency, affirming that what we do as individuals *matters*, even in the face of a complex global challenge that requires broad systemic change.

I am not aiming to whitewash the crimes of those who use religion to justify the oppression of fellow human beings or the exploitation of the natural world. But I do want to convince you that religion is worth paying attention to. "Religion" has civic, social, political, economic, psychological, and ecological consequences, and we ignore it at our peril. After nearly three decades, I continue to study and teach about religion because I am convinced it is where the very best, and the very worst of us show up. And it is worth knowing how that very best and very worst might save us from (or condemn us to) the mess we've made of this planet. I want to challenge those hegemonic worldviews that enable an extractive, exploitative economy, by uplifting alternative ways of being in the world. And when it comes to facing climate chaos, religious and Indigenous traditions have rich resources for processing grief, for living in and working through trauma, for centering ourselves and connecting with the sacred, and building resilient and compassionate communities. These prophetic voices call us to account, demand that we courageously confront injustice, and offer pathways for radically regenerative ways of living. These are tools we'll need if we want a livable future.

Spiritual resilience is radically relational

In a recent class at Yale's Center for Business and Environment, Peter Boyd defined spirituality as "having coherent beliefs about the higher purpose and meaning of the universe; knowing where one fits within the larger scheme." The Pew Research Center appears to have drawn from a similar definition for their 2023 study, which reported that 70 percent of Americans say spirituality is important in their lives. But here's how they defined it: believing "there are some things that science cannot possibly explain" (74 percent), "there is something spiritual beyond the natural world, even if we cannot see it" (81 percent), or in the existence of a spirit or soul (83 percent).[14] The common element? The reduction of spirituality to *individual belief*. Here, spirituality is merely personal philosophy. This is an understanding that makes sense in the context of the (mostly) Protestant, (largely) white (and very) individualist American religious landscape. But it doesn't reflect the ways spirituality plays out in the sacred traditions I study. (And I'd argue it really doesn't work so well for white, Western, Protestants, either!)

The definition of spirituality that guides this book is different. It's directly informed by Indigenous leaders, African American womanist theologians, Quaker philosophers, Hispanic folk traditions, and Zen Buddhist teachers. And it has very little to do with individual belief.

Theologian and professor of Africana studies Layli Maparyan explains that, "spirituality is not to be confused with religion. Religions exist to deliver people to a spiritual knowledge and its application ... For womanists, spirituality is an acknowledged *relationship* with the divine/transpersonal/cosmic/invisible realm, while religion is a culturally organized framework for experiencing that relationship."[15] Indigenous scholar Lyla June Johnson (Diné/Cheyenne) defines spirituality as *experiential engagement* with "the animating energy of creation." Parul Rishi describes "spiritual intelligence" as a higher *state of consciousness* that enables one to make meaning, cope with day-to-day challenges, and subsume personal interest for the greater good. In the Coast Salish traditions of Puget Sound where I live and work, "spirituality" is fundamentally about being engaged in *dynamic relationships* with one's ancestors, with future generations, with the spiritual entities or persons that inhabit the natural world. It is about attending to and being guided by the Spirit that unites these beings.

My use of the term spirituality thus has less to do with what one *thinks*, and much more to do with the actual lived relationships that enable us to transcend the individual, material, and strictly human. This understanding of spirituality is a fundamental challenge to individualism, inviting us to move beyond intellectualizing or personal mission statements. Instead, it reminds us that spirituality is first and foremost about restoring relationship with something (or someone) beyond our finite, individual selves. And that is another reason why attending to spirituality is essential for addressing climate change, because the origins of our climate crisis lie in broken relationships. Nuu-chah-nulth elder, hereditary chief, and professor Umeek (E. Richard Atleo) explains that Nuu-chah-nulth spirituality "sees the global crisis in relational terms, in terms of a creation filled with mutually interdependent life forms that require mutually acceptable protocols in order to maintain balance and harmony. From this point of view, the global crisis is one of relational disharmony."[16] I'm with Atleo on this one: if we want to solve the climate crisis, we've got to begin with a reexamination of the relationships that sustain us—and this is spiritual work.

If you're a concrete thinker, perhaps all this "spirituality" talk is a bit off-putting. But rest assured, this is borne out in scientific studies as well. Spiritual practices change our brain chemistry and structure, building the resilience and capacity for empathy we will desperately need when confronting the challenges to come. Researchers have found that meditation and other forms of contemplative practice build more resilient brains. While cognitive intelligence is associated with the left brain, and emotional intelligence with right, subjects who engaged in regular meditation or contemplative practices showed greater degrees of synchronization and communication across brain hemispheres. Contemplative practices appear to strengthen existing brain networks, build new networks, and reduce the neurotransmitters that generate fight or flight responses. Higher levels of engagement in spiritual practices have been associated with higher levels of creativity, intuition, empathy, compassion, and positive social interaction. Neurological imaging studies have also shown that regular meditation produces neurochemical changes that reduce the severity of anxiety and depression. Lisa Miller, professor of clinical psychology at Columbia University's Spirituality Mind Body Institute, found that individuals who engaged in spiritual practice had healthier neural pathways, increased activity in the parts of the brain associated with love and empathy, and decreased activity in parts of the brain that disassociate from others. In other words, spiritual experiences have the potential to heighten our care for others, and our ability to be in relationship with them.

In the natural sciences, the term *resilience* is used to refer to those systems or organisms that bounce back after experiencing stress. In psychology, it refers to the individual's ability to identify dangers and manage the stress responses they evoke well enough to respond effectively. In contrast, Indigenous philosopher Kyle Powys Whyte (Citizen Potawatomi) argues that resilience is not grounded in individual fortitude, but in *moral relationships*. Whyte's work emphasizes ecological and collective resilience as "a society's capacity to learn from and adapt to the dynamics of ecosystems in ways that avoid preventable harms, promote the flourishing of all human and nonhuman lives, and generate wisdom to sustain future generations." Whyte draws from Anishinaabe origin stories: tales of migration and prophecy. Such stories "tell us how the people adapted to new environments by developing moral relationships, including responsibility, spirituality, and justice, which are at the heart of how we understand resilience."[17]

Indigenous philosophical and spiritual systems center those moral relationships that link human beings to each other and to the more-than-human world, and these are living relationships that are intrinsically adaptive and responsive. But, as Whyte explains, colonialism used every tool in its arsenal to disrupt those moral relationships. Because of this, enacting them—particularly within a society grounded in colonial ideals of individualism, extractivism, and human exceptionalism, is an act of resistance. As Kaitlin Curtice (Citizen Potawatomi) explains in her book *Living Resistance: An Indigenous Vision of Seeking Wholeness Every Day*, because colonialism upended these systems, any effort to reclaim relational resilience is an act of resistance. Such efforts are "the way we use our everyday lives to exert energy against the dangerous status quo of our time," and can take numerous forms: creativity, mindful presence, embodiment, or caring for the vulnerable.[18]

Indigenous philosophers, climate scientists, ecologists, and ecopsychologists all appear to agree that the roots of our climate crisis are severed relationships: with living landscapes, with ancestors, with future generations, and with each other. Real, transformational resilience—the resilience we need if we are to build a just and sustainable world—requires reclaiming that radically relational way of being. This is deep work. It's spiritual work, and it's ceremonial work.

To understand what I mean when I talk about *ceremony*, let's consider what theologian and ritual studies scholar Tom Driver has to say. For Driver, ritual is powerful stuff. He even uses the word *magic*, arguing that if ritual and ceremony are done right, they can change the world. How? Because ritual and ceremony tell a story. More than this, they are opportunities for us to *enact* the story—to *become part of it* through physical participation. We give voice and form to the world as it *should* be. We give flesh to the vision, drawing it closer. Symbols—those words, images, and actions that represent our highest values—are the key ingredients in this alchemical formula. We don't simply think about those values, but bodily enact them. Ceremony brings them to life.[19]

For Driver, ritual and ceremony are particularly vital "to those in need, especially those who, having little social power, and being the victims of injustice, have a need for the social structure to be transformed." The magic of ritual, he argues, is that it serves to express and transform social relationships, not just changing what we think or feel about the world, but our actual relationships with humans and other-than-human beings. Of course, not all rituals are good—a ceremony can inspire conformity or obedience to unjust systems. But there is a reason that autocrats suppress ceremonies, and outlaw symbols. There's a reason that the United States and Canada outlawed Native American and First Nations ceremonies—imprisoning and denying food to people who dared gather in prayer, in defiance of a colonial regime. There is a reason that slave-holders violently suppressed the religious freedom of enslaved people and sought to control Black-led independent churches. There's a reason that segregationists were terrified of activists sitting in at lunch counters, or crossing a bridge. A reason that apartheid-era South Africa outlawed prayerful gatherings. As Driver argues, "ritual magic is the principal technique available to oppressed peoples for the transformation of their historical situation. Rational political methods alone cannot bring about the transformation of society from a less to a more just condition, because they cannot fuse the visionary with the actual as rituals do, thus profoundly affecting moral life .... Ideas require flesh and blood performance."

Ceremonies are powerful because they gather us together—a collective space where we stand side-by-side with others, affirming our commitment to a world we want to see. In a good ceremony, we become part of a sacred story. And we come to see that each one of us has an essential part to play in the work of healing and renewal. In ceremony, we are not just actors playing a part, but are also sharers in a sacramental reality.

One of the best parts of my job is advising senior capstone projects. Recently, I got to work with Abigail Carr. A passionate gamer, she wanted to explore the therapeutic potential of first-person-player video games. Knowing that Abi is Diné (Navajo), I suggested this might also be an opportunity to learn about the role of first-person narrative in Diné chantways. We talked about how chantways reenact sacred stories—often a hero's journey. Patients identify with the story's hero, repeating the tale in first-person-present, seated within a sandpainting that illustrates the story and its key players, invoking the presence of the *ye'ii*, or holy people. Through ceremony, patients identify with an ancestor, one who struggled with similar challenges, and survived. And that has powerful potential. As Abi wrote:

> With that narrative shift, it becomes a lot easier to talk about the problem. There is less shame and guilt associated with struggling. You get to see how others also struggled, and overcame it. It no longer becomes an impossible part of you to overcome, but instead

> a hurdle along your own hero's journey. You can and will recover. Many have done so before you, and will continue to do so after .... The story tells you, in plain words, that death is not the escape you seek. The only way to recover is to move forward .... You are the player and the character. You are the one overcoming these trials, which once again connects you to these struggles and your place within the narrative.

Abi was on to something really important here. Because in ceremony, we have the power to write, and re-write the sacred narrative that is to come. And at the heart of that story, is a rediscovery of our place within a greater whole.

The only way forward is through

In my darkest moments, when the reality of climate change is simply too much for me to bear, I do not just feel sad. I feel *bereft*. What a perfect word. Because to be bereft is to be deprived of, or lacking in, something fundamental. In those moments, I feel the absence of that *Something Other*, that which is both me and not me, both greater than the troubles of this world and also deeply engaged with them.

Now, I'm of the opinion that who or what that Something Other will be differs in beautiful and complicated ways, depending on who's doing the talking. For adherents of African diasporan religions like Yoruba, Vodun, or Santeria, that *Other* may be orishas, ancestral guardian spirits, Olodumare, or saints. For Native folks active in their Indigenous traditions, that *Other* may be ancestors, spirits of the natural world, the Creator, or the spirit/wind/breath that animates and unites all things. For Muslims it may be Allah. For Jews, the Shekhinah, the collective recorded wisdom of the Jewish people, the Torah, or *Hashem*. For Buddhists, it may be Buddha Nature, or the profound truth of our constantly changing and intricately interdependent world represented by Indra's Web. For Hindus, it may be Brahman, any number of national or highly localized deities, or sacred groves, rivers, or mountains. For Christians, it may be Jesus, the Holy Spirit, the saints, the Virgin Mary, or simply God. And, of course, there is so much diversity within each of these traditions as to stagger the mind. Whatever that *Something Other* is, real resilience—the resilience we need right now—is rooted in our relationships with those beings that sustains us, those relationships that takes us beyond our individual, material, and merely human selves. It is a turning toward and reconnecting with a sustaining Source.

But if there's anything religious traditions seem to agree on, it's that remembering this Sacred Other isn't easy. And it's a particular challenge in a society that worships at the altar of material wealth and individualism, and whose sacred mythologies extol the virtues of the lone superhero who saves the day—usually through ecstasies of violence. But our survival depends on our remembering the truth that we human beings exist only insofar as we have a place within an intricate web of kinship with other living beings: plant people, animal people, mycelium people, those who came before, and those yet to be born.

Looking ahead

A couple of important points about this book. While I draw from a wealth of different traditions, you'll find I prioritize the voices of communities who have experienced colonialism and systematic oppression. I do so because I believe these are the voices from whom we most need to hear. Heather McTeer Toney puts it well:

> Mainstream America ignores hard-learned lessons from a people who, enslaved and forced to travel across the Atlantic under unimaginable conditions, to work a land they did not know, figured

> out how to make things thrive and grow using their wisdom of nature and spirit. We all face a climate crisis that threatens our very existence. The ability of my ancestors to adapt to wholly new environments offers wisdom to embrace.[20]

In the chapters that follow, we'll be turning to that wisdom to build spiritual resilience for purposeful action. My point is this: when hope is a ceremony, it is a way of living, infused with reverence and care. It is a story we tell. And more, it is a story we enter into, one in which we take part, and which we have the power to change. It is a story of a radically relational way of living, cultivated in daily acts of (self)care, connection, and attention.

In Chapter 2, we'll take a closer look at what psychologists have to say about eco anxiety and climate grief, identifying the practical tools they offer for building physical and emotional resilience, and consider how those tools might be integrated into a ceremonial approach to climate hope. Chapters 3 through 6 will consider lessons gleaned from comparative religious and Indigenous traditions for grieving, eating, resting, and moving in ways that help us build personal, collective, and ecological resilience. In these chapters, we see that when resilience is grounded in moral relationships, acts of care for the planet and for ourselves can be one and the same. Chapters 7 through 9 invite us into deeper reflection on the nature of those moral relationships, exploring comparative approaches to contemplative practice, the importance of kith and kin, and the foundational role of justice and decolonization. Chapters 10 through 12 invite us into purposeful action, as we consider how to respectfully listen to and learn from other cultures and traditions without engaging in religious appropriation, and explore comparative understandings of vocation. We'll see that hope is a ceremony, one that empowers us to write and take part in a new story of a more just and sustainable world.

Key takeaways

1 Climate change is a threat multiplier. Extreme weather events threaten lives, lead to forced migration, and disrupt access to food, water, healthcare, and education. People who experience extreme weather events suffer from PTSD, increased rates of anxiety, depression, domestic violence, suicidal ideation, and exacerbation of existing mental health conditions. Psychologists also note rising levels of climate anxiety or eco-grief among the general population. Such anticipatory dread, particularly among young people, is exacerbated by perceptions that political leaders are failing to take action.

2 Most of us are worried about climate change. We know what's causing it, and we also know what we need to do to solve it. So why aren't we taking action? A lot of it has to do with emotional overwhelm and unresolved grief. Climate change isn't just a technological problem, it's a profoundly spiritual one. And it's going to require spiritual solutions.

3 "Religion" is a category of human experience, and one we ignore at our peril. The best and the worst of human activity happens here. Some religious institutions and beliefs have contributed to this problem by justifying extractive and exploitative systems. But other religious and spiritual traditions offer counter examples, ways of living that affirm the value of Earth and care for all her creatures.

4 While often described as one's personal philosophy, in this book, we define spirituality differently: as the practices and orientations that make it possible for us to be in relationship with someone (or something) bigger than our finite,

individual, human selves. And spiritual resilience is the ability to return to and draw strength and guidance from those relationships—even in times of crisis.

5 Ritual and ceremony—when done well—have the power to change the world. In ceremony, we come together with others to tell a story, a story that grounds us in who and where we are. In ceremony, we enter into and gain the power to write a new story, to represent the world as it should be. And through that sacred performance, we bring what is hoped for into the here and now.

Invitation for further reflection

1 Do you find it difficult to talk with others about climate change? If so, why do you think this is?

2 What comes to mind when you hear the words "religion" or "spirituality"? Is spirituality a creed or code of ethics? Or is it something you experience? Or an orientation to life?

3 What would emotional or spiritual resilience look like for you? What are the relationships that sustain you now?

4 Have you ever participated in a ritual or ceremony that changed you, or the way you see the world?

Want to learn more?

Visit our website at https://bloomsbury.pub/climate-spirit where you'll find recommendations for further reading and resources for individuals, reading groups, and educators.

2

Retrain your brain: Lessons from climate psychology

I've already tripped over my words, and my feet, so when my I drop my dry erase pen for the third time, I figure I should just give up on my lecture. Facing the room full of students, I also drop whatever remains of my professorial demeanor. I grimace. "Sorry guys. No sleep last night. The Pacific Garbage Patch had me up at 2am." Blank stares greet me in return, and I start to regret my life choices. Then Kelly meets my eyes: long hair, serious expression, front row, by the windows. Lips pursed to one side, she nods. "I get you," she says, quietly. "That Garbage Patch is a bitch."

This was not the first time I'd been kept awake by ominous environmental disasters I could do nothing about. Nuclear meltdowns in Fukushima. Wildfires in Australia. And Canada. And Oregon. Heat-stressed cedars. Declining salmon runs. The polar bears. Jesus, will someone please think of the polar bears?

I'm not alone in this. Overwhelmed with a deluge of bad news, many of us are in a constant state of alert, alarm, and dis-ease.

Psychologists Lise Van Susteren and Stacey Colino describe this as a state of *emotional inflammation*, the symptoms of which include hypervigilance, constant low-level distress, nameless dread, anticipatory anxiety, sleep disturbance, poor eating, difficulty concentrating, and emotional hyperreactivity.[1] Any of that sound familiar?

This chapter introduces us to the work of climate psychologists who help us understand why we struggle to respond to climate change, and how we can retrain our brain to respond more effectively to the crisis before us. These are the kinds of lessons we'll take with us as we explore what a ceremonial approach to climate hope might look like. Because here's what we need to remember: while unbounded grief and anxiety are debilitating, when *bounded* and *transformed* they can inspire resistance, adaptation, and care for others. Consider, for instance, one 2013 study which found that habitual ecological worry rarely evolved into pathological worry. Instead, it actually correlated with a higher likelihood of pro-environmental behaviors, imagination, and openness to new ideas. Similar findings were reported in a 2024 study that found that while climate change is having an increasingly serious impact on our mental health, and can be maladaptive, it is also the case that adults reporting climate-related psychological distress are more likely to engage in climate action and activism.[2] Finding ways to effectively manage climate anxiety or eco-grief, then, is an essential part of a broader approach to climate action. In a synthesis of numerous studies, Susan Craydon and Tara Crandon identify three broad categories of climate resilience: problem-focused coping (which includes activism and making personal lifestyle changes); emotion-focused coping (processing emotional responses), and meaning-focused coping (exploring values, finding purpose).[3] We'll consider each of these in the chapters that follow. But first, we need to understand why so many of us struggle to wrap our heads around the facts and feelings of climate change. According to climate psychologists, the answer has a great deal to do with the way our brains are wired. As it turns out, we're really not built for this kind of crisis.

We're just not built for this

Our brains are incredibly well equipped to respond to many different kinds of threats, but, unfortunately, climate change isn't one of them. Evolved to protect us from the saber-toothed tiger at the mouth of the cave, our brains are really good at identifying immediate hazards and responding quickly to those enemies that are right in front of us. And while climate change is already harming many human and other-than-human communities, the more privileged of us are still able to regard it as a distant danger. Consider, for instance, what Anthony Lieserowitz and his colleagues at Yale School of the Environment found: a growing number of Americans are increasingly concerned about the impacts of climate change on our health—but a majority also believe it is more likely to impact *someone else, somewhere else.*

A second reason has to do with the double-edged sword that is human adaptability. In his book *Don't Even Think About It: Why Our Brains Are Wired to Ignore Climate Change,* George Marshall, founder of the Climate Action and Information Network, explains that we as a species are fantastic at figuring out how to live in challenging conditions.[4] Provided crises or stressors arise slow enough, we adapt. The problem is, our skill at adaptation, coupled with our desire for normalcy and reassurance, means we're quick to forget that things were ever any different. While this can be a great survival mechanism when it comes to short-term threats, it puts us right in the path of that slow-rolling juggernaut of climate change.

In the summer of 2023, my spouse and I were grabbing breakfast at a cafe in Northern California. While waiting for the barista to work her magic, we struck up a conversation with a woman in town to visit her grandchildren. She nodded toward the smoky haze outside. "I guess this is just the new normal," she said with a resigned shrug. "Amazing what we can adapt to, isn't it?" I tried to hold my tongue, I really did. And I did manage to force a smile as I responded, "Hopefully we don't just adapt. Hopefully we also get mad." At that moment I couldn't have told her who we were supposed to be mad at. Oil executives? Settler colonialism? Frequent fliers? Meat eaters? Fast fashion wearers? Barbie? Ourselves? I only knew I didn't like the cheerful resignation on her face. I only knew there was nothing "normal" about that smoky haze.

But our resigned grandmother also has a point. Atmospheric change is happening fast enough that we feel internal pressure to do something about it, but also slow enough that our brains convince us we can wait. With just enough time to adapt before the next wave of crises hits, we downplay the immediacy of the threat and delay our response. We see the bus bearing down our children, but we convince ourselves there's still time to pull them out of the way.

Hans Rosling's book *Factfulness: Ten Reasons We're Wrong About the World—and Why Things Are Better Than You Think* gives another reason for our inaction, explaining that our brains are hardwired to misperceive facts in very particular ways.[5] First, our brains have a simplicity bias, instinctively dividing perceptions of problems into two distinct categories (what he calls the gap instinct): good guys and bad guys, right answers and wrong answers. Faced with a problem like climate change, our brains want to find single causes with simple solutions, and we really, *really* want to have someone to blame. While this instinct can be useful, it's a liability when facing complex, multifaceted problems that require collaboration and cooperation to fix.

Second, the longing for a simple narrative inspires what Rosling calls our "straight-line instinct," a desire to locate a unilinear progression of time, a clear trajectory, where the state of the world is either moving toward perfection, or in a state of decline and decay. Our brains love to group information into categories that reaffirm our existing assumptions: civilization is either on the verge of collapse, or we're marching toward a techno-utopia. Because of this, it's hard for us to grasp that both of these things can be true. In the case of complex global challenges like climate change, things are nearly always getting a whole lot better, and a whole lot worse, at the same time.

But our perceptions of the climate crisis are also distorted by our negativity bias. For our ancient ancestors, surviving in a hostile environment required a keen fear instinct, and our brains evolved to overemphasize negative information. It helped them survive. But the problem is that our brain reacts the same way to a tiger in the bush as it does to an alarming click-bait headline. The result is that a single piece of bad news can take up far more cognitive space than a multitude of good, leading to a sense of doom, even when there's great cause for hope. Too much negative news (and there's plenty of it out there) and we conclude it's too late to make a difference. And that's when civilizational collapse just might become a self-fulfilling prophecy.

And, finally, our responses to climate change are stymied by our aversion to cognitive dissonance. We dislike holding conflicting ideas or values, and we suffer when we are forced to act in ways that are contrary to our conscience, experiencing what psychologists working with veterans of war have called "moral injury." Climate change demands that we confront those internal contradictions, and environmental catastrophe forces us—particularly those of us in positions of privilege—to confront the fact that we are complicit in our own destruction, that the lifestyles we have (or aspire to have) are simply not sustainable. And most of us will go through truly remarkable mental gymnastics to avoid that kind of moral discomfort.

The desire to avoid cognitive dissonance often means we take mental shortcuts, rather than suffer through the hard work of critical thinking. One of those shortcuts is groupthink. As climate scientist Katharine Hayhoe explains, our response to climate change often has more to do with our identity than with facts.[6] Simply put: we want to believe that we are good people in a community of good people. So if your facts suggest I am a bad person (or that my kin-group is in the wrong) my brain will reject your facts. Psychologist and economist Per Espen Stoknes comes to similar conclusions, pointing out that most of us are motivated to align with our identity group, and more likely to trust those messengers who come from our group.[7] If climate communication inspires a defensive posture, our brains are far less likely to take it seriously, or be motivated to act on it.

All of this helps explain why we find it so difficult to talk about, let alone act to solve, climate change. And it's why gaining the emotional resilience to face the feelings that climate change evokes is so essential to our survival. In her book *Climate Crisis and Consciousness*, Sally Gillespie argues that only by turning toward the difficult feelings that our environmental crisis evokes can we begin to face the reality of our situation, and take the necessary steps to address it. That includes facing our complicity in unjust and destructive systems. But, as she notes, this is easier said than done. The climate crisis triggers terrible and terrifying emotions—and the emotional backlash can be severe.

In 1999, I was a teaching assistant for an undergraduate course on Black, Hispanic, and Indigenous women's literature at UC Santa Barbara. On this particular day, we were listening to an introductory lecture on the ways race and gender shape our experience. To a former US history major, this was pretty standard stuff. So, I was startled when a young woman rose to her feet, interrupting the professor with an angry interjection.

"*Stop making me feel guilty!*"

The lecture hall fell silent, and our professor, caught off guard, struggled to respond. The student, shaking with outrage, grabbed up her things and stormed from the hall. I'd almost forgotten about this exchange, until I read Sally Gillespie's description of a similar moment. In her story, it was an Australian climate researcher whose talk was interrupted by an abrupt and highly revealing shout: "*Stop frightening me!*"

It strikes me now that neither of these individuals were objecting to the *content* of what was being said—but to their mind's aversion to pain and fear. And the more I think about these individuals, the more I appreciate both of them—for their sheer emotional honesty. They were not disputing the facts, but their emotional impact. In short: if we do not like the way information makes us feel—and particularly how it makes us feel *about ourselves*—we are far less able to integrate what's being said.

All this helps explain why we, as a species, are frozen like deer in the headlights. Climate change is complex, multifaceted, and difficult to predict. It is not a single problem with a single solution. It doesn't operate on a predictable unilinear projection. It feeds our negativity bias, so that we lose sight of a hopeful future. It fails to provide us with an enemy to eradicate: while some of us do more harm than others, we are all caught up in destructive and extractive systems. And perhaps most importantly, the notion of ecological collapse is simply too terrible for our minds to comprehend. All this leaves our brains stewing in a cauldron of cortisol and other stress hormones, a chemical bath that makes us vulnerable to depression, anxiety, mismanaged rage, helplessness, and behavioral paralysis.[8]

The good news that climate psychologists offer, is that while our brains aren't built for a crisis like this, we can *retrain* our brains, building the strength we need to do the work that needs to be done. In his book *Transformational Resilience*, social theorist Bob Doppelt describes three steps to preventing climate disruption.[9] First, we need to mitigate climate change by reducing emissions and improving energy efficiency. Second, we need to adapt to the changes we can't avoid, building more resilient systems and stronger communities. And, third, *we need to build our capacity to cope with the stress and trauma that will come with rising temperatures*. This last task is akin to what psychologists Richard Tedeschi and Lawrence Calhoun call "post traumatic growth": the personal and collective transformation that comes from attending to and learning from the experience of trauma.[10] In the rest of this chapter, I'll describe four ways to do just that.

#1: Retrain your brain

"*I would like some attention, please.*" I turn away from the produce aisle and kneel down to give my two-year-old a hug. After a few seconds I feel his anxiety melt away under my arms. Glancing up, I make eye contact with a woman stocking carrots a few feet away. "Did he just say what I think he said?" she asks with an incredulous laugh.

My son started to talk before he could crawl, and well before he could walk. It was a gift, cutting temper tantrums in half as he learned to articulate his desires. But, as with all things, it had its downsides: it's tough to lay down the law with a child who learns to out-debate you by the time he is seven. As he's grown into a young man, I remain impressed by his ability to look inward and describe what he's feeling. We may need to wait for a wave of emotion to pass, but soon, he'll be there to explain it to us. Fourteen years later, that phrase, *I'd like some attention, please* remains a staple in our family. It's our code-red for *Drop Everything and Come and Give Me a Hug*! It's a phrase that often comes to mind when I'm reading the latest dire predictions about climate catastrophe, both because the changes we're seeing are the Earth's way of shouting out that *she'd like some attention*, and because, after reading the news, I definitely need a hug. Here's my point in all this: in order to face our grief about ecological catastrophe, we first have to acknowledge what we're feeling. As systems theorist Joanna Macy explains, feelings like climate anxiety are far from pathological. They are a moral and *humane* response to suffering. It is denying, downplaying, or seeking to numb those feelings that can be harmful—not only because it prevents us from taking action, but because long-term suppression of emotional pain has serious consequences for our mental health.

African American theologian Barbara Holmes writes in her book *Crisis Contemplation*, "as those of us raised in communities under siege can tell you [the first step of coping with crisis is to] take a big gulp of reality."[11] This means we have to stop running, and acknowledge the reality of climate change, and the terrible potential it holds. Then we need to be honest about how it makes us feel. For many of us, that kind of emotional honesty can be terrifying.

But emotional resilience begins when we stop turning from our pain, and instead turn *toward* it. This is a tough one for those of us who have grown up in a culture that equates "happiness" with the absence of discomfort, and who may fear that, once acknowledged, pain may move in for good. However, mental health professionals agree that the acknowledgment of our emotions has a remarkable ability to defuse their power. For example, the simple act of naming one's feelings increases neural activity in the prefrontal cortex—the part of the brain responsible for integrating emotions with critical thinking—and reduces activity in the amygdala, our brain's emotional response center, and command central for our fight, flight, or freeze response. Those reflexive reactions to danger can be helpful, but, detached as they are from the rational, thinking part of our brain, they can also be deeply *unhelpful*. If our amygdala takes over, we're not problem solving. We're fighting (blame someone else!), running away (deny it's happening! find a distraction!), or freezing (assume the fetal position!). The first step in getting us out of our amygdala and back into our prefrontal cortex, is to simply be present with our emotions: observe them objectively, and describe them. As neuroscientist Lisa Feldman Barrett explains in her book *How Emotions Are Made: The Secret Life of the Brain*, the more nuanced your descriptors, the more powerful the brain response. We need to go beyond "sad," to identify the "fifty shades of crappy," then consider how you might put those feelings into words, images, music, or action.[12] In her book *Emotional Resiliency in the Era of Climate Change*, psychologist Leslie Davenport suggests we think of emotions as guests in our home.[13] Be a good host: welcome them, greet them by name, work the room. Don't get stuck talking to one emotion for too long. Get to know them all. Be curious. Ask why they stopped by. (And we may need to be prepared to show disruptive guests to the door if they overstay their welcome.)

#2: Find your why

Getting to know our emotions is important because it defuses their power, but it's also important because our emotions are valuable sources of data, providing a window into who we are, what we value, and what needs our attention. As Steven Hayes points out in *The Liberated Mind: How to Pivot Toward What Matters*, pain is an opportunity to learn: What does this pain suggest I care about? What would I have to stop caring about for this pain to go away? In our pain, we find what we value. The fact is, our emotions are some of our best data, and paying attention to what triggers them helps us identify danger, alerts us to unresolved business, and shows us what we truly care about. We may go through remarkable acrobatics to avoid feeling or acknowledging our emotional distress, but the tragic result of those acrobatics is a *disconnect* from our values. Climate psychologists help their clients name their values, and find therein a sense of purpose or calling, a way to participate in the work of transforming our world. This entails finding the intersection of what we are good at, what gives us joy, and what needs to be done. For some, this can mean making a life-changing pivot. Finding our *why*, our deepest and non-negotiable values, is the first step in translating our values into action.

Climate communications scholar Britt Wray takes this point even further, arguing that not only are feelings of grief and anxiety healthy, normal responses to climate chaos, but they reflect our deepest motivations—and those can be "super fuel," mobilizing us for personal and cultural transformation. As she argues: "If we don't recognize our eco-distress, and learn to purposefully and justly transform it, we'll miss the opportunity we have to use all this restless energy for a deeper purpose: to bring forth the future we owe each other by promoting solutions that have co-benefits for all people and the planet."[14]

#3: Expand your window of tolerance

There is never enough time to do all the work that needs to be done. Or at least it certainly feels that way. And, as I meet more people committed to doing the work of caring for our planet and its most vulnerable citizens, I also encounter more and more people struggling with burnout. Riddled by a constant fear that we can never do enough, we skip food, sleep, or time with family. If we are not simply exhausted, how do we know when we've done enough? But sacrificing our health and well-being for the sake of work—no matter how meaningful that work is—not only shortens our own life, but undermines the very impact we're trying to have.

Caring for our mental health in times of crisis helps expand what psychiatrist Daniel Siegel calls our "window of tolerance," the state in which we are best equipped to respond to stress and in which we're maximizing use of our prefrontal cortex.[15] Expanding that window requires good self-care: rest, nutrition, exercise, connection. Otherwise, that window shrinks, and even minor stressors can cause us to lose contact with our reasoning, problem-solving prefrontal cortex as our brain function shifts toward our crisis-prone amygdala.

#4: Acknowledge the bad, attend to the good

As we've already seen, our brains have a negativity bias that, if unchecked, can leave us in a perpetual state of agita and despair. Constantly scanning for bad news, our brains seize upon it, then release a flood of cortisol and other stress hormones to make sure we never forget it. "Our brains are like Velcro for bad experiences but Teflon for good ones," says Rick Hanson, psychologist and Senior Fellow at UC Berkeley's Greater Good Science Center.[16] Some researchers suggest it may take *three to eight times* more positive stimuli than negative to keep us in emotional equilibrium. That's why even one bad encounter can ruin an otherwise good day.

But there's reason to be optimistic: by training ourselves to pay attention to positive events, sensations, and emotions, we can counteract that bias. In his book *Resilient*, Hanson suggests we learn to critically and thoughtfully engage with bad experiences (what can I learn from this?), and then let them go. And equally important, he advises us to train our brains to fully attend to good moments, to create space in our mind for them, be fully present with them, and adopt tools for imprinting them, such as mindful breathing or gratitude journaling. And, indeed, studies show that cultivating gratitude has real therapeutic benefits. Taking time to reflect on those people, things, and experiences for which one is thankful changes our brain chemistry, shifting activity to the prefrontal cortex, and resetting the dial, moving our mindsets from scarcity and toward creative possibility. Gratitude can also expand our sense of justice, recentering equity and reconciliation within climate work, because it subverts our tendency toward self-centeredness, an essential shift in a time when our survival may depend on our ability to recognize our interdependence with and responsibilities toward others. All this helps rewire our brain to have a more balanced view of our world and our experience in it. And what's even better? You don't need to live in a perpetual tropical paradise for this to work. It only takes mindfully attending to the joy found in the smallest of things: that first sip of morning coffee. The pleasure of a loving hug. The satisfaction of a cat choosing your lap. The beauty of the sun reflecting off the water. A small act of kindness. Small changes can have a big impact in countering our negativity bias. Acts as small as switching the music you're listening to, or taking ten seconds to look at a photo of a happy memory, can actually change our brain chemistry, helping us see our experience with greater accuracy, and reducing the damaging impacts of stress on our brains.

Looking ahead

We'll be returning to these themes in later chapters, as we consider guidance from sacred traditions that support the work of learning from our feelings, identifying our values, expanding our window of tolerance, and cultivating gratitude, all essential tools in metabolizing our grief, and cultivating a ceremonial approach to hope.

Meanwhile, if you are struggling, be encouraged: there is a wealth of resources within the growing field of ecopsychology, including more and more mental health practitioners trained to support clients struggling with climate anxiety and eco-grief. I've linked to more resources below, but if you're struggling, now is the time to find a therapist or supportive group. Because this is not work to do in isolation. Remember that climate change is a threat multiplier—if your brain chemistry inclines toward clinical depression or chronic anxiety, then know this: getting good care is part of your climate activism. Because the climate movement needs you at your best. We need you doing the work that only you can do. If you've been needing encouragement to see a doctor, or find a mental health provider, here it is. You matter. You are essential. Take care of yourself, so you can take care of others.

Key takeaways

1. Despite knowing that climate change threatens life as we know it, and despite knowing what we need to do to address it, we are still slow to act. Psychologists tell us that this has to do with the way our brain is hardwired: we adapt to slow-moving and distant threats; we demand simple explanations; we overemphasize negative news; and we're averse to cognitive dissonance or self-recrimination.
2. Ecopsychologists offer a host of tools to "retrain our brain" so that we can better cope with the stressors of climate change and find the courage to take action. These include (1) naming

your feelings; (2) finding your why; (3) expanding your window of tolerance; and (4) mindfully attending to joy and gratitude.

Invitation for further reflection

1 Take five full minutes (set a timer) and write down every word or phrase that comes into your mind when you hear the words climate change. You might also consider "meta-emotions," or what you feel *about* your feelings. Does feeling a certain way make you feel guilty? Proud? Confused? Try not to judge your feelings—just observe them. If at all possible, do this exercise with a friend or in a group, so you can share what you wrote down. Try to be as specific as possible. You might even invent your own words or phrases that better describe your very personal sensibilities and experiences.

2 What are some of the ways you try to avoid the feelings you listed above? What are some different ways you could engage with those feelings that might be more helpful?

3 What do these painful feelings suggest you care about? What would you have to stop caring about, to not feel this way?

4 What kind of world do you *want* to leave for future generations?

5 How can you cultivate gratitude and attention to good moments throughout your day? Can you pause and breathe deeply, mindfully considering even small opportunities for joy? Could you snap a photo? Keep a journal? How about a 24-hour-gratitude-date with a friend, in which you commit to

text each other throughout the day any time you encounter a simple thing that brings you joy?

Want to learn more?

Visit our website at https://bloomsbury.pub/climate-spirit where you'll find recommendations for further reading and resources for individuals, reading groups, and educators.

3

Lament can change the world

For millennia, Indigenous people from throughout the inland Northwest gathered at *Shonitkwu*—also known as Kettle Falls—on the upper reaches of the Columbia River. A center for fishing, trade, political alliances, and ceremony, it was second only to the mighty Celilo Falls. But, in June 1940, the people came together for a different reason: The Ceremony of Tears. For three days, they mourned the anticipated loss of this sacred site. In the days that followed, the Grand Coulee Dam was completed, and the people watched as the falls were inundated. For the first time in thousands of years, fish could not migrate upstream. An ancient economy built on a people's relationship with these sacred waters came to a halt.

But the people kept coming back. Each year, they held a ceremony, remembering the salmon who were no longer there. As Aaron Fitzpatrick (Colville) explains, "It's hard not to tear up and cry because before the dams, there would be many thousands of Indigenous people gathered there. … Now we're not even allowed to camp unless we have our archaeologists with us. We have to seek permission to be there." But, for Fitzpatrick, returning is a pilgrimage. "Coming to Kettle Falls, for us Indigenous people, is like going to Mecca or the Vatican. It's a symbolic and spiritual experience."

The direct descendants of those who attended the Ceremony of Tears are now conducting different kinds of ceremonies. Sometimes, that looks like writing a grant or building trust with state agencies. Sometimes, it's trucking salmon around dams, releasing them into their natal waters with prayer and song. Sometimes, a ceremony is learning from traditional knowledge keepers, who point engineers and fish biologists in the right direction. In 2024, Sinixt tribal member and chairman of the Colville Confederated Tribes Jarred Erickson told reporters why those ceremonial acts matter. "The push has never stopped. All of our life revolved around the river and the return of the salmon .... It's taken this long to get here, but I'm glad we're actually getting some groundwork done."[1] And now, eighty years later, salmon are once again swimming beyond the Grand Coulee Dam.

Our relationships with places sustain us physically and spiritually. They shape our collective memory, and our identity. They enliven us, and give us joy. But climate change poses an existential threat to beloved species, waterways, and landscapes. And when that happens, the fear, anger, and sorrow can seem too much to bear.

How do we stomach this grief? Or, if I may suggest a more helpful phrasing: how do we *metabolize* it, transforming sorrow, fear, and anger into the energy we need to do the multigenerational healing work required of us? This isn't an easy question to answer. We may have some sense of how to grieve a loved one. But how do you grieve a forest? A species? Who declares the time of death, when such losses occur slowly, over time, and out of sight? Who is the next of kin for an eroding coastline? A vanishing species? A diseased stand of trees? Who officiates a funeral for an aquifer? How do we say goodbye to family reunions, canceled because of smoke, or drought, or storm? More often than not, ecological sorrow goes unspoken.

And that's a problem, because unacknowledged grief is dangerous.

It leads to shutting down, numbness, inaction, avoidance, floating anxiety, chronic stress. Unresolved grief doesn't go away—it festers.

That's why we need new ways of thinking about what it means to grieve, to move us through our darkest moments, and toward restorative action. I'm far from the first person to think about this. Environmental Humanities professor Jennifer Atkinson advises her students to acknowledge their grief, take action, build community, and get outside. The Good Grief Network, founded by LaUra Schmidt and Aimee Lewis Reau, offers a Ten-Step Program and healing circles. And psychotherapist Francis Weller offers workshops on what he calls the Five Gates of Grief. This chapter is informed by their work, while also considering what comparative religious and Indigenous studies might offer to that larger conversation. I want to think about the ceremonial work of grieving, and how it can help us metabolize our sorrow and turn it into purposeful action, because comparative ritual studies can help us see how rites of grieving guide us through our sorrow and, when done right, change us for the better. And when we bring a spirit of *ecological lament* to those rites, we don't just change ourselves, we also change the world around us, restoring our relationship with the species and ecosystems we have lost, and embodying the kind of moral relationships that can rewrite national narratives, and transform global politics.

The five stages of climate grief

An elected leader strips the word "climate" from government websites and fires climate scientists, insisting it is all part of a mass global conspiracy—even as unprecedented hurricanes and floods destroy communities, coastlines erode, and wildfires rage unchecked.

A college student, overwhelmed by the existential threat of climate catastrophe, simply shrugs. "I've gotta work extra shifts just to buy textbooks. The billionaires have all the power. What can I do? We're doomed anyway."

A marine biologist is exhausted. Budget cuts threaten a lifetime of determined research and advocacy, and she feels like giving up. No matter how hard she works, the problems keep getting worse, and some days it's hard just to get out of bed in the morning.

As different as these three stories may sound, they actually all have something in common: they are all expressions of climate grief.

You're likely familiar with Elizabeth Kubler-Ross's five stages of grief: denial, anger/blame, bargaining, depression, and acceptance. While usually applied to grieving the loss of a loved one, they can also help us understand our responses to climate change. *Climate denial* might look like insisting the science is a hoax, or that it's overblown. Or like insisting it's someone else's problem to solve. It may be the person who says, "I need to take care of my own life, my own family, and let the rest of the world take care of itself." It might even take the form of religious apocalypticism: "No need to change how we're living! Jesus will save us!" (If you're one of the chosen few, that is.)

Climate anger can manifest in different ways as well. It may be doubling down on conspiracy theories, or it may look like the outrage of climate activists who've lost patience with a world that insists on business as usual in the face of ecosystem collapse. We often conflate grief with sadness: it's good to remember that grief has as much to do with rage as it does with weeping.

We certainly do our share of *climate-bargaining*. The wealthy bargain with rockets to Mars, changes to their investment portfolios, or a survivalist cabin in the woods. We bargain with desperate prayers: "I promise I'll be good, God, just let this storm/wildfire/tornado pass us by." Or perhaps it's the hope that we can carry on with our consumer lifestyle—if we just switch to the "greener" brand.

If you're reading this book, you probably already have an idea of what *climate-depression* might look like. Maybe it looks like despair. But it's important to distinguish between despair and sorrow. Despair is sadness stripped of hope. Despair is paralytic. It's the young person who cannot envision a future and sees no point in even trying. It's the adult who lunges for the bottle—anything to numb the pain. It's the body-and-soul exhaustion of burnout. But this stage of grieving may also look like sorrow. As poet and essayist Ross Gay reminds us, sorrow retains its footing in love and hope. It offers a glimpse of a way forward.[2]

Climate acceptance is not the same as surrendering to our fate. Rather, it's making peace with not knowing what the future will hold. It's acknowledging there are no guarantees—but determining to do what we can anyway. It's the realization that giving up isn't an option—that we will and must create a livable world for future generations. It's a determination to create joy and nurture life, because the alternative is unthinkable.

Eco-grief can overwhelm us. We need to envision and work toward a better world. But we can't if we're stuck in anger, denial, and despair. Joanna Macy and Chris Johnstone have challenged the notion of a linear journey through grief, preferring instead the image of a spiral, arguing that eco-grief is a cycle we return and grow through, with each loss and setback. Macy and Johnstone invite us to first hold moments of grief with gratitude—for what we love and our desire to protect it. Second, she asks us to honor and acknowledge our pain. Third, to draw on that engagement with what we cherish to see the world with new eyes. Finally, to go forth, taking from that insight new energy to transform the world. But how ought we create that ceremonial space for metabolizing our grief, to ensure we are indeed moving up that spiral staircase, and not merely spinning in circles?

Five lessons for metabolizing grief

I was in the midst of researching this chapter when the idea of grieving became all too real. Within a matter of weeks, my family experienced one loss after another, as we grieved two aunts, two uncles, two friends, and parents of dear friends. It was a painful constellation of loss, and particularly strange that it came at a time when I was spending my days reading about comparative grieving traditions. When it came time to plan my aunt's memorial, the question of how we grieve became unavoidable. My aunt had no church-home, and left no instructions or requests for her funeral. Would she have preferred cremation? A traditional burial? A natural burial? Did she want a church service? Or a joyful party to celebrate her life? We stumbled through, hoping that decisions made in love would be the right ones. The experience became all the more striking when contrasted with the experience of my husband's family in Bantry, Ireland. There, everyone followed a familiar and meaningful pattern of custom and tradition. What a gift, I thought, to know what one is supposed to do during such times.

Because here is the thing: grief *bewilders* us.

In its literal definition, to be *bewildered* is to "*be thoroughly led astray*." How fitting. Because we so often become *lost* in the wilds of our grief. We lose our beloved, but we also lose track of our place in the world. It's why we human beings create rites of mourning—we need those well-lit paths to walk when we are adrift in our sorrow. In a similar way, the impacts of climate change and ecological destruction leave us bewildered. As coastlines erode, seasons change, and 100-year storms become more and more common, we lose our sense of place. We ache for the certainty we once had, and feel lost in the face of an unpredictable future, rife with dire predictions, painful news of rising temperatures, threatened species, or the terrible violence that human beings visit upon each other. Entire ecosystems are vanishing before our eyes.

How do we grieve that scale of loss? How do we tell the stories of melting glaciers and eroded coastlines? How do I enshrine memories of predictable summer weather? Of a June when rainforests dripped wet, and cedars thrived? Where do we enshrine the species that came before us, the species we have lost, the species who have made us who we are, and remain spiritually, genetically, molecularly with us? And in the midst of this loss, how do we find ourselves again? Or rather, how do we find the selves we are called to be in this terrible time of mass extinction? How can we transform our grief into transformative action? I don't have all the answers, but in the rest of this chapter, I'd like to offer five lessons that just might illuminate the way forward.

#1: Grief is a rite of passage

Contrary to what we might think, grief is not just about ending and loss. We grieve because we have to go on, even in the face of loss. When we experience loss—of a person, a species, a place, an ecosystem—we are forced to confront the question: *now what*? Who am I, in this new world? In *A Field Guide to Getting Lost*, Rebecca Solnit describes the dual nature of loss.[3] We are losing something or someone—and that just plain hurts. And we are also *lost*, trying to figure out who and where we are in this alien world, where familiar landmarks have been obliterated. That's why funerals are, at heart, rites of passage, ceremonial, communal means of transporting us through incredibly scary periods of liminality. *Liminality* comes from the Latin word *limen*, meaning threshold. When we are in a liminal state, we are in-between—neither outside, nor inside, but in a state of transformative potential, where our choices determine our future. In those moments, we are incredibly malleable, able to be transformed in good or bad ways. It's why human cultures tend to surround liminal spaces with care.

Many religious traditions talk about the end of the world. But we often forget that there's always another world on the other side of that ending. Indeed, the notion that we move through periods of death and rebirth is one of the most common themes found throughout the world—likely inspired by observing the cycles of nature. Diné (Navajo) and Pueblo communities in the southwestern United States describe creation as a series of worlds, the destruction of one leading to emergence into another. Hinduism describes the cycles of samsara—a series of renewals. Even Protestant Christian traditions with their emphasis on "the end times" aren't really talking about the end—but the end of one era, and the beginning of another. This is not to put a rosy picture on things—loss is loss, and death is death. It is painful, and often awful. But never *the end.* Climate change is already happening. We have taken too long to act, and we are already experiencing warming of our planet that will result in great loss: species, human lives, coastlines, ecosystems, and homelands. But so much remains to be saved, and so much yet to be created. And because of that we are *obliged* to do the work of grieving, because we must arrive at the other side equipped to envision what that new world is going to be.

Consider the example of an Irish wake. In his work, folklorist Ray Cashman describes a funeral in the township of Aghyaran in County Tyrone as a rite of passage. The funeral wake is a liminal, transformative time wherein the dead become ancestors, and recollections help the living understand who they must become in light of that loss. Bookended by evening and morning mass, Irish wakes are famous all-night affairs. A member from every household in the township is expected to attend, temporarily setting any differences aside. Hosts provide food and drink, while guests are expected to bring the chat—memories and good stories. Historically, church officials did not approve of wakes, describing them as "feast and riot," that would go on "to their undoing forever," with their "excessive drinking and disorder." But as Cashman explains, the festivities serve important social and spiritual functions. "Wake guests expected the departed soul to participate in feasting and drinking at the wake," and in doing so to be fortified, strengthening the "soul to successfully travel the long and hazardous journey to the next world." The bereaved are able to "disengage from normal time by stopping clocks, and from the wider world by covering televisions, turning off radios, and leaving newspapers unread." Liminal spaces require pre-liminal rites (activities that separate us from normal life) and post-liminal activities (those that help us return to a sense of normalcy). In this case, that gradual return to normalcy happens with morning mass, burial, and funeral lunch. It continues with the "month's mind," a memorial mass held one month later, and the annual memorial mass that will later mark the one-year anniversary of their passing.[4]

Japanese Buddhist traditions may look very different, but they are also a rite of passage, replete with rites of separation, transformation, and reintegration. After experiencing a loss, the bereaved leave off their normal lives, entering into a state of mourning. The tradition also includes a wake, referred to as "passing the night," during which a priest will chant sutras in honor of the dead, and the family will receive visitors. The morning of the funeral, elaborate flower displays are placed before the casket, priests continue to chant sutras, and family members receive names, symbolic of their new identities, social positions, and obligations. The deceased is cremated, a tradition that honors Buddhist teachings of impermanence, and follows Buddha's example of releasing ties to the material world. A return to the new-normal begins as mourners gather together for a vegetarian meal, sharing stories of the departed, and continues as prayers are offered each day for seven days, then every seventh day for seven weeks, and finally in a one-year anniversary ceremony—which includes burning of food and offerings for the dead.

My point here is this: grief can feel like forever. When we're in it, it is all consuming. But we need to remember that grief is actually a step in a transformative process, a becoming and emerging into something new. It's also a sacred space—set aside—when the normal rules do not apply. Climate psychologists call us to attend to our feelings around climate change. To sit with them, and learn from them. The wake gives us a model of intentional space, time out of time, to be with one's feelings, to listen to the stories they have to tell, and from them gain new insight into who we are called to become, in this new and changing world.

When asked how her father endured the loss of his family in the Holocaust, Jewish historian and theologian Dr. Susannah Heschel answered: "There is a phrase in the Zohar that says only someone with a broken heart is a whole person. It is a very cryptic statement, and one of the interpretations is that when the heart is broken, then the Shekinah, God's presence, comes and fills it."

Lesson #2: Grieve together

A second lesson that comparative grieving traditions offer, is that we must grieve, and we must grieve in community. In traditional cultural contexts, participation is required. Grief demands that we attend to it, and our obligations to each other mean that we show up. In Native North America, a death draws everyone back home. Attendance at funerals—even if they are not a close relative—is expected. And rarely are these half-day affairs. Instead, loss often calls the community together for a week or more. In her book *The Art of Ceremony*, Rebecca Dobkins cites Warm Springs tribal member Rosalind "Rosie" Johnson's description of her community's traditions.[5] When death takes place, family and community immediately come together. The bereaved are surrounded with support. On the day of the funeral, extended family members are there to help the bereaved change into new, black clothing, and cut their hair. They help to prepare the body, which will be wrapped, put in a casket, and placed on a tule mat in the ceremonial longhouse. Emotions are expected and encouraged, and a particular ceremonial time and space is created to help mourners express their sorrow. The Cry Service "opens up their hearts to cry, releasing themselves of hurt .... Those gathered weep and let go of their grief, knowing that to do otherwise could make them sick."

But while sorrowing is necessary, the bereaved are not left in that heavy place. Ceremony helps lift them up and out. In this case, the Cry Service is followed by a meal, conducted with reverence by a spiritual leader and centered on traditional first foods. Songs are sung to acknowledge their non-human relatives, to express gratitude, and remember the many ties that bind the extended family of creation. "A small tule mat with eating utensils is placed at the head of the table for the deceased, whose food is served first before the rest of those gathered may eat. The mat and utensils are later placed at the head of the freshly covered grave."[6] Then, stories are shared, eliciting both tears and laughter, and a giveaway concludes the gathering, thanking those who have helped. A spouse will be in mourning for a year, but on the anniversary of their death, a memorial giveaway will be held to honor the dead, express gratitude to the community, and signal an end to that time of mourning. It is at this time that family members will be formally asked to take up new roles, and names will also be passed on.

Grieving demands a degree of interiority, of bare honesty that can be hard to find in the company of others. But every religious and spiritual tradition the world over will tell you that grieving is not meant to be done in isolation. Grief is powerful and perilous, with potential to determine the course of our future. Caring community helps ensure that grief does not become despair. In times of loss, we are reminded of the relationships that sustain us.

African American theologians Rachel Elizabeth Harding and Rosemarie Freeney Harding describe a childhood in which

> The dying were never left alone, and children were included in the process of comforting and encouraging them ... I grew up with a great respect for death, but no fear of it. It was a very sacred time .... It gave me a sense of how one balances one's own grief with the need to encourage a dying person to leave amid as much happiness as possible ... We learned to laugh and joke and have a good time in life, and simultaneously to understand that life means mourning too.

The authors describes death as a time for gathering, where the wake and the funeral dinner replace loss with a sense of shared abundance, where familial ties are reestablished, relatives (re)introduced. "It is as if in compensation for the loss, we use the time of death as an opportunity to assert the continuity of life, the line going on."[7]

If we want to metabolize our climate grief into purposeful action, remember the lessons offered here. First, this is not an optional activity. We all need safe spaces to give expression to our grief—whether we are feeling angry, or lost, or filled with sorrow. Emotions need to move through us. But those emotions are powerful, and potentially dangerous. So we need safe, culturally appropriate spaces where that can happen. We need the supportive arms of community—whatever that community looks like for you. We need elders, mentors, and teachers who can help create that safe space, and guide our movement through it. And we need to include food, story, and laughter, knowing that we can return to spaces of sorrowing if and when we need to.

Lesson #3: Temporal boundaries

Britt Wray writes that, "in this time of ecological unraveling," we need "times out of time that we can step into together, where it is acceptable to say, 'I'm not personally okay with this. I'm feeling absolutely devastated.'"[8] Reflecting the dangers of *uncontained* grief, human beings the world over have sought to create safe spaces for the anger, confusion, and despair of loss. Comparative religious studies can help us see how different traditions create *sacred time*, and how they set those times apart. There may be strict protocols for proper behavior, including restrictions on activities, clothing, or food. Or, the normal rules of everyday life may be temporarily suspended, amidst excesses of drink or emotional expression. But always, these are understood to be times of intense vulnerability, so we surround each other with protection and care.

The Jewish tradition recognizes the dangers of uncontained grief. After the loss of a loved one, grieving families will *sit shiva*: seven days of deep mourning at home. Mirrors are covered: mourners are not expected to worry about their appearance—in fact, it's discouraged. A constant stream of visitors will stop by, but there is no requirement that grieving family members speak to guests, or perform the duties of a host. Guests simply sit in companionable silence, speaking only if mourners want to talk. The bereaved are permitted to simply grieve, however they need to do so, supported by their community.

But this unrestrained grief is not unbounded. At the end of those seven days, mourners are expected to dress, go outside, and walk around the block. It's a simple gesture, but a clear symbol of the call to begin gradually re-entering the world. This begins the *sheloshim*, a 30-day mourning period during which close family members will continue to restrict their behavior, not worrying about physical appearance, and avoiding social engagements. The one-year anniversary of death—the *yahrzeit*—marks the end of formal morning. Mourners are encouraged to get a haircut, put on new clothes, and attend services, where the *kaddish* will be recited in honor of the dead. Novelist Anita Diamant describes this movement through the stages of Jewish mourning as a series of concentric circles.

"The innermost circle is the darkest, but as the weeks pass, mourners move from the dimness of remembering and weeping, to the light of rejoicing in memory and to life itself."[9]

We need to create containers for our anger, bewilderment, and despair; safe spaces where those raw wounds of grief won't grate against the world's rough edges. The reality is, we need ritual spaces in our lives for grieving ecological loss, spaces that are marked by a clear beginning and a clear end. Not because grief ends, but because we need to learn to live alongside our grief—and not be consumed by it. Considering traditions like these reminds us that we move through the concentric spheres of grief—sometimes pausing in the darkest center, and sometimes moving outward, finding strength to support others. These are reminders that we need outlets for our grief, so as not to be consumed by it.

When Angie sat down to talk with me after a recent speaking event, it was clear that she was exhausted. A marine conservationist, she had been working nonstop. Worried that funding could be cut at any time, she was desperate to do as much as possible, while she still could. But it was clearly taking a toll, and she was close to tears. "I don't have time to lose it," she told me. "I've got kids at home, work to be done." But she decided to start giving herself one half-hour a week. She'd set a timer, maybe light a candle. Meditate, collage, scream into a pillow if that's all she could do. This would be alone-time, but she wouldn't be alone. "I'm going to tell my girlfriend to be on standby," she explained. "When the time is up, I'll give her a call. Maybe we can go for a walk. It's not much," she said, "but it's a start."

Being intentional about creating bounded space for feeling the feels will mean different things for all of us. It might mean 15 minutes for prayer and meditation each day, maybe marked by a timer or the lighting of a candle. It may mean showing up to a weekly gathering or meditation group. It may mean making time for creativity, a hike, or a cathartic run. When my friend Imam Jamal Rahman finds himself struggling with grief or worries, he offers them a gift of time. "Alright, my worries," he says. "You have twenty minutes. I will sit with you and ask Allah to help me carry you. But at the end of those twenty minutes, we will go our separate ways. I'll see you again tomorrow." If there is one clear lesson from grieving traditions, it is that the health of our souls and our communities depend on acknowledging that we need time out—to come to grips with what we have lost, and who we are now called to be. And, that such times must be bounded. Grief is potent stuff—with power both creative and destructive. To channel our grief into work that heals, we must make sure to border it—with limits of time, and a community of care.

Lesson #4: Tell the stories

Maya Lin is one of the United States' most well-known architects and designers. She was just twenty-one when she created the design for the national Vietnam War Memorial, and since 2010, she has been building a digital monument to commemorate lost species. *What is Missing* (whatismissing.org) is a web-based memorial, existing in many forms and engaging with locations, communities, and species around the world, using sound, media, and science to tell the story of the sixth mass extinction, and the projected loss of 50 percent of our biodiversity by 2050. The site evokes grief, it expresses sorrow, and it also turns us with renewed fervor toward the creation of solutions.

To metabolize something is to digest it, to turn food into fuel. We take the sacrifice of life—after all, every bite of food is a sacrifice of some kind or another—and transmute it into energy and action. In the same way, metabolizing grief is a fundamentally creative act. And when it comes to transformative grief, that creative work is often the work of story-making. We tell the stories of those we have lost, and in doing so we are also constructing our future. Implicit in the story is the question: *because they were, who am I now? Who must I now become?* It's the storytelling that happens in the "chat" at the Irish wake, the stories at the Buddhist funeral meal, or in the laughter that follows the cry ceremony at Warm Springs.

We also tell these stories through the creation of memorials—both public and personal. Many sacred traditions include the creation of centering spaces in the home—focal points for personal prayer and meditation that ground us in values and connect us with ancestors and sources of spiritual power. In Japanese Buddhism, *butsudan* are home shrines to honor ancestors that serve as centers of domestic religious life. Simple ritual gestures—offerings of incense, food, or tea—contain a wealth of meanings: the continued presence of ancestors and how those ancestors have shaped the present, obligations to uphold familial values, and a sense of continuity between generations. Adherents to the tradition of Yoruba likewise build home altars. Here, members of the African diaspora create a sacred center that represents unnamed ancestors, invoking their presence, and requesting their assistance. On the Day of the Dead, Oaxacan families in Mexico build beautiful altars, lavish works of art that sustain memory and affirm the relationship between the living and the dead, the individual and their community.

Rather than a physical shrine, Coast Salish communities of Puget Sound keep the memory and presence of ancestors by passing on their names, songs, and stories. In naming ceremonies individuals take up the responsibility to "wear" their ancestor's name, to "keep it clean," and respect it through living an honorable life. Songs are likewise gifted, and when sung, the breath of ancestors are present once more.

But how do we memorialize *collective* losses? How do we grieve ecological devastation? And why should we? In her essay "Precarious Life: The Powers of Mourning and Violence," Judith Butler argues that collective, public mourning has the potential to create a "political community," one that cares for each other, while demanding the transformation of unjust systems. Collective ceremony—rites of remembering—are powerful, because they transform not just individual understanding, but collective identity. Such ceremonies may happen in physical spaces, such as the Vietnam War Memorial, Ground Zero, or Stonewall. But many of the most impactful memorials are built in time. In Israel, *Yom Hashoah v'Gevurah* is a day set aside to commemorate the Holocaust and the Warsaw Uprising. At 8:00 a.m., a two-minute air raid siren sounds throughout the country. Cars come to a stop. Drivers exit. Everyone stands in silence. Those two minutes are "the one ritual text shared by all in Israel .... For the very act of commemoration provides a common experience for a population otherwise divided by innumerable disparate lives."[10] Or consider Canada's Truth and Reconciliation Day, which falls on September 30, also known as Orange Shirt Day. It is marked by marches and vigils commemorating the thousands of First Nations children lost to the abuses of residential boarding schools. Sacred time, symbolic clothing, and movement through space coalesce to honor the lost, acknowledge the harm caused, and recognize the country's obligations to those who survived. In other parts of Native North America, memorial walks honor and remember victims of genocide on the Cherokee Trail of Tears, or the Navajo Long Walk. Memorial horseback rides honor Nimiipuu (Nez Perce) Chief Joseph's flight from the US Army, Nisqually Chief Leschi's last ride before his assassination, or the tragic journey of Dakota warriors executed by the US government. But we have also begun creating public memorials for ecological losses as well.

November 30 is Remembrance Day for Lost Species, a day when growing numbers around the world gather to lament what we have lost. In August of 2025, Greenpeace activists scaled a gas rig in the North Sea, and unfurled a massive blood-stained canvas. (The "blood" was beetroot powder and seawater.) Designed by sculptor

Anish Kapoor, the piece was titled "Butchered," and it was both a memorial and a protest, an effort to tell the story of "the destruction—the bleeding—of our globe and our state of being," and an attempt to disrupt our "collective amnesia around the real causes of climate breakdown."[11] In works of art, parades, protests, funerals, and rites of collective grief, participants acknowledge where humanity has fallen short, and demand a different kind of future.

Here's what we must remember: these rites of remembering are also rites of creation. They are acts of mythopoesis, ceremonial reenactments of our origin stories, those powerful stories that tell us who and why we are. In the midst of climate change, we must hold dear each loss, we must remember the places and species that gave us life. We must wrap ourselves in those stories, daily make offerings at their altars, so that we remember our relational obligations, the debts we can never repay. This, I think, is the work of artists, and novelists, and poets, of scientists, and journalists, this crafting of our eco-memorials, this work of sacred storytelling.

Lesson #5: Lament can change the world

In 2018, people throughout the Salish Sea and around the world grieved with Tahlequa, a mother orca who carried her dead calf, Tali, for seventeen painful days, traveling over 1,000 miles as she did so. Every parent who had lost a child, or feared losing one, could share in that horrible grief. It was a heartbreaking story, and sadly one that would be repeated in 2024, when Tahlequa lost another baby. Tribal members and many within the general public accompanied her in grief, creating works of art and ceremonies of solidarity. And, in doing so, they began to tell another story of life in this region, planting seeds for a different way of seeing ourselves in relation to our Salish Sea. We began talking more about declining salmon runs, pollution, dam removal, and sea lion overpopulation. Governor Jay Inslee committed to doing more, and new legislation was passed, aiming to protect orcas and restore dwindling salmon runs. Because of this new, emerging story, the boundaries between land and water parents have grown a little thinner, and our solidarity with other mammal-mothers has become a little stronger.

Tahlequa's story invites us to ask: how do we turn personal grief into collective transformation? For me, the answer centers on the idea of lament—creative, collective, expressions of sorrow grounded in a belief in justice, and a faith that the world must rise to become what it is intended to be. The transformative potential of lament is profound. Because the fact of the matter is this: the stories we tell about the dead have political and social consequences.

The funerals of enslaved African Americans were restricted in the antebellum South: no more than twelve people were permitted to attend. They were told to rein in their emotions. Only allowed to wear signs of mourning for a few days. (And even that was outlawed after Denmark Vesey's attempted uprising in 1822.) Slave holders knew that funerals had political power to create solidarity, to affirm one's humanity—and so to undermine an economic system that depended on the dehumanization of others.

During the Irish War for Independence (1919–21), Irish soldiers executed by the British were honored with lavish public funerals, processions that filled the streets and were attended by thousands, documented in photographs, covered by the press, and memorialized in song, obituaries, and testimony. Dramatic enactments of collective mourning, these public funerals united Irish people of all faiths and helped to shape a modern, independent, national identity. As literary scholar Allan Hepburn has argued, each revolutionary death came to represent "an archive of loss—lost citizens, lost heroes, lost opportunities, lost aspirations for the nation."[12]

When Emmett Till was murdered by white supremacists in 1955, his mother insisted on an open casket funeral, "Let the people see what they did to my boy," a bereaved Mamie Till said. More recently, in the wake of the killing of George Floyd, protests across the country brought anger and despair into the streets. Known as the "Mothers of the Movement," Mammie Till (Emmet Till's mother), Sybrina Fulton (Trayvon Martin's mother), and Lucia McBath (Jordan Davis's mother) brought their private grief into the public sphere, and in so doing issued an indictment against unjust systems that devalue the lives of Black people—and young Black men in particular. As Fulton said, "If they refuse to hear us, we will make them *feel* us .... Feeling us means feeling our pain; imagining our plight as parents of slain children."[13]

In 2010, Nuu-chah-nulth wood carver John T. Williams was murdered by a Seattle police officer. His family responded by carving a memorial totem pole, and leading a public procession of that pole from its carving site on the waterfront to Seattle Center, where hundreds of people gathered for its raising. (In Native Northwest culture, memorial poles are carved to honor the dead and their life; they are typically raised on the one-year anniversary of their passing.) The pole now stands in a place of prominence below the Space Needle, a testimony to Williams's life, his art, and the continued presence of Indigenous people in Seattle.

I share these examples, because they illustrate a lesson that climate activists should take to heart: the power of lament to change the world. Lament happens within public, heart-felt, creative ceremonies of outrage and pain. Lament is an artform, often extemporaneous, often gendered, that speaks truth to power. In Biblical studies, it is described as a dialogue with God, one that includes both penitence and protest. In lament, we acknowledge where we have fallen short, but we also call God—and others—to account. Lament takes us from personal sorrow to collective grief, to solidarity, justice, and joy.[14]

Lament is biblical. Job. Lamentations. Psalms.

Jesus lamented.

Brutally honest, lament makes clear what we value, and demands that the world live up to its promise. And because of that, lament has more to do with stubborn hope than despair. W. E. B. DuBois described African American spirituals as "sorrow songs," within which "there breathes a hope—a faith in the ultimate justice of things," even while "such hope does not, however, entail an expectation of fulfillment." It is "hope against hope," "both a lamentation and an expression of resistance." Where "the *ought* and *should*, prevailed over the *was*."[15]

My favorite essay on lament is by the luminous Cole Arthur Riley, who describes the relationship between lament and hope:

> In lament, our task is never to convince someone of the brokenness of this world; it is to convince them of the world's worth in the first place. True lament is not born from that trite sentiment that the world is bad, but rather from the deep conviction that it is worthy of goodness.
>
> Lament is not anti-hope. It's not even a stepping-stone to hope. Lament is itself a form of hope. It is an innate awareness that what is should not be. As if something is written on our hearts that tells us exactly what we are meant for, and whenever confronted with something contrary to this, we experience a crumbling. And in the rubble, we say, God, you promised. We ask, Why? And how could we experience such a devastation if we were not on some mysterious plane, hoping for something different. Our hope can be only as deep as our lament is. And our lament as deep as our hope.[16]

Lament is a force of change that is both spiritually and politically charged—because it is an expression of *relational* grieving. Ceremonies of lament are technologies of connection, and they are the means by which our pain becomes the immutable force of moral relationships, the means by which those relationships are restored to harmony. Lament is where we enter into dialogue between God and me, between me and other human beings, between me and this precious Earth that I have failed, and that I feel failing around me. Lament is an invitation to face the reality of one's situation with bare honesty, in all its emotional weight—and to do so knowing that one is not alone, but in the presence of Spirit, and in the midst of the lamenting crowd.

The lament tradition rests on the assumption that such expressions of grief have power to move God to action, and to change the world in which we live. In Jewish scripture, lament is so powerful, it can change God's mind. In the book of Job, his lament is a wailing *why*, a demand that God be present with his grief. Lament is the opposite of giving up—it is where we wrestle. Even at its most bitter, lament is still an act of faith, and an insistence that change is possible.

Looking ahead

"The Irish funeral howl is notorious," wrote one nineteenth-century observer. And, indeed, Irish wakes were infamous for their lamentations. Professional keeners, women skilled at this loud, public, improvised song, led the lament. One observer wrote: "Each old woman, as she took her turn in the leading recitative, seemed possessed for the moment with a profound ecstasy of grief, swaying to and fro, and bending her forehead to the stone before her, while she called out to the dead with a perpetually recurring chant of sobs."[17] The most famous of these compositions was first written down in 1800. Four-hundred lines long, it is a tour de force, in which the singer curses her husband's murderer, unleashing "love, loss, guilt, grief, pity, family pride, anger and revenge."[18] In a patriarchal society governed by a male-dominated church, the lament was one space where women could, quite literally, have the last word. Keeners publicly accused murderers, and sometimes even shamed the dead for their lives of abuse or neglect.

The climate movement needs keeners. Skilled poets and musicians whose broken hearts have made room for the spirit of loving sorrow and righteous anger. Our grief for a wounded world bewilders us—we become lost in the wilds of it, unable to find our bearings. And keeners—prophetic voices that express our pain and demand recompense—help us find our way back to ourselves and each other. They remind us that grief is not pathological—but an expression of love, an acknowledgment of our intertwining, and an opportunity to draw from that love to insist upon a future that honors what we have lost.

Such keening may look different these days. Earth Day marches, student strikes for climate, a lone protestor scaling a tree, a ceremony for a mother orca. But do not underestimate their power. Because, as African American theologian Barbara Holmes explains: "Lament is risky … because it challenges power structures, it calls for justice, and it makes demands on our relationships with the 'powers that be,' one another, and God. Once lament is released it cannot be recalled."[19]

Members of the Confederated Colville Tribes continue to gather at *Shonitkwu*. The falls still lie beneath 70 feet of water. But each year the people remember their relationship with salmon. Their songs and prayers are an expression of pain and loss. They call on the Creator, and settler colonial society, to right a historic wrong. Their lament manifests through construction projects that build alternative salmon passage around the dams, in prayers that accompany the release of fry, and in first salmon ceremonies that celebrate the first fish to return to their natal waters in decades. But eighty years is nothing to salmon—they've inhabited this part of the world for *millions* of years after all.

The people who have cared for them since time immemorial are still here. And dams do not last forever.

This chapter is about grief, and it is about hope. When we create safe liminal spaces for climate grief, surrounded by community, and bounded by time, when we tell the stories of what we have lost, and when we call the powers that be to account, we perform a kind of magic. It's the kind of magic that Tom Driver talked about, the magic of ritual and ceremony that changes our relationship with the world, and our other-than-human relatives. Climate change and its impacts will be with us for the rest of our lives. We will continue to experience new losses. This is not something to *get over*, but a sorrow we will continually return to, with care, reverence, and remembering. Because when we grieve together, we have an opportunity to re-write our collective stories: and those stories can change the world.

Key takeaways

1. Climate grief is complex, and isn't just about being sad or anxious: it encompasses denial, anger, bargaining, sorrow, and determination. And those emotions can turn up in many different ways.
2. Grieving is not optional—religious and Indigenous traditions help us see that it's essential we show up for ourselves, and to support others. Our mental and spiritual health demands that we attend to the difficult feelings that climate change evokes.
3. Grieving is a rite of passage—it marks both an end, and a beginning. It's a liminal experience that—if done well—helps guide us into a new identity and a new way of being. In an era of climate change, we need to ask: who are we called to become in this new, emerging world?

4 Grieving is powerful, and potentially transformative. And because of that, it should be approached with care. Set aside bounded time for grief. We may at times sorrow alone, but don't grieve in isolation. Find your community, and show up to support those who are in pain.

5 Grieving is about the stories we tell—about where we come from, and how we've been shaped by those we've lost. We need to memorialize the people, seasons, ecosystems, and species we have lost, to honor their memories, and consider what they have to teach us.

6 Public grieving, and traditions of lament, are ways of speaking truth to power—they are expressions of sorrow, outrage, and hope, and they provide a means of accessing the transformative power of ceremony.

Invitation for further reflection

1 Think about how you might name or express the feelings you have around climate change. This might be speaking with someone you trust, journaling, or another form of creative expression.

2 How might you carve out intentional time in your day, week, month, or year to do the work of grieving? How can you find places to do this with others? For some of us, this might look like a collective ritual. For others, it may simply mean an honest talk with a friend. Or it may mean time alone, but making a plan to connect with loved ones afterward.

3 Are there creative ways you or your community might grieve the loss of species or places that matter to you? Brainstorm a grieving ritual, or design a memorial for a lost species or a

particular place. It could be an event, an activity, a physical memorial, a performance, or a work of art. Remember to include spatial and temporal boundaries, and to include community.

4. Do you have knowledge or expertise in a particular religious or cultural tradition, or access to that knowledge? What does that tradition teach us about mourning, loss, lament, and healing?

Want to learn more?

Visit our website at https://bloomsbury.pub/climate-spirit where you'll find recommendations for further reading and resources for individuals, reading groups, and educators.

4

Feeding resilience

The final scramble of this mountain trail rewards us with a stunning view of Mt. Rainier's southern flank, gleaming in the distance. I've scarcely reached the top when vertigo hits me hard. *Well, this is new.* I've always been eager to reach a peak, hungry for that rush you get standing at a cliff's edge, sweat cooling in the blast of an updraft. But today my head swims, heart clenching in my chest, and I make a quick retreat. Becoming a mother has changed me in ways I'm only just starting to realize, and this appears to be one of them. I have zero interest in being anywhere near that cliff edge.

I take Declan from the carrier on my husband's back, and we head back down the trail, stopping when we reach a sheltered spot, overlooking alpine meadows rich with bluing lupine. He fusses, so we settle in to nurse. I've grown used to the painful ache of milk letting down, so I clench my teeth and let it pass, knowing it will be followed by that luscious full-body wave of oxytocin—a warm rush of intoxicating affection. I understand the chemistry involved, but I still call it love.

Up above, our friends are laughing, hollering for their boys to come back from the edge. I breathe deep, thankful for the Earth solid beneath me. From up here I can see snow-capped Pahto (Mt. Adams) and Lawetla'la (Mt. St. Helens), and remember a story about how these mountains were once the wives of Tahoma (Mt. Rainier), sisters who scattered their dowries of salmon and huckleberries across undulating hills. Nisqually teachings describe these volcanoes as lactating mothers, feeding the landscapes with white rivers, rich with glacial silt. I think about mothers, and this soul-deep need to feed our children.

It reminds me of Robin Wall Kimmerer's essay "Epiphany in the Beans," where she comes to a similar revelation—right smack in the middle of her garden.

> Maybe it was the smell of ripe tomatoes or the oriole singing, or that certain slant of light on a yellow afternoon and the beans hanging thick around me. It just came to me in a wash of happiness that made me laugh out loud, startling the chickadees who were picking at the sunflowers, raining black and white hulls on the ground. I knew it with a certainty as warm and clear as the September sunshine. *The land loves us back.* She loves us with beans and tomatoes, with roasting ears and blackberries and birdsongs. By a shower of gifts and a heavy rain of leaves. She provides for us and teaches us to provide for ourselves. That's what good mothers do.[1]

I'm not sure there's any expression of love more fundamental than food, this primal human need that feeds body and soul.

And maybe what's why I so often think, when faced as we are with the anger, disbelief, despair, and exhaustion of environmental grief, that the first thing we need to do is *eat something*.

In his work on managing stress and traumatic experiences, psychologist Dan Siegel advises us to expand our "window of tolerance," the conditions in which we can remain firmly rooted in our prefrontal cortex, able to respond to stress with our greatest degree of emotional resilience and creative problem solving. The tools for keeping that window wide open are no big secret: eat, sleep, exercise.

Of course, it's not about eating *just anything.* What and how we eat matters. In fact, we're learning more and more about the relationship between a healthy gut biome and mental and emotional health. Turns out, our gut creates and regulates vital neurotransmitters and hormones like serotonin, dopamine, norepinephrine, and gamma-aminobutyric acid (GABA). Serotonin and dopamine regulate our mood, norepinephrine triggers our fight, flight, or freeze response, while GABA balances those triggers, lowering anxiety and quieting the nervous system. The interaction between our digestive system, mood, and mental clarity is so strong that some researchers refer to it as our "gut brain." What we eat has big impacts on our brain chemistry.[2]

But food isn't just about our gut biome or blood sugar levels. Food lies at the heart of religious and spiritual traditions the world over. (I have a working hypothesis that our need to eat is the origin of every religious tradition in human history, that our ancestors' necessity for nourishment inspired their earliest ceremonies.) Paying attention—really paying attention—to what we eat and where our food comes from, is truly illuminating. Is there any more visceral way to realize our interdependency with the natural world? Spiritual resilience relies on restoring moral relationships with our human community, ancestors, Earth, and Spirit, and that can feel like a pretty lofty goal. But the good news is, every time we sit down to eat, every bite we take, is an opportunity to restore and renew those relationships.

And besides this, eating with purpose and meaning has climate consequences. Globally, industrial food systems account for twenty-two percent of the world's greenhouse gasses, and are the largest driver of habitat and biodiversity loss. Fertilizer runoff is the world's biggest water polluter, more than doubling the amount of nitrogen and phosphorus in our waterways. Food systems are also the thirstiest, drawing 85 percent of our consumptive water use (although AI data centers may soon outpace them).[3] Changing the way we produce and consume food is essential if we're to build a sustainable world.

Of course, this isn't the only way to feed ourselves. Indigenous food systems sustained people for millennia, without polluting waters or depleting soil. To understand how they did it, Environmental Humanities professor Mariaelena Huambachano (Quechua) conducted a comparative study of Māori and Andean food systems, finding that they are both "based on a kinship-centric system wherein all community members, human and non-human (deities, rivers, mountains), have duties and responsibilities to respect Nature and care for one another." Huambachano explains that the Quechua term *allin kawsay*, often translated as "living well," actually means a great deal more than that. It means "showing respect, love, and care with your community members, your family, and with *apu* (Andean deity) *Ausangate*, rivers, lakes, animals and plants." At heart, it's an understanding that our well-being is intricately and inseparably tied to our waters and soil, that, "if this land is healthy, our foods will be healthy, and our physical and spiritual bodies will be healthy."[4] In short, Indigenous food systems are grounded in moral, harmonious relationships with a sentient world. Moral relationships are guided by values of reciprocity, reverence, and responsibility, which ensure a healthy overall ecosystem.

This is not the stewardship or dominion model of nature care that is often found in monotheistic traditions. Rather, it's a model in which human beings act in partnership with other species. As Yurok tribal member and forestry professor Seafha Ramos explains, "Yurok people and wildlife collaboratively strive to create and maintain balance of the Earth via physical and spiritual management in tandem."[5] From Zuni waffle gardens and dryland farming in New Mexico, to Swinomish clam gardens in Puget Sound, to Koyukon hunting protocols in central Alaska, Indigenous food systems exemplify a world in which what and how you eat is grounded in relationality. This is something we need to pay attention to. Because Indigenous food systems provide a model for a way of feeding ourselves that also nourishes our plant, animal, and water relatives.

To help us get there, this chapter introduces four ways to think differently about how we eat, cultivating spiritual, social, and ecological resilience along the way. These are different practices, from widely varying traditions, but they all do the work of restoring moral relationships with the natural world. They all provide pathways for transmuting climate grief and anxiety into purposeful action, building internal resilience, while connecting us to wider systems of transformative care.

#1: Mindful eating

A 2025 study published in the journal of *Food Science and Nutrition* has found a positive association between mindful eating, improved psychological well-being and climate change awareness, highlighting ties between sustainable nutrition and mental health.[6] According to the findings, when a heart-healthy and climate-friendly diet was accompanied by mindful eating practices, individuals reported both a growing awareness of climate change *and* improved mental health. Here, mindful eating was defined as "focusing on the food to be consumed at that moment, being aware of why and how eating behavior occurs, internal (such as emotion, thought) and external (such as situation, event) factors that affect hunger and awareness." The study raises the question: how can paying attention to one's experience of eating help us transform our climate grief into purposeful action? A closer look at Buddhist traditions of mindful eating may help us begin to understand just that.

We already know that climate change is bad for our mental health. It exacerbates existing concerns and elevates risks of depression, anxiety, and suicidal ideation, while triggering our brain's trauma responses. In her book *Occupy This Body: A Buddhist Memoir,* Buddhist studies scholar Sharon Suh explains how Buddhist meditation and mindful eating aided her recovery from childhood trauma, abuse, and disordered eating. For Suh, body scan meditation, and mindful cooking and eating empowered her to assert her right to take up space, to trust her body, and feel safe in the world. Rather than seeing food as an enemy, she came to see it as an opportunity for care, and a space of joy. Mindful eating offered a path toward restoring relational harmony with her body and the world around her.[7]

Mindful eating also provides a simple path toward reclaiming the ceremonial within our everyday lives. In his book *No Recipe: Cooking as Spiritual Practice*, Zen Buddhist chef Joseph Espe Brown encourages us to restore a degree of ceremony to our table. Rather than eating mindlessly, he invites us to create space for being fully present with our food, and with each other. But Brown also cautions against *over ritualization*, reflecting on his own experience in community when rituals around food became so time consuming that he and his fellow monastics were forced to eat at a frantic pace, scarcely aware of what they were putting into their mouths. Now, as an elder in his community, he simply asks those he serves to "please enjoy your food."[8]

Helpfully, Brown goes on to define what he means by "enjoy." Brown's understanding of joy in the Buddhist tradition is: "awareness resonating with or being moved by the object of awareness .... Joy offers a way for our awareness to connect with objects," and to do so in a way that is "profoundly satisfying, so that we feel truly nourished."[9] Mindful eating can thus become an embodied meditation on the interconnected and interdependent nature of all beings, inspiring gratitude, compassion, and purposeful action. As we acknowledge the labor, gifts, and sacrifices required for each bite we take, we awaken to the radical relationality of our world. Brown explains that Buddhist teachings advise us to eat with awareness and to minimize the suffering of other beings whenever possible; to be fully present in the moment so we can receive the insight our food can provide.

According to the Plum Village Zen Buddhist tradition and the teachings of Thich Nhat Hanh, we are not only sustained by food, but also by *the four nutriments*: food and drink, sense impressions, volition or will, and consciousness or states of mind.[10] In this teaching we are encouraged to be mindful of what we eat, but also of those things that feed our insight, compassion, and awareness. What sounds, sights, tastes, and smells do we seek out? What perspectives or information do we take in? While we cannot isolate ourselves from the world and its challenges, we also have myriad opportunities to choose to what and whom we bring our attention. This aligns well with the advice of many climate psychologists who recommend adopting a "media diet," to be mindful of what, when, and how much media we consume. Neuroscientist Daniel Levitin, author of *The Organized Mind*, argues that media consumption can have real impacts on brain function: when we enter a state of information-overload our brains lose their capacity to distinguish between the trivial and the important. Even the smallest bad news can break our heart or send us into a rage.[11] In an era when negative climate news comes fast and furious, being mindful about the media we ingest may be more essential than ever. Thich Nhat Hanh advises his students to "feed what you want to grow," fueling those values, motivations, perspectives and states of mind that sustain us, and starving those that do not.

Jan Chozen Bays is a pediatrician and Zen teacher. In her book *Mindful Eating: A Guide to Rediscovering a Healthy and Joyful*

Relationship with Food, Bays provides both practical guidance and an exploration of the ways in which mindful eating can support a life of attention and practice.[12] As Bays' work helps to show, mindfulness practices—and mindful eating in particular—are powerful because they ground us in the present moment, freeing us from our fixation on the past and from our catastrophizing of the future. They restore us to the immediate, to this bite, this taste on my tongue. And, in doing so, they free us to live *now.*

But eating is different than other mindfulness practices, because it also grounds us in the relationships that sustain us. Each bite is an opportunity to be mindful of the myriad elements coalescing in this miraculous moment: Nutrients and microorganisms in the soil. Wind, sun, and rain. Generations of seeds and seed-keepers. Pollinators and propagators. Sowers and harvesters. Pausing to acknowledge each bite, to contemplate the food web upon which this taste depends, helps us realize our interdependency and interconnectedness with the world around us. The food nourishes us, but it is also an embodied remembering of the relationships that sustain us. Mindful eating is a practice with the potential to inspire climate-friendly food choices and to mobilize us to work for systemic change.

#2: Sacramental eating

On this brilliant August day, I'm a guest at the Squaxin Island tribe's first salmon ceremony. Squinting into the sun, I watch as the canoe casts off from the rocky shore. Only an hour or so before, the crew brought Mother Salmon to us, welcomed like an honored guest, greeted with song on a bed of cedar branches, and carried up a path lined by cedar fronds (the Salish Sea version of a red carpet). Carefully filleted, the salmon was prepared so that everyone present could have at least one sacramental bite.

In traditional teachings, salmon people come from a village under the sea, putting on their salmon cloaks and traveling to their natal rivers to visit their human relatives, offering up their lives so that those distant cousins can live. In return, the human people promise to care for the waters, to clear the way, and to return their bones to the sea, so they can travel back home, and be reborn. It's a sacred covenant between people and salmon. And on this day, I watch as the young woman in the canoe leans over its edge, carefully returning the salmon's remains to the water. Goosebumps shiver down my arms. This is what resurrection ecology looks like.

It's also an example of what I call sacramental eating: moments when food embodies—not figuratively but in a material, ingestible way—a profound spiritual truth. In this case, that truth is the covenantal relationship of kinship. Origin stories throughout the Pacific Northwest describe the moment when Creator made human beings. Other species were concerned, to say the least. These new creatures were feeble and helpless, without fur, feathers, or scales. They didn't have claws or speed. They were nearly blind, could scarcely hear, or smell. How in the world would they survive? Creator responded by asking for volunteers to help these (pretty pathetic) cousins. In many stories, salmon were the first to volunteer, offering their bodies in exchange for a promise that the humans would show them respect, honor their sacrifice, and place their remains in the river, heads pointed toward the sea, so that they could return to their ocean-homes and be reborn. In some traditions, the salmon also gave the people their voice, in return for the promise that humans would speak for the salmon, advocating for their needs. For Coast Salish people, kinship means a sacred obligation of respect, reverence, and care.

Albert Raboteau, professor of African American religious history, defined "sacrament" as those instances in which a spiritual reality "coinheres" with the material, when it takes physical form.[13] *And then we eat it.* We bring that spiritual reality into our bodies. Through the fleshy experience of chewing and swallowing it *becomes* us. How amazing is that? When a Christian participates in the eucharist they are bringing God-made-manifest into their very own bodies, and, in that act, their own body becomes an extension of a Creator who is present within creation, who is manifest in grain, grapes, sun, soil, water, bread baker, wine maker, and congregation. When a Jewish person joins a sabbath seder, they are affirming through bread and wine their people's covenant with God, and the commandment to rest. When they participate in Passover, eating each symbolic food on the seder plate, they are affirming their part in the common history of their people, that they "were once slaves in Egypt," that they longed for a homeland, and so understand the suffering of others. Each food on the plate becomes a doorway to a story, each a spiritual truth to be taken in, consumed, transmuted into energy.

In Native North America, the term "First Foods" refers to the traditional foods of their ancestors, and in many communities these sacred foods are honored in ceremonies that affirm reciprocal obligations, and remind the people of their kinship with and obligations to care for the land. These are not considered merely resources, but teachers and relatives. On the Columbia Plateau, the Confederated Tribes of the Umatilla went so far as to integrate their natural resources and cultural resources departments, re-organizing their work around their four sacred foods: roots, salmon, berries, and game. In Plateau traditions, foods are categorized by social and geographic location: women are responsible for plant foods, men for fish and game, and each are honored in a seasonal ceremony, always accompanied by water—the first and most sacred gift from Creator.

Among the Rarámuri of northern Mexico, corn is honored as an ancestor. In one origin story, a great catastrophe took place, and the people were nearly extinct. Only two children remained. Their community was restored when new relatives were born from an ear of corn. On Haida Gwaii, off the coast of British Columbia, Raven finds the first people in a clam shell. Among the Skokomish of western Washington, the last survivor of a devastated village is transformed into a salmon, marries into a salmon clan, and returns to her human form in time to give birth to human children—with salmon ancestry. In the southeast, stories of Corn Mother describe a matriarch who sacrifices her own life to feed her people. The first corn plants emerge from her grave. In the Northwest, camas bulbs are the gift of a grandmother, transformed into food as she grieves for her starving grandchildren. Throughout Turtle Island, ancestral foods and heritage seeds are considered relatives and ancestors, and sacramental eating, framed with sacred ceremony, keep these lessons alive. Sacramental eating happens when we reenact the stories at the heart of who we are and who we hope to be. Usually, this is a sacred rite. But a sacramental *approach* can be taken up anytime, in any meal, offering a daily opportunity to perform a mini-miracle: transforming grief into gratitude, loss into energy for action.

What might this look like? First, remember that sacramental foods—these most sacred expressions of profound truths—are usually the *least special foods*. They're the daily, sustaining foods, the ones accessible to even the poorest among us. Jesus didn't eat bread and wine because he was rich, but because it was simple, widely available food. Before settler colonialism devastated our rivers, Native people in the Northwest might eat salmon three times a day. Corn was and is a staple that sustains nations. Anishinaabe people founded their homes and their communities where wild rice (*manoomin*) was abundant.

This is important, because a sacramental approach to eating is *our invitation to find the holy in the daily*, the revelation within the mundane. The mystery in the Top Ramen. Anytime we pause in a spirit of humility and gratitude to acknowledge our dependence on the cycles of the natural world, its seasons, plants, animals, and sustaining spirit, we bring the sacred into our lived experience. We reorient ourselves toward our relatives, and remember that even in the midst of climate crisis, we are not alone, but richly supported by a vast web of relations.

Coast Salish people have never stopped holding first salmon ceremonies. But those ceremonies are increasingly threatened by the impacts of commercial overfishing, rising temperatures, ocean acidification, and melting glaciers. Salmon runs are a tiny fraction of what they once were. Some years, communities have had to use Alaskan salmon because they could not fish from their own waters. But the ceremonies continue—because these rites are sacred fuel, empowering and reminding tribal communities to speak for their salmon relatives.

#3: Ancestral eating

Mesquite bean pudding squashes through my fingers, warm and visceral. It's 1999, and I am in a cooking tent on the Mescalero Apache reservation, helping to prepare food for the crowd attending *Isanaklesh Gotal*, the girls' coming of age ceremony. I arrived just last night, collapsing into my tent after a fifteen-hour drive from Santa Barbara where I'm working on my PhD in religious studies. My advisor is Inés Talamantez, a renowned scholar of Native American religious traditions, whose life's work has centered on this ceremony and the spiritual traditions of her father's Mescalero Apache people. And I'm here today at her invitation. This morning, she's nowhere to be seen, so I follow her instructions: when in doubt, find the kitchen, and get to work.

At first, the aunties are cautiously polite. (Who is this white girl, and where did she come from?) But soon, they are teasing me for not knowing how to cook tortillas on a hot stone beside an open fire. *Tsking* at my general ineptitude, they put me to work mashing mesquite beans instead—apparently, this is harder to mess up. And I am eager not to mess up, to be a good guest, thankful for the invitation to this beautiful ceremony, and already in love with these pine forests, Sierra Blanca rising behind them. The cooking tent is full of playful banter, but there's one rule that is absolute: don't prepare food if you're not bringing a good spirit. "That bad energy gets in the food," the elders say. "And everything we do here needs to bring good things for that girl. This is her life."

Later on, I will join the line of others seeking a blessing from male *gahe* dancers, embodiments of mountain spirits who are here to support *Isanaklesh* during her ceremony. Standing in front of them, I actually go weak in the knees. They are awe inspiring: headdresses making them impossibly tall, faces obscured, other-than-human sounds emerging from their throats.

At the end of the four-day ceremony, the young girl will give each of us cattail pollen blessings, daubing brilliant yellow and white clay on our faces. She is a manifestation of Changing Woman, the one who gave the first humans their medicines and taught them how to live, and she is radiant. For her, the ceremony will continue for another four days of quiet seclusion and reflection, accompanied by her mother, auntie, and the medicine man who directed this sing. But for the rest of us, the ceremony ends as it should: with food. More than a hundred people are gathered here, most have been here through the night. And they are all hungry.

Food has the power to transform our climate grief into purposeful action when it restores us to our ancestors and reminds us of our accountability to future generations. Ancestral eating is one way to do this: it happens when we eat our heritage foods. And it happens when we feed those spirits that sustain us—including when we feed our dead. To a secular person in the twenty-first century, feeding the dead may seem like a strange practice. But it's a profoundly human one. Food is offered to the dead, placed on elaborate altars during Oaxacan Day of the Dead celebrations. Irish families once burned food in the hearth to feed the departed. African diasporan traditions such as Vodou and Santería venerate the ancestors and spirits by offering their favorite foods during Saints' Day celebrations, laid out on elaborate altars. Fruit, rice, or sake are placed on butsudan in Japanese Buddhist homes. In many Indigenous North American communities, plates of food are offered to the dead—by setting out spirit plates, or burning. In all of these instances, food becomes a site of memory, of connection with ancestors and ancestral lands, memory made material and transmuted into energy.

Climate grief and anxiety overwhelm us when we feel alone. But when food evokes the presence of ancestors, when it reminds us of our obligations to future generations, we recall that we are a link in a chain, that we are supported by a host of beings we cannot (yet) see.

#4: Not eating

Charlene is concerned. She and I have been working together on this afterschool program for unaccompanied minor refugees, and today's event was supposed to be special. We'd surprised them with an ice-cream sundae bar—usually something that got them excited. But today, a whole group of teenagers from Eretria and Ethiopia were quietly opting out.

"What's going on?" She asked. "They loved this last time."

I shook my head, equally confused. Then, it occurred to me. "Didn't we do this on a Thursday before?" She nodded, and I snapped my fingers. "That's it," I said. "Friday's a fast day. No dairy!"

Ethiopian and Coptic Orthodox Churches have more fasting days than any other major religious tradition: 180 days a year in which they eat just two meals a day and forgo meat and dairy. Of course, they're not alone. Observant Catholics abstain from meat, eggs, sugar, and fats for the forty days between Ash Wednesday and Holy Week. Muslims honor Ramadan, a month fasting from food and water from sunup to sundown, to cultivate spiritual clarity and inspire *zakat* (charitable giving). Jews observe Yom Kippur, a day in prayer and fasting to mark the new year. In the American Southwest, Choctaw and Cherokee communities keep the Green Corn Ceremony, honoring harvest and planting through ceremonies of fasting and purification. Among the Lakota and other vision quest cultures, fasting enables spiritual insight, and communion with the natural world.

Of course, fasting can be dangerous, exacerbating or even celebrating disordered eating. Some Christian saints were revered for starving themselves to death, after all. Perhaps for that reason, many traditions place guardrails around fasting, to protect health and well-being. Broadly speaking, fasting is nearly always done in community, for a limited amount of time, and certain folks are excused altogether. For instance, daily fasting during Ramadan is often bookended by large, celebratory meals shared with family in the morning and evening. And, while all Muslims are expected to participate, exceptions are made for those who have not yet reached puberty, are ill, injured, breastfeeding, pregnant, suffer from an eating disorder, or are traveling and require extra nourishment.

Or consider that many religious traditions build sacred intention around eating by avoiding certain *kinds* of foods. For instance, some Buddhists adhere to vegetarian or vegan diets in an effort to reduce suffering of other living creatures. Muslims abstain from alcohol and insist on meat that is halal (which excludes pork, and requires that animals be killed in ways that minimize suffering). The Nation of Islam—a twentieth-century new religious movement inspired by Islam and most often associated with the civil rights leader Malcolm X—eschewed what it referred to as "white man's food," and called for its followers to take up a vegetarian diet. Jews who keep kosher do not eat pork or shellfish, mix meat with dairy, and eat only animals that have been slaughtered in a rabbinically approved manner.

We know that solving the climate crisis requires that we shift our food systems away from carbon-intensive foods like meat and dairy and lean into eating locally and seasonally. What this section helps to show, is that opting out of certain foods can be more than a sacrifice—it can be a path toward spiritual insight and growth, one that is good for our minds, bodies, and the planet as a whole. It requires a ceremonial approach, one in which "opting out" is done safely, joyfully, and in community. Consider, for example, the growing movement of eco-kashrut (or eco-kosher). Here, climate-conscious Jews infuse sustainable food choices with spiritual significance, reframing keeping kosher as a way to eat lightly on the planet. The term "kosher" (literally: "fit" or "allowed") is expanded to emphasize eating locally, organically, seasonally, and avoiding carbon-heavy foods like meat and dairy.

Now, one person's choice to give up beef, or dairy, or strawberries in the dead of winter will not single-handedly solve the climate crisis. But sacred fasting traditions are a place where that magic of ritual can happen—because they are moments when taking such steps can change the individual, shifting one's personal location in the sacred economy, enlivening values of charity and care, and deepening awareness of the relations that sustain us. Such practices alleviate the psychological distress of living in conflict with our values, and they also bring body and spirit in alignment with a world in need of healing.

#4: Justice eating

The previous three examples have focused on the ways that eating can transform our relationship to the world around us. Our need to eat provides us daily opportunities to rediscover our interdependence with plant, animal, and human beings, and can encourage us, bring comfort, and inspire gratitude. Eating is also an opportunity to radically rethink what it means to live into our values. What would it look like, if we ate in keeping with our conscience? What does it mean to eat for climate justice?

When we practice justice eating, every meal becomes an opportunity to live out lives of purposeful compassion—for all people and the Earth. In his book *The Spirit of Soul Food: Race, Faith, and Food Justice*, African American theologian Christopher Carter explores the transformative potential of food. For Carter, food justice is "a state wherein the benefits and risks of where, what, and how food is grown and produced, transported and distributed, accessed and eaten, are shared fairly." Here, Carter weaves together history, theology, and his favorite recipes in his vision for Black veganism, which, he explains, differs from mainstream veganism in four ways: it is motivated by the "radical compassion of Christ," accountable to marginalized communities of color, aimed at decolonization, and celebrates African American cuisine.[14]

What does that radical compassion of Christ look like for Carter? It means "loving one's neighbor," and "doing unto others as you would have them do unto you." It means getting real about the racial disparities of our food system. It means fulfilling biblical commandments to feed the hungry, recognizing that Jesus' miracles were nearly always about healing and feeding the poor and the suffering. While the actual recipes may change, Carter argues that "soul food" is what it is because it grows from the collective wisdom of ancestors: the values of compassion, care, resourcefulness, community, and hospitality stay the same. For Carter himself, that call to be in a real relationship with Christ and creation meant adopting a vegan diet. Because that is what it looks like, when he brings his values to the table.

Food justice demands that we rethink the hierarchical systems that have created the climate crisis in the first place. In the Sikh tradition, food justice means feeding the hungry: gurudwaras (Sikh temples) house food pantries and host free community meals. Sikh values of egalitarianism, hospitality, and care are exemplified in the tradition of *langar*, a celebratory meal open to all, and where everyone eats from the same pots, sitting together as equals. An explicit rejection of the Hindu caste system, such meals are a way to celebrate personal milestones through joyful service to others.

Looking ahead

This chapter had a lot to say about the upsides of bringing spirituality back to our food. But I'd be remiss if I didn't note the dangers in doing so. Food practices can be intrinsically exclusionary. They can be weaponized to enforce spiritual purity or defend ethnic superiority. Fasting and purity codes can feed body shaming and self-loathing, and are frankly hazardous for individuals without supportive communities or careful guidance. With those caveats in mind, there are still valuable lessons to be learned here. Because multiple times a day we are offered opportunities to ingest our values, transmuting them into energy for action, opportunities to set our table with radical relationality, justice, and good trouble.

Industrial food systems are some of the biggest contributors to climate change. If we're going to survive, we have to change how we eat, and what it means to eat well. I know that good nutrition expands my window of tolerance, making me more physically, mentally, and emotionally resilient. But this chapter shows that food is more than just fuel. When our approach to food is grounded in reverence, respect, and reciprocity, it can restore our relationships with the natural world and each other. Eating mindfully and justly builds spiritual and relational resilience. We are reminded that we are not solitary, isolated individuals, but deeply enmeshed in and tied to the broader human community, to soil, and water, to microorganisms, to plants and animals and ancestors. Gratitude and reciprocity are not just nice—they are transformative values, values so powerful they can restructure economies, rebuild communities, and restore ecosystems.

Key takeaways

1. What we eat has real implications for our physical, mental, and spiritual health, and our ability to expand our window of tolerance.
2. Eating mindfully can provide insight into the interconnected nature of life and help us cultivate gratitude.
3. Eating sacramentally enables us to embody spiritual truths, and provides an opportunity to remember the miraculous within the every day, the holy in the things that sustain us.
4. Feeding our ancestors reminds us that we are part of a chain of life, that we are sustained by our ancestors, and obligated to sustain future generations.
5. Choosing not to eat—for a period of time or abstaining from certain foods—provides an avenue for centering

justice and sustainability, and being more mindful about the meaning of food.

6 Justice eating challenges us to invite our values to our dinner table. How differently would we eat if we insisted on the rights of workers? On reducing the suffering of other creatures? On living in sustainable relationship with our world?

Invitation for further reflection

1 How do you "eat your values"? Are there ways you might eat more mindfully, sacramentally, or justly?

2 Identify one food that is culturally or personally meaningful for you. Get to know more about it. Then have some! Approach eating it as a meditative/reflective practice. Begin with gratitude, considering everything and everyone involved in bringing this food to you. Think about your relationship with that food, then write about it, or discuss with others.

3 How might we reflect on sacramental foods to bring the sacred into the mundane? The holy into the everyday?

4 Feed your ancestors! Create a space, set out photos or other symbols to represent those who have gone before you. Honor them with a symbolic food. Consider what foods sustained them, and how these foods help connect you to your ancestors, and the Earth we share.

5 Trying going meat-free or vegan for a single meal or a whole week. Or, try eating locally and seasonally. What values or insights might this spark?

Want to learn more?

Visit our website at https://bloomsbury.pub/climate-spirit where you'll find recommendations for further reading and resources for individuals, reading groups, and educators.

5

Sleep is sacred

Once again, I've been asked to change the assignment.

It's too hard. Takes too much planning and preparation. And, the student finally admits, it makes them anxious.

What is this terrible task I've set?

To take a day off.

I'm teaching a class on the history of Judaism in America, and I've asked my students to take a sabbath. They're not to copy Jewish rituals, but to carve out one twenty-four-hour period without work, driving, spending money, or technology. It's the last item that has them concerned: twenty-four hours without internet, computers, tablets, or cell phones? Um, no.

We talk preparations: get ahead on homework, pre-cook your meals. Don't go solo. If there's one constant over the years, it's that students who keep a sabbath alone are far more likely to spend it depressed and anxious. But those who invite friends over for dinner and boardgames, or take a day with their family? They have a great time. I'll never forget the student who reported having her first real conversation with her parents in *years*. Some get creative: collaging, drawing, or playing music. Unplugging for even one day shows students how challenging real rest can be. For my students—all of whom have jobs and many of whom work to support their families—rest feels like an indulgence. Not what the Jewish tradition says it is: *a requirement.*

In the midst of the Vietnamese civil war, Thich Nhat Hanh's Zen Buddhist monastic community worked tirelessly for the cause of peace, even in the face of violent reprisal. But as the situation became more dire, they realized the need for daily sitting meditation, balancing activism with stillness. African American theologian Barbara Holmes expresses a similar sentiment in her book *Crisis Contemplation.*

> When the crisis strikes, the response from the village must be a pause. There is little that we can do, but we can be. We can listen. We can love our neighbors, and we can host the s(S)pirit that flutters over every dawning day .... When the crisis occurs, the only way out is through, so we take a cue from nature and relax into the stillness.[1]

Real rest is not the same as *entertainment.* As a society, we excel at distractions. We scroll Netflix, plan vacations, go to Disneyland. We chase that dopamine, on the lookout for The Next Big Thing. I love funny cat videos, but they do not restore my soul, or ground me in Spirit. (Well, maybe sometimes they do, but not always.) Real rest brings us back to what we value and to the relationships that sustain us. It is where we remember the *why* behind our labor, the meaning behind the work, the purpose we are pursuing. Climate psychologists tell us that getting good rest is essential for our mental health, and a key way to ensure we are resilient enough to handle both climate crises and anticipatory dread of what may yet come. But the truth is, most of us have forgotten how to rest in a world where one's value is based on productivity, and headlines drive a constant sense of urgency. The answer lies in reclaiming a *ceremonial* approach to rest, one in which we renew not just ourselves, but also the relationships that tie us to others, to rest in a way that is not just good for us, but the

Earth. In this chapter, I offer four reasons why rest needs to be part of every climate activist's toolkit.

First, rest is essential for expanding our "window of tolerance," ensuring we're doing our best critical and creative thinking. Faced with a challenge like the climate crisis, rest is not optional. It's a requirement. When we're rested, we can *respond*, not just *react*. We need to rest, so we can think clearly, even in the chaos. Second, rest is revolutionary. Choosing to rest is a way to reclaim our independence from a consumer society, declaring that while we may be ensnared by fossil fuel economies and systems of exploitation, we are not defined by them. Sacred traditions show us models for rest that include reducing our consumption and our climate impact in ways that are practical, achievable, and also deeply meaningful. Third, human beings have always surrounded rest with prayer, ritual, and meditation. Sleep offers daily opportunities to center ourselves in gratitude, and remind ourselves of what we truly value. For those of us concerned about our ecological future, such grounding moments help to counter the emotional overwhelm, settle the outrage, and nurture the longer-term vision we need to keep going. And, finally, in this chapter I argue that those of us struggling with climate anxiety and eco-grief need to (re) learn how to pay attention to our dreams. Throughout human history, sleep has been a source of insight and clarity—particularly during periods of grief or confusion. Rest is the realm of visions, moments of insight when we discover new solutions, new ways of understanding, and new possibilities for renewing the world. And if ever there was a time when we needed to dream a new future, this is it.

#1: Rest is required

Having a baby gave me a whole different perspective on rest. For the first year, my son rarely slept for more than two hours at a stretch, and at times I felt my sanity slipping away. The stack of books I read on sleep training were useless, and in the end I had to give in and follow his lead. He was a contact sleeper—it was simply who he was. We donated the crib and bought a full-size mattress—a good one, because I'd be sleeping there as well. At last, we both got a full night's rest.

Sleep is sacred. And I know from first-hand experience, going without it has real consequences for our mental and physical health.

Ecopsychologists remind us that real rest is essential for managing the anxiety and grief of climate chaos. Along with diet and exercise, getting good sleep is key to maintaining our "window of tolerance," the amount of stress we can endure while remaining rooted in our prefrontal cortex, doing our best thinking, empathizing, and problem solving. Chronic fatigue, stress, and overwork are incredibly bad for us, creating a toxic stew that impacts all of our bodily systems, mental clarity, critical and creative thinking, and emotional resilience. Psychiatrist Lise Van Susteren explains that the allostatic load of continually elevated adrenaline, cortisol, and related elements of our internal stress response system (the hypothalamic–pituitary–adrenal, or HPA pathway axis) reinforce destructive thought patterns, damage our overall health, accelerate aging, alter behavior, and stimulate anxiety, foreboding, and hyper-responsiveness. Lack of sleep impacts nearly every system in our body. Circadian rhythms monitor essential hormones, including cortisol (a primary stress hormone), melatonin, serotonin, blood pressure, pain response, allergic responses, digestive functions, immune responses, mood, alertness, energy, and metabolism of food and medications. Long periods of inadequate sleep can lead to system-wide inflammation, increasing risk of stroke, heart disease, and type 2 diabetes. Sleep supports our parasympathetic nervous system, which helps to ensure that we respond to stressors with our cerebral cortex—using our best and most creative, critical thinking—rather than reverting to our amygdala and its fight/flight/freeze response. Rest is not optional. Because if we want to be effective agents of change and renewal, we need to be operating at our best—otherwise we risk just making things worse.

As we learned in Chapter 2, we are hardwired to seek out clarity. We long for predictability. We dislike ambiguity and cognitive dissonance. But the climate crisis requires us to see multiple (sometimes conflicting) truths and potential outcomes at the same time. Our present situation is dire, but it is also full of possibilities. And to see and act on those possibilities we must use our best creative and intuitive thinking. We need to rest, because *burnout is real*—particularly for those working in conservation or responding to crises exacerbated by climate change. Preventing burnout requires that we prioritize moments for renewal in our daily, weekly, and seasonal lives. Without rest, we simply can't care for the vulnerable, heal the hurt, rebuild what is broken, or resist the powers that be.

If sleep is a moving target for you, good sleep hygiene can help. Avoid looking at screens for at least thirty minutes (ideally two hours) before bed. Follow a consistent sleep schedule, including on the weekends. Dim lights one or two hours before bed, and engage in calm evening activities. Avoid stimulating food or media. No doom scrolling. In the morning, get in some bright, natural light going for a walk upon waking is ideal for calibrating circadian rhythms. Of course, for some of us, it's a little more complicated.

#2: Rest is resistance

"It's never enough," I lament to my therapist. "There just aren't enough hours in the day to do everything I ought to do."

"What does *enough* look like to you?" She asks, giving me pause.

"When I get to the end of the day completely exhausted," I finally say. "When my body physically can't do anymore. *That's* enough."

As a child, my favorite author was George MacDonald. A founding father of the fantasy genre, MacDonald was inspired by Celtic folklore and Scottish egalitarianism, and in his book *The Lost Princess* MacDonald writes of a cruel, spoiled princess stolen away by a Wise Woman. Locked up in a magical cottage, she is outraged: there are no servants to attend to her, and no food unless she finishes her chores. She learns that if she works, she will eat, if she shows kindness, she'll receive it in turn. Oh, lordy, did that story lodge deep in my soul. To this day, I abhor a hierarchy. Princesses should clean their own bathrooms, thank you very much. And while I still love this story, I've also had to reckon with how it fed into my own rather obsessive (and self-destructive) tendencies. For many years I believed that only if I finished all my work, did I deserve to eat. Only if I was exhausted, did I deserve to rest. Only through constant productivity could I justify my existence. It took me a long time to realize that our capitalist system relies on this fallacy, that the creation of wealth for the few depends on reducing human beings (and the natural world) to tools to be used, stripping a sentient world of intrinsic, sacred value.

All this is to say—the burden of what sociologist Max Weber called the Protestant Work Ethic has always laid heavy on my shoulders.[2] And when it comes to climate change, I never feel like I'm doing enough.

Then I remember. Rest is revolutionary.

We rest because it is an act of resistance against a world that tells us we are nothing more than our productivity, where rest is a privilege reserved for princesses, out of reach for many, and where access to it is shaped by gender, race, culture, and class. Many of us forget that real rest requires *safety*—a door to lock, a home free of violence, a place where one can let down their guard, where the bombs are not falling, or tempers flaring. And that, unfortunately, is a privilege many do not have. The unequal access to rest should concern us all—because if we are going to survive as a species, we need everyone operating at their best. And if you are someone who takes the Bible seriously, it really ought to concern you: because *rest is a commandment*, one required not just of the wealthy, but of everyone. In a radical turn, the God of the Hebrew Bible doesn't just command his chosen people to rest, but also their servants, the foreigners among them, their animals, and the very Earth itself! *All of creation* has a biblical right to rest. And that is nothing short of revolutionary.

In her groundbreaking book *Rest Is Resistance*, Tricia Hersey calls our attention to this social inequality of rest, arguing that Black and Brown women have disproportionately borne the brunt of capitalism and the exploitative environmental and labor systems on which it depends. In short: their overwork enables the leisure of others. In that context, insisting on everyone's right to rest is an act of resistance. Hersey emphasizes that the purpose of rest is not to make us better workers, but enlivened human beings. As she writes,

> The Rest is Resistance framework does not believe in the toxic idea that we are resting to recharge and rejuvenate so we can be prepared to give more output to capitalism. What we have internalized as productivity has been informed by a capitalist, ableist, patriarchal system. Our drive and obsession to always be in a state of 'productivity' leads us to the path of exhaustion, guilt, and shame. We falsely believe we are not doing enough and that we must always be guiding our lives toward more labor ... We are not resting to be productive. We are resting simply because it is our divine right to do so.[3]

When my students have mixed feelings about taking a day of rest, I invite them to read Abraham Joshua Heschel's book *The Sabbath: It's*

Meaning for Modern Man. The only member of his family to escape the Holocaust, Heschel became one of the most important Jewish theologians and civil rights advocates of the twentieth century. Like Hersey, Heschel emphasizes that we do not rest so that we can work: we work, so that we can rest—and, in that rest, we restore our relationship with the eternal. "Man is not a beast of burden, and the Sabbath is not for the purpose of enhancing the efficiency of his work." In *The Sabbath,* Heschel acknowledges the lure of material possessions and modern technology, and the dangers of being enslaved to profit. We must learn, he explains, to live in the world without being controlled by it. "There are many who have acquired a high degree of political and social liberty," he explains, "but only very few are not enslaved to things. This is our constant problem—how to live with people and remain free, how to live with things and remain independent."

Heschel argues that the solution can be found in the sabbath. At first glance sabbath observance can seem like a list of negatives: no work, no burning fossil fuels, no technology, no shopping. But Heschel tells us that the purpose of such restrictions is to usher us into "the realm of time where the goal is not to have but to be, not to own but to give, not to control but to share, not to subdue but to be in accord." By opting out of technology and consumer economy for just one day in seven, we reclaim our true nature, one not defined by *things*, but *relationships*—to God and each other. As Heschel explains: "Six days a week we wrestle with the world, wringing profit from the earth; on the Sabbath we especially care for the seed of eternity planted in the soul. The world has our hands, but our soul belongs to Someone Else."[4]

Heschel's words have inspired a new generation of Jewish ecologists, many of whom argue that Shabbat provides a pathway toward more sustainable living. Jonathan Neril, founder of the Interfaith Center for Sustainable Development, makes the case:

> Air pollution. Species loss. Climate change. These are problems not of the environment, but of a society bent on doing and producing seven days a week. On Shabbat, we are to walk on the earth without asserting our mastery over the earth, in order to acknowledge the sovereignty of the Creator. In this way, we will remember that we are only the custodians of the earth with the responsibility to work it and to guard it.[5]

African American essayist Cole Arthur Riley also considers the liberatory potential in rest, when she reflects on the remarkable fact that rest is God's answer to crisis.

> It seems like anytime God is talking about salvation in the Bible, he makes a point to name rest. 'I'll refresh tired bodies' (Jeremiah 31:25). 'Find rest for your souls' (Matthew 11:29). And, in Psalm 23:2, we have 'He makes me lie down.' What a peculiar answer to the valley of the shadow of death. You might expect God's response to be to have people rise, to empower them to fight. But God's answer is unapologetic care for the body. The deepest yet most neglected of needs ... Rest is not the reward of our liberation, not something we lay hold of once we are free. It is the path that delivers us there.[6]

Rest is the way we reclaim the sacred stuff of which our lives are made. Riley puts it this way: "People think the sabbath is antiquated; I think it will save us from ourselves."[7]

The English language seems to have an antipathy toward time, viewing it as a finite resource (at best) or something to be done away with (at worst). We kill it, waste it, spend it, use it, and invest it. We've reduced it to a commodity, a resource. But I want to *attend* to time, to *dwell* in it. To *abide* in it. I want us to remember when time was all we had. Maybe reclaiming the wisdom of the sabbath is a way to do just that.

#3: Grounding in gratitude

Neuroscience has uncovered a lot about sleep. Did you know human beings are the only mammals that choose to delay sleep when they're tired? That being awake for sixteen hours straight decreases your ability to function equivalent to a blood alcohol content of 0.5 percent? But despite all we have learned, sleep remains a mystery. And the comparative study of religion shows us that we've always approached sleep with a degree of uncertainty and even fear. How many generations of us went off to bed praying, "If I should die before I wake, I pray the Lord my soul to take ..."? But we human beings have also seen sleep as a nightly journey into Spirit, and restful states as opportunities for communion with the divine. Because sleep is both mysterious and wonderful, we surround it with ritual.

Around the world, we mark sleep as sacred by bathing, praying, and creating spaces of peace and safety. We meditate on the day and set intentions for the next. Islam advises a series of bedtime recitations—prayers that acknowledge the presence and mercy of Allah. When researching ancient Celtic and Hebridean traditions, Alexander Carmichael learned that women bowed to the moon, and men to the rising sun. In many Native American communities, elders teach that we ought to greet the sun at sunrise and sunset, with gratitude, intentions, and prayer. It was a practice my graduate advisor, Inés Talamantez kept, greeting the sun and blessing herself with cattail pollen, a sacred element in her Mescalero Apache tradition. St. Ignatius Loyola authored *The Examen*,[8] a nightly reflection still practiced by Jesuits that begins by centering in God's presence, followed by reflecting on the day with gratitude. Adherents then review the day, paying attention to moments when strong emotions rose—considering what they might reveal, before making intentions for tomorrow.

Karen Armstrong calls such forms of nightly reflection a form a "daily kenosis," or emptying the self. "Every day, first thing in the morning and at night, for just a few moments we should consider three things: how little we know; how frequently we fail in kindness to other beings; and how limited are our desires and yearnings, which so often begin and end in oneself."[9] For its part, Orthodox Judaism advises three prayers before bed: the *shema*, a prayer to forgive others, and a prayer of repentance. Upon waking, the prayer is simple: "I offer thanks to You, living and eternal King, for You have mercifully restored my soul within me; Your faithfulness is great." It's akin to the morning recitation common in Plum Village, the Buddhist community led by Thich Nhat Hanh: "Waking up this morning, I smile. Twenty-four brand new hours are before me. I vow to live fully in each moment and to look at all beings with eyes of compassion." By marking sleep as sacred, we tell our minds and bodies that it's time to rest. But we also ground ourselves in what we value, re-connecting us to spirit.

For those of us overwhelmed by climate anxiety and eco-grief, or struggling to stave off burn-out as we do the creative, caring, and confronting work of climate action, such traditions offer an accessible and simple way to bring contemplative practice into one's life. For a few moments before and after our rest, we can ground ourselves in gratitude, return to what we value most, and set intentions for the day to come. Such simple actions have transformative power.

#4: Dreams and visions

When I was offered a position at Pacific Lutheran University, I knew it would mean moving to the rainy Northwest, leaving behind the idyllic home Michael and I had made together in Santa Barbara, California. This was the job of my dreams, the one I'd been working toward for over a decade. So, when I got the offer, I was elated. The problem? Michael *did not* want to leave paradise. (Did you know it's always 70 degrees and sunny in Santa Barbara?) We were at an impasse. One night, I dreamt I was standing under a rain cloud—the Saturday morning cartoon variety, just big enough to douse a single person. Damp, shivering, and wearing a frumpy sweater, I watch as Michael pedaled by on a tandem bike, a gorgeous blonde riding behind him, both laughing in sunshine bliss. The woman's name? Barbara. And if you're wondering, yes, my dreams are always that literal. My subconscious lies pretty close to the surface.

While this particular dream may not have inspired profound insights (though I did rethink my frumpy sweater collection), the idea of dreams and visions as sources of insight is important. Building a ceremonial approach to hope in which we metabolize our climate grief and anxiety into purposeful action requires a turning toward deeper sources of knowledge, insight, and intuition. And throughout human history, dreams and visions have been a key part of that work. If we're to write a new story of our climate future, we need our dreamers and our visionaries at their very best.

To some of us, this may sound too farfetched. But most religious and Indigenous traditions emphasize the importance of paying attention to dreams. Within Catholicism, saints appear in dreams, offering comfort and guidance. Protestant charismatics take dreams seriously, examining them for possible communication from the Holy Spirit. Hinduism, Jainism, and Islam all have complex systems for interpreting dreams, seeing them as potential tools for anticipating luck, pregnancy, sickness, or death. Religious traditions also provide cautionary guidelines for dream interpretation. Islam emphasizes the dangers of taking dreams too seriously, distinguishing between three kinds of dreams: *Ru'yaa* (dreams from God), *Hulum* (dreams from Satan), and common dreams that stem from one's own mind. Noting the potential to be misled, Islamic teachers advise consulting with spiritual leaders, ensuring all interpretations align with Qur'anic wisdom, and proceeding with humility.

In their work on the Black religious experience in America, womanist theologians Rachel Elizabeth Harding and her mother Rosemarie Freeney Harding explain that

> there is a vast tradition among African Americans of dreaming and paying close attention to dreams. Dreams can be auguries of coming good or ill. Dreams of deceased relatives and friends are often interpreted as forms of communication with them, and the sharing of dreams within a household or among friends is a way to connect with a collective wisdom regarding the meaning of a particular feeling or event.[10]

Harding and Harding remind us that dreaming can offer insight—whether from Spirit, ancestors, or from our own subconscious, freed from the constraints of the day and given the time to process.

Within African diasporan religions—including Yoruba, Santería, Vodou, and Candomblé—the power of dreaming reflects a broader belief that ancestors are an active presence in peoples' lives, offering chastisement, guidance, and protection. While powerful dreams don't happen all the time, ancestors may choose to communicate through them. Professor of African Culture and Civilization Onukwube Anedo argues that this respect for dreams has its roots in West African traditions of ancestral veneration. It's a practice that survived the diaspora, endured centuries of enslavement, and persists today within African American and Afro-Caribbean culture. While ancestors can communicate through spirit possession, divination, conjuring, or prophecy, according to Anedo that communication takes a more personal, intimate expression in dreams, which serve as "a mechanism of continuous revelation."[11]

Within Afro-Caribbean traditions, dreams take on particular potential, when initiates choose to sleep alone one night a week in the hope of receiving a dream communication from an ancestor, *lwa*, or *orisha*. As African American Studies scholar Adam McGee has argued, dreaming as a source of insight has been key to Haitian Vodou's ability to adapt within a rapidly changing world. Dream interpretation plays a central role in Haitian healing work, helping those who are struggling to correct course or make sense of tragedy.[12]

Among those Indigenous North American cultures that place a high value on vision quests and personal relationships with spirit powers, dreams are powerful and respected sites of insight and revelation. In Coast Salish cultures, both spirit powers and ancestors communicate through dreams, offering guidance, or gifting people with spirit songs. In Northern Plains cultures, dreams and visions are taken seriously, inspiring new ceremonies, rituals, songs, and may even reveal a change in gender identity. The famous text *Black Elk Speaks* describes the Lakota spiritual leader's own vision, received during a serious illness, which became the basis for a new ceremony. Kaúxuma-núpika, a Kutenai scout, warrior, and prophet who lived at the turn of the nineteenth century, was born a woman, but received a vision midway through his life that announced that he would henceforth be a man. His community took him at his word—because such dreams were powerful, and not to be questioned. He went on to marry a woman and changed his name: Kaúxuma-núpika means Gone to the Spirits, a testimony to the spiritual transformation he experienced while in a powerful dream state.

I share these myriad examples to make this point: When we reclaim rest, we also reclaim opportunities for insight and inspiration. Whether they provide clues to our subconscious, insight from ancestors, or spiritual inspiration, human beings have learned to attend to dreams with care. Climate psychologist Sally Gillespie likewise offers an invitation to consider the importance of dreams in the face of eco-grief and climate anxiety. In her book *Climate Consciousness*, Gillespie writes, "When we run into an impasse, dreams can show us 'the unvarnished, natural truth' delivering insights which radically alter the attitudes that led us into the impasse." Attending to dreams helps us hold complex and contradictory truths at once, and see a path forward.

> To find our way in a climate disrupted world we must pay heed to the margins of consciousness, to the dreams, visions, and imaginings that are vehicles for instinctual awareness, intuitive insights and emergent understandings that reveal possibilities for a wildly different kind of life … In times of crisis, when breakthrough is the only way forward, paying attention to our dreams and imaginings is crucial evolutionary work.[13]

Metabolizing climate anxiety and eco-grief into purposeful action requires that we reclaim real restorative rest. The problem is, it's hard for us to turn off our brains, put aside distractions, and be truly present with others and ourselves. As Heschel writes, "labor is a craft, but perfect rest is an art." When we take a ceremonial approach to rest, we reclaim it as a holy right and obligation. We refuse to offer up our lives on the pyre of production and consumption. We insist on rediscovering rest that is joyful, communal, and playful. We lay ourselves down, not afraid to dream up a new kind of future.

Key takeaways

1 Rest is essential for our physical, mental, and spiritual health, and key to expanding our window of tolerance, so that we can effectively respond to the climate crisis.

2 Insisting upon real rest is an act of resistance against fossil fuel economies built on extraction, consumption, and social inequality.

3 None of us can entirely escape our consumer society, but we can refuse to be enslaved to it. One way to do so is to reclaim a sabbath tradition: regular respites from technology, consumption, and labor, accompanied by a return to those things that matter most.

4 Sleep is sacred, and religious traditions around the world provide examples of the ways in which human beings surround sleep with ritual reflection. Such simple, daily actions help combat burnout by grounding us in gratitude, restoring perspective, and connecting to what really matters.

5 Throughout human history, dreams have been sources of insight and inspiration, from ancestors, spirit, or our subconscious. In the face of our climate crisis, we need to make space for intuitive insight, visionary thinking, and inspiration.

Invitation for further reflection

1 If you are part of a religious or cultural tradition, take some time to learn about how your tradition creates space for meaningful rest. What does that look like?

2 What are ways you might incorporate meaningful rest into your life? What's the right balance for you between "doing the work" and "caring for yourself"?

3 Do you think we work so we can rest, or that we rest so we can work? How do these mindsets shape your approach to how you live?

4 What are ways we can help make rest a right for everyone—and not just the privileged few?

Want to learn more?

Visit our website at https://bloomsbury.pub/climate-spirit where you'll find recommendations for further reading and resources for individuals, reading groups, and educators.

6

Mindful movement

I'm laughing out loud when the wave of water hits me in the face. It leaves me sputtering, but I don't mind. After decades of back pain, I have finally found a form of exercise that doesn't hurt. It's water aerobics, ladies! I flail about, not at all sure I'm doing this right. But then I realize: it doesn't matter. Because it's *fun*. There are so few places in my middle-aged professor-mom life where I get to *play*. After slipping off my noodle for the third time, I bob back to the surface, a smile plastered on my face. There are a thousand things I ought to be doing, so many emails in my inbox. But this hour with the retirees at my local YMCA is exactly where I need to be.

I was eleven when I was diagnosed with scoliosis. When I was twelve, doctors strapped me into a metal and plastic corset, cinched so tight I struggled to breathe and even the smallest meals made me ill. The thing *hurt*, chafing my skin and bruising my hipbones. I didn't take it well, withdrawing from friends, and sliding into a severe depression. I don't remember ever encountering a female physician during that time. Perhaps she might have empathized with an adolescent girl who was being taught through the language of x-rays, and metal, and plastic, that her body was her enemy, something to be forced into submission.

The brace became my full-time companion, with just one exception. For six hours a week, I was permitted to hide the brace away in my ballet bag, and *move.* Free of constraints, dance class was a temporary reprieve from my personal prison. I suppose most people think of ballet as a discipline of rigid control, but, for me, it was the only time I breathed freely.

Two decades later, my husband and I decided to have a child. I was in my thirties, up for tenure, with a sabbatical on the way. If we were ever going to try, this was the moment. I'd received conflicting advice from physicians (none of whom were scoliosis experts), but I was healthy, strong, and decided to take the risk. Our pregnancy was easy, until the third trimester when my back could no longer sustain the weight I was carrying. Muscles frayed like worn rope, and I spent the better part of two months confined to bed. I had one respite: a hand-me-down VHS of *Yoga for the Hugely Pregnant* (not its real title). Breath and movement combined once again to help me find my way back into my body, offering a space of mutual forgiveness for the pain we inflicted on each other.

There were "complications" with the birth. My memories are hazy, but I recall the midwife hitting the panic button, staff scrambling, the color draining from Michael's face as they whisked me away to surgery. Declan and I were lucky. We had excellent care and we came through it okay.

But after he was born, I came to loathe those parenting books and blogs, all full of fit and fabulous mums frolicking about with their babies. No one wrote about what happens when your body isn't built for pregnancy, or natural delivery, or schlepping a baby around. I cried with frustration when I struggled to lift him, or couldn't carry him for more than a few minutes. But I *could* walk, and our all-terrain stroller became my salvation. Every day, no matter the weather, Declan and I headed out, in search of big trees and board walks.

When I turned fifty (good lord, how did that happen?), my body caught up with me once again. Back pain become a chronic presence

I couldn't ignore. But more than just physical discomfort, I soon realized it was also triggering my climate anxiety by amplifying my sense of powerlessness. *How can I save the world if I can't even weed my garden?* That was when I stumbled on the work of early twentieth-century German physiotherapist Katharina Schroth. At fourteen, Katharina was diagnosed with scoliosis and given a brace. It looked a lot like my own—the technology hadn't changed much in a hundred years. But she pushed back, designing a different approach focused on building strength and flexibility instead of passive acquiescence to an external force of control. While the brace left me struggling for air like a fainting Victorian, her approach begins with deep, expansive breaths. Instead of surrendering bodily autonomy, hers is a path toward personal agency.

It was my Schroth-certified physical therapist who recommended I take up water aerobics—a great way to build strength and elongate the spine, she said. She was right. But I found something else that was also pretty wonderful: a community of women who cheer each other on, and who are boldly and joyfully present in our aging bodies. It's not about perfection, but breathing, moving, and laughing.

As I researched this book, I also discovered that aerobic exercise is key to regulating my brain's stress responses. Exercise raises serotonin levels and releases a protein, neurotrophic factor BDNF, that actually *blocks our stress-hormone receptor sites*, so that cortisol can't find a purchase in our brain. As Lise Van Susteren puts it, aerobic exercise protects us from the impacts of stress like "wearing a waterproof raincoat in a downpour."[1]

Physical exercise also helps close the stress response cycle. Our ancestors evolved to respond to physical threats with a physical response. When we encounter a threat—real or imagined—our amygdala tells the hypothalamus to trigger our sympathetic nervous system, releasing adrenaline to enable our fight, flight, or freeze response. Taking action to address the problem helps move those stress hormones along, and once we're safe, our parasympathetic nervous system takes over, returning us to equilibrium. But what if today's threats require creative, intellectual responses, rather than physical ones? What if we never feel safe? If the triggers keep coming? Without that physical response, those stress chemicals can remain at unhealthy levels, disrupting our sleep, appetite, mood, and elevating risks of heart disease, stomach ulcers, and burnout. One way to complete that stress cycle? Get physical: laugh, cry, create, exercise, and play.

But I often find it hard to justify making time for movement: there is so much work that needs to be done. When the world is falling apart, how can I possibly take time to *play*? With so much pain in the world, how can I think about *fun*? I find it helpful to remember this insight from Thich Nhat Hanh:

> The Buddha advises us to create the feeling of joy and happiness in order to nourish ourselves before we deal with the painful feelings. Just as a surgeon may judge that a patient is too weak to undergo surgery, and recommend that the patient first get some rest and nourishment so she can bear the surgery, so we need to strengthen our foundation of joy and happiness before focusing on our suffering.[2]

So we already know exercise is good for us. But in this chapter I want to argue that it can also be good for the Earth, that it is an essential step in metabolizing our climate grief, and transforming eco-anxiety into purposeful action. Restoring a sacred, ceremonial spirit to our movement builds resilience, because it can restore relationships with the natural, the spiritual, and the interpersonal. I don't want to just work out—I want meaningful movement that supports my well-being and also contributes to the healing of the Earth. In this chapter, I want to consider how movement can facilitate spiritual clarity, cultivate subtle energy, and change the world for the better.

#1: Go outside, and learn to listen

Clinical therapists agree that getting outside and around green and growing things is good for us. Studies have found that the relative density of green spaces and tree canopy in urban neighborhoods has a direct correlation with crime rates, overall physical and mental health, and the vibrancy of social support networks. Children attending schools near green spaces exhibit better self-control behaviors, and numerous studies have found that time outside in natural settings improves cognition, memory, flexibility, attention, and focus. Psychologists have a variety of theories for why this might be the case. For instance, the "biophilia" hypothesis holds that we have an innate need to be in nature—and around trees in particular—because our ancestors evolved in those spaces. Others note the chemical impact, with brain studies showing lower stress hormones and increased dopamine, serotonin, and oxytocin after time spent in natural spaces.[3]

Indigenous North American traditions demonstrate that physical activity outside is not just good for our bodies, but also supports mental clarity, spiritual insight, and deeper relationship with an animated landscape. In his book *Standing Ground: Yurok Indian Spirituality from 1850–1990*, anthropologist Thomas Buckley describes Indigenous spiritual practices of physical training in the natural world, including long-distance running and purification.[4] Women climb to sacred lakes high in the mountains, bodies of water set aside for them by the Creator for ceremonial bathing, while young men participate in sweat baths and cold plunges in streams and rivers. Such physical training prepares them for the intensive spiritual work to come: time spent in high places in the mountains seeking spiritual power. The end goal of such training is thus not physical fitness but spiritual insight, which requires mental clarity and the strength to access remote places. Or, consider the role of physical stamina in Native Northern Californian world renewal ceremonies. In these traditions, the people bring down dances that are always occurring in the spiritual realm. For several days, the people gather, don ancestral regalia, and affirm their place within an ancient agreement. Drawing on the spiritual relationships and the physical stamina they've gained in their training, these dances restore the world to balance, and keep things going. Physical training is a means of cultivating mental clarity and the agility necessary to do the work of restoring relational harmony with the natural and spiritual world.

A similar claim could be made of the revitalization of traditional canoe culture in the Pacific Northwest. Since 1989, an intertribal canoe journey has been held each August. Today, more than a hundred canoe families from dozens of tribal communities paddle hundreds of miles, culminating in a week-long celebration of song, dance, and ceremony. For many, the experience is transformational. Participants share stories of receiving spirit songs while on the water, or powerful encounters with whales, eagles, and other sea creatures. Paddling requires physical stamina, and a commitment to learn one's language, songs, dances, and traditional arts of carving, weaving, and navigation. Endurance, clarity of mind, and common purpose support the people as they reconnect with community, ancestors, and waterways. Squaxin Island tribal member Charlene Krise describes tribal journeys as a "modern day soul retrieval ceremony," through which Native people reclaim their spirits and heal from intergenerational trauma.[5]

Communities in the Pacific Northwest also have traditions of bathing in frigid seas, streams, or lakes, scrubbing themselves with cedar branches, to cleanse body, mind, and spirit. Nuu-chah-nulth hereditary chief and professor Umeek (E. Richard Atleo), explains that Nuu-chah-nulth people engaged in this strict physical and spiritual training in order to gain insight, and be better equipped to listen to and learn from the plant and animal people around them.[6] It was part of *uusumč*, a discernment practice that includes bathing in cold water, fasting, prayer, and seclusion. Steam baths, or sweat lodges, play a similar role in many Native cultures. In the twentieth century, Lakota-style sweats were adopted in intertribal settings, and have been adapted into Indigenous-led mental health and recovery programs. With their intense heat created by pouring cold water over heated stones, sweats are emotionally cathartic, physically challenging, and spiritually powerful, often described as entering the womb of Mother Earth.

While non-native folks should not appropriate Indigenous traditions, these examples are a challenge to go beyond mere "outdoor recreation," and to instead seek real relationship with a sentient world. In these practices, the goal is not about perfect abs, but mental clarity and spiritual insight. It is about getting to know one's land, so as to better hear what it has to say. Climate psychologists agree that one of the best remedies for climate anxiety is getting outside and into nature. Time spent out of doors builds resilience, reminds us of what we love, and enlivens our determination to care for what remains. We recall that we are part of a living world, one that demands our care, reverence, and respect.

#2: Renewable energy

If the previous examples encourage us to turn outward and build relationships with the natural world, other movement traditions challenge us to turn inward, to raise subtle energy and connect with Spirit. The traditions in this category employ movements and breathing techniques to cultivate mindfulness and integrate mind and body. Built on Chinese Daoist principles of inner transformation, ch'i-kung and tai-chi are systems of movement intended to raise and direct the flow of *chi* (subtle energy), bringing the individual into harmonious alignment with the natural world. Even better known, yoga has its origins in Hinduism and combines physical postures with breathing meditation to facilitate the movement of energy (*prana*) along pathways (*prana vayus*), with the goal of aligning and balancing energy at constellation points (*chakras*) in the body. In the Western world, however, yoga studios usually have more to do with getting fit than spiritual practice. Religious studies scholar and yoga instructor Liz Bucar explains that while yoga in the West has maintained some of its cultural foundations—such as the intersection of breath and the movement of energy—it tends to obscure or ignore its spiritual foundations. It is actually more traditional, she explains, to begin with ethical and moral teachings, followed by lessons in meditation, before progressing to physical postures.[7] Despite this, it's also true that many practitioners in the Western world see yoga as a pathway for spiritual growth. In his 2025 book *Yogalands,* religious studies scholar Paul Bramadat explores the spirituality and politics of yoga, finding that many practitioners see yoga as part of their spiritual life, and a means of integrating mind, body, and spirit.[8]

Sacred dance is another form of meditative movement found within the comparative study of religious traditions, one that also rests on highly nuanced theological or epistemological foundations. For example, whirling dance in Sufism is grounded in the recitation of prayer, and intended to facilitate the surrendering of ego or conscious self (*nafs*) and union with Allah. Or, consider Afro-Caribbean traditions like Santería, in which spirits (*santos*) are invoked through their own percussive rhythms. Here, music and dance quite literally bring the spirits into the room.

Discovering an integrative approach to mind, body, and spirit helps individuals struggling with climate anxiety and eco-grief by mitigating the physiological impacts of trauma on the body. Such practices change our brain chemistry, and regulate stress hormones. But these traditions, rooted as they are in rhythmic breath and mindful movement, do much more. They remind us that we inhale and exhale alongside a breathing Earth. When we stand in mountain pose, we feel our feet on stone contiguous with those very mountains—even if they are far away. When we dance in rhythm with others, we remember we are not alone, and when those rhythms evoke the spirits of ancestors or S/spirit, we are rewoven into the tapestry of our human and more-than-human relatives. As Cole Arthur Riley argues, the liberative potential of African American worship is inseparable from its embodied nature.

> To be people capable of extending welcome to the body, even those bodies the world discards and demeans, is to be people of profound liberation. By this we will know our faith: We will stay whole ... You want to tell me to love God? Ask me when I've last eaten. Come now, you want me to tell you a prayer? You'll find it in the blood beating from heart to head to toe and home again.[9]

Manifesting justice

"Now I'm in ceremonial mode," Wendsler Nosie declares, having laced up his running shoes. Nosie is a political and spiritual leader of the San Carlos Apache, and he is about to begin a forty-mile run from the San Carlos Reservation to Oak Flat, Arizona, in an effort to raise awareness of threats to their ancestral ceremonial ground from an international mining conglomerate. The proposed land transfer would reduce Oak Flat—the site of Apache sunrise ceremonies for centuries—to a massive sinkhole. Apache activists are using every legal and ceremonial tool at their disposal to stop that from happening.

Running is traditional. It's part of the girls' coming-of-age ceremony that takes place at Oak Flat. Initiates train for a full year, building the stamina needed to dance through the night. Physical resilience is also required of the male *gahe* (mountain spirit dancers) who accompany her. For Apache, running is a demonstration of spiritual power and physical strength. Today, running shoes and Lycra are an alternative form of regalia, and long-distance runs a new kind of ceremony. But they tell an old story: this land is theirs, and they will fight to protect it.

It's not just an Apache thing. Long-distance running is a venerated part of many Indigenous cultures, a pre-colonial means of communicating across great distances during times of crisis. So, it's fitting that Native water protectors and climate activists have made a kind of ceremony of relay running, a means of raising awareness about threats to their lands and waters. Many of us are familiar with the 2016 protests at Standing Rock, but fewer know that the movement began with a group of Cheyenne River and Standing Rock Sioux teenagers, and a 500-mile relay protesting the Dakota Access Pipeline. Buoyed by their success, they did it again, this time covering 2,000 miles, all the way to Washington, D.C. The runs were rich with ritual and symbol, bringing the fight at Standing Rock into national and international news. But perhaps even more importantly, the relays transformed the lives of those young people, enabling them to connect deeply with their culture and spirituality, to identify as warriors and culture-keepers, and build a community committed to healing.

Each year, Klamath River tribes hold a three-day 260-mile relay from the mouth of the Klamath River on the Yurok reservation in Northern California up to the river's headwaters in Oregon. The run was first held in 2002 after a mass fish kill: more than 60,000 salmon died in overheated waters. Since then, runners have followed ancient trails, praying for the health of the river. In 2024, after twenty-two years of tribally led political activism, four major dams on the Klamath came down, opening up 400 miles of salmon habitat, and creating a new era for Klamath River tribes who are working together to heal the ecosystem. And in 2025, a group of tribal youth were the first to kayak the length of the river, from source to sea. One of them was "Ducky" Franke Colegrove, born in 2002—the same year as the fish kill. "I've been involved with river warrior work my whole life," he said. "Ever since colonization, we've been living with little pieces of who we're actually supposed to be .... I'm hoping with these dams down, all of us will be able to reconnect once more."[10]

This third way in which physical movement can help metabolize our climate grief into purposeful action is through the transformative potential of ceremonies of protest, like those at Oak Flat, Standing Rock, and the Klamath River. To understand how protest can be a ceremony, we need to understand the power of ritual performance. In sacred rites, symbolic movement gives physical form to that which is assumed to be spiritually true. When Christians kneel in prayer, or Muslims perform *rak'ah*—the prescribed movements associated with *salah* (prayer)—they are physically enacting the deeper truth of their orientation to their Creator. When we bring our body into alignment with our beliefs, we bring abstract ideas into the realm of experience. Among the Tlingit and Haida of the northern Northwest Coast, for instance, potlatches and other winter ceremonial dances enact spiritual realities, making them present. Elaborate masks transform mid-dance: raven, killer whale, or thunderbird open to reveal the ancestor mask within. The Kwak'wak'wakw Hamatsa dance and the Nuu-chah-nulth Tlukwana ceremony reenact mythic stories wherein young men are taken by the spirits of warfare and aggression, but restored through prayer, dance, and ceremony. They give physical expression to very real spiritual struggles, representing them through metaphor and movement.

When ritual is functioning as it should, it changes us, and the world around us. How? Because within ritual we give voice and form to the world as it should be, performing it in community and with our own bodies, and in so doing we affirm that vision, and draw it closer. Entering into and transforming the story is how, according to Tom Driver, the marginalized "confront one kind of power with another, and rehearse their own future."[11]

In the same way relays, walks, marches, bike rides, creative street art, witty protest signs, songs, dance, and determined expressions of joyful movement can all become revolutionary acts with transformative potential. When we bring protest off-line and into the streets, when we stop worrying in the abstract about climate change and instead take a mindful walk in the woods, we remember that we are not alone. That we are part of a living world. When we care for our bodies, we build our resilience, we reclaim our agency. And when we do that in the company of our human and more-than-human relatives, we find new sources of insight and transformative potential.

Key takeaways

1. Exercise is essential for our mental and physical health, and eco-psychologists recommend that those struggling with climate anxiety take every opportunity to get outside and connect with nature.
2. Many Indigenous traditions use physical training and purification to build relationships with the other-than-human world. Here, physical fitness is not the end goal, but a means toward mental clarity, spiritual insight, and deeper intimacy with the natural world and its Creator.

3 Some contemplative practices combine movement, breath, and meditation. Yoga, tai chi, and sacred dance cultivate subtle energy and affirm the interrelationship between body, mind, spirit, and cosmos.
4 Collective, creative, ritual, and ceremonial movement can change in the world. For instance, activist long-distance running facilitates connection with Earth, alignment of breath and rhythm, and demonstrates the political power of symbolic actions.

Invitation for further reflection

1 If you are familiar with a religious tradition or physical discipline, consider how it connects with the ideas in this chapter. What opportunities does your tradition offer for mindful movement? For embodied practice within ritual and ceremony? What ways might your tradition bring those practices to the work of advocating for a just and sustainable world?
2 Do you have an exercise regimen? Does it provide you opportunities for connecting with the natural world? With your community? To bring your mind, body, and spirit together? How might you change what you're doing to make this more possible?

Want to learn more?

Visit our website at https://bloomsbury.pub/climate-spirit where you'll find recommendations for further reading and resources for individuals, reading groups, and educators.

7

Climate contemplation

When I picked my eight-year-old son up from summer camp, all signs pointed to a good day. He was muddy, weary, and had a grin on his face. The sun was shining; a cool breeze rippled the water. Perfect weather for hiking wooded trails and exploring tide pools.

"How'd it go?" I asked, anticipating a joyful reply. His face fell.

"It was the *worst*," he moaned. "They made us sit and *listen*. For like *ten minutes!*"

I'd been forewarned that campers were going to be experimenting with mindfulness exercises today, so I nodded in empathy, biting back a smile. "That must have been pretty tough."

"It was sooo boring. They better *never* make us do that again, or I'm going to be *so mad*."

Why contemplation?

Sitting quietly while paying attention to one's breath isn't something that comes naturally to most adults—and it's definitely tricky for eight-year-olds who would rather be building mud forts. But, my son's feelings about mindfulness meditation aside, his camp counselor may have been on to something.

It's often said that action is the antidote to climate anxiety. And to some extent, this is true. But it's also true that we cannot simply out-work or out-hustle all our problems. Frenetic activity, when not balanced with rest and renewal, is a quick path to burnout. Action can be a welcome distraction from generalized anxiety or sorrow—and, believe me, I can spin my wheels all day long—but history is full of the well-intentioned rushing off to save the world, only to make things worse. Good intentions don't guarantee good outcomes. As Thich Nhat Hanh said: "We do so much, we run so quickly, the situation is difficult, and many people say, 'Don't just sit there, do something.' But doing more things may make the situation worse. So you should say, 'Don't just do something, sit there.' Sit there, stop, be yourself first, and begin from there."[1] We need to act, and fast. But before we act, we need to think. And before we think, we need to listen: to marginalized communities, the natural world, and the still, small voice of the spirit within.

The truth is, my addiction of choice is over-working. But I'm trying to get better at making sure the actions I'm taking are the right ones, in the right way, and at the right time. And that means forcing myself to pause, and breathe.

In *Zen and the Art of Saving the Planet,* Thich Nhat Hanh writes that each of us has three aspects to our person: a meditator, an artist, and a warrior. "Our inner meditator brings us lucidity, calm, and deep insight." Our inner artist brings creativity, playfulness, and healing. And our warrior brings courage, and the determination to keep going.

> You should allow all three aspects to be active at the same time in order to have balance. We have to mobilize them all and never let one of them die or become too weak .... You have to know how to cultivate these three aspects within yourself so you can offer balance, steadiness, strength, and freshness for those around you.[2]

For those of us faced with burnout or struggling with the emotional overwhelm that comes from facing up to the climate crisis, contemplative practices offer a path for renewal, and a means of moving forward. By caring for our inner meditator, nurturing our inner artist, and providing wise guidance for our inner warrior, we can enter into the transformative work that climate change demands.

The psychology of mindfulness

It turns out, even a few minutes of mindful breathing lowers blood pressure, reduces cortisol levels in the brain, and calms our flight, fight, or freeze response. In fact, as few as ten mindful breaths can lower stress hormones, shifting our brain activity from the amygdala to the prefrontal cortex. Neuroscientist Jill Bolte Taylor explains that after shock or confrontation, our initial jolt of stress hormones typically only lasts for ninety seconds. Ride out those ninety seconds, she suggests, breathing deeply and watching the clock. After they have passed, we can then choose if we want to stay with that emotion, or begin to take steps away from it. As Taylor writes, "When I allow myself to remember that all of my thoughts are fleeting physiology, I feel less moved when my story-teller goes haywire and my circuitry is triggered."[3]

To better understand the relationship between mindfulness practices and mental health, it helps to consider their impact on our parasympathetic nervous system. Psychologist Rick Hanson explains that our sympathetic nervous system is fueled by adrenaline, cortisol, and dopamine. It demands that we respond to threats by *doing something*, and to pleasure by demanding *more*. By contrast, our parasympathetic nervous system thrives on oxytocin and serotonin. It responds to threats with problem solving, and to pleasure with gratitude, contentment, and a feeling of satiety. Our parasympathetic nervous system helps us slow down, repair, refuel, and center. It lowers our heart rate, eases digestion, activates the amygdala's ability to process and regulate emotions, and supports the part of the brain associated with motivation. To be healthy, we need our sympathetic and parasympathetic nervous systems to be in balance. The problem is, we live in a world that constantly triggers our sympathetic nervous system—with news alerts, media feeds, click-bait, and a consumer culture driven by fear of missing out or being left behind. The solution, according to Hanson, is to nurture our parasympathetic nervous system—and the best way to do this is with real rest, mindfulness, and gratitude.

An engaged parasympathetic nervous system is vital for effectively responding to existential challenges like the climate crisis. Here's why: Our sympathetic nervous system is triggered by stress, but how it responds to those stressors depends on our emotional state. If threats are met by positive emotions (happiness, love, security), our sympathetic nervous system responds with resilience, creativity, and determination, supercharging our prefrontal cortex to do its best work. However, if threats are met by negative emotions (anger or fear), our sympathetic nervous system responds by pivoting toward fight, flight, or freeze. We don't respond, we *react*. There's a huge lesson here: stressors in themselves aren't inherently bad. In fact, in the right circumstances, they can be good for us—inspiring a creative, resourceful response. The more we ground ourselves in love, confidence, and happiness, and the less we feed our fear and anger, the more effective our brains will be at solving problems when they arise. But it's our *parasympathetic* nervous system that builds those positive feelings of happiness, love, and confidence.

This explains in part why researchers at Johns Hopkins University found that mindfulness practices improve outcomes for patients suffering from chronic anxiety and trauma. Chronic stress inhibits children's physical, emotional, and mental development, and adults who suffer trauma experience higher morbidity and mortality. Professors of Pediatric Medicine Robin Ortiz and Erica Sabinga have found that participants in mindfulness interventions have "reduced depression and anxiety, reduced trauma-related symptoms, enhanced coping and mood, and improved quality of life." They conclude that, "high-quality, structured mindfulness instruction may mitigate the negative effects of stress and trauma related to adverse childhood exposures, improving short- and long-term outcomes, and potentially reducing poor health outcomes in adulthood."[4]

Psychologist Steven Hayes likewise recommends mindfulness exercises within Acceptance and Commitment Therapy to help his patients move from avoidance of difficult thoughts and feelings, and toward mindful acceptance of them, engaging them with openness and curiosity. In his work, Rick Hanson describes this as a three-step process: *let be, let go, and let in.* First, let our emotions be: accept and compassionately hold them. Name them. Let go of self-defeating or unfounded fears. Let in whatever good can be taken away from this situation, or whatever tools you have to heal from it. Clinical psychologist and well-known teacher of meditation Tara Brach uses the acronym RAIN to describe a similar technique for mindful engagement with emotions: (R) recognize what's happening; (A) allow ourselves to feel, (I) investigate the emotion with gentle attention, and (N) nurture ourselves with self-compassion. Mindfulness techniques can also help strengthen our emotional and mental resilience by helping us pay attention to small moments of joy, love, or connection throughout the day.

The power of attentive presence

We know that mindfulness techniques impact brain function and emotional regulation. But, as Thich Nhat Hanh has said, "Mindfulness can only help reduce our stress and tension if it provides us with insight." For the rest of this chapter, we'll take a closer look at how contemplative practices help adherents stop *reacting* to crises like climate change and begin *responding*. While varied in their techniques and philosophies, contemplative practices all offer tools for quieting the mind, being centered in the present, and transcending the finite self to realize our interrelationship with cosmos/Creator. By stepping into these moments of the eternal present, practitioners can regain balance within a world that is increasingly unpredictable. As extreme weather events, climate migration, and the downstream effects of social disruption become more common, our ability to quiet the mind, connect with what matters most, and discern the relationships that sustain and connect us will become more and more essential.

If we want to build spiritual resilience, we've got to get centered—and contemplative practices can help us do just that.

What is contemplation?

Very broadly, *contemplation* refers to culturally specific practices that quiet and focus the mind so as to become conscious of a greater presence, spirit, or order to the cosmos, and a realization of one's place within this greater whole. There is enormous diversity here—both between and within religious traditions. For instance, we may talk about "Buddhist meditation," but there are enormous differences between Japanese Zen Buddhism, Tibetan Vajrayana Buddhism, and Chinese Mahayana Buddhism, and within each are many different schools of thought and practice that have evolved over time. The same can be said of Hinduism, Jainism, Daoism, Sikhism, Islam, Christianity, and Judaism. Likewise, each Indigenous culture has their own approach to private and public contemplative practice—and often those practices differ from family to family. The idea that one can even talk about "contemplation" as a unified *thing* is pretty audacious—but scholars of contemplative studies try to do just that.

Hinduism scholar Lorelei Bernacki describes the heart of contemplative practice as "becoming aware—aware of oneself, aware of one's surroundings, just being attentive to one's reality. And it's something that basically comes through practice. It's this capacity to be more attentive, be more aware of what's happening. A contemplative practice changes a person's being in the world."[5] Muhammad Faruque explains that in Islam, contemplation is "a cognitive, spiritual activity in which the mind, body, and spirit work in unison to transform the self." Islamic contemplative practice includes *fikr* (meditation) and *tafakkur* (contemplation), and "*murāqabah*, which means basically watching yourself at every moment. And there is a further word called *muḥāsabah*, which translates roughly as self-accounting or something akin to 'self-examination.'"[6] Mary Virginia Rojas (Yurok) grounds her definition within Native Northern Californian spiritual practices when she argues that "meditation is the moment-to-moment awareness of self within the cosmos."[7]

Thus, we might define contemplative practices as techniques for focusing attention—both to our external and internal worlds—with the goal of transformation. Disrupting a narrow self-centered focus, we (re)realize our interdependence with God, Spirit, ancestors, cosmos. As Oludamini Ogunnaike, professor of African religious thought at the University of Virginia explains,

> the Real is witnessing itself through you, and you are nothing other than the Real. That's al-mushāhada .... The Qur'an, for example, repeatedly tells Muslims: *tafakkurū fī ayat Allāh*—to meditate upon the signs of God in creation. This could be the night and the day, the rain, the trees, the waves, the growing of plants, the

turning of the seasons. You fix your attention so that the deeper meanings, the symbolism, of these things are revealed to you.[8]

Mindfulness meditation

Contemplative practices aren't just good for our brain chemistry. They also help us cultivate a mindset essential for climate resilience. Contemplative traditions are often pragmatic, with concrete strategies for achieving alert, wakeful consciousness. For instance, some mark the beginning and end of contemplative practice with symbolic actions, such as lighting candles or snuffing them out. Others set physical boundaries, restrict some activities, require others, or incorporate ritual movement, to avoid distractions and focus concentration. A range of practices quiet and engage the mind: breathing techniques, recitations, visualizations, mantras, prayers, music, or percussion. And practices may look as different as you can imagine: from total stillness and silence to raucous movement that might include twirling, dancing, swaying, clapping, or singing. But always, the goal is experiential insight.

In Buddhism, contemplative and mindfulness practices are often aimed at cultivating awareness and presence. As Thich Nhat Hanh explains,

> The opposite of mindfulness is forgetfulness. Forgetfulness means that you are pulled away by the past, by the future, by your projects, by your anger, by your fear. You're not truly alive. Every one of us has a seed of forgetfulness and a seed of mindfulness inside, and if we train ourselves a little bit … after a few days the seed of mindfulness in us will become stronger.[9]

Buddhist traditions offer practices such as walking meditation, mindful eating, and seated meditation that can include focus on the breath, recitation of mantras, or visualization—all opportunities to attend to body and mind, moment by moment and without judgment, observing thoughts and feelings with compassion and with curiosity.

One goal of Buddhist contemplation is greater understanding of the Four Noble Truths. The first truth is suffering. Or, more specifically, that we experience stress, dissatisfaction, anxiety, and suffering in life, and the cause of this suffering is impermanence. All things emerge through interdependent co-arising, and all things are impermanent. Second, we suffer because of attachment, or desire. Third, we can escape from suffering by releasing our attachment, and letting go of desire. And, fourth, the means of freedom from attachment comes through following the eightfold path: right view, right resolve, right speech, right conduct, right livelihood, right effort, right mindfulness, and right *samadhi*, or meditative absorption. Mindfulness is thus not simply a stress reduction technique, but a means to facilitate insight and realization into the interdependent, co-arising nature of the universe.

In his work, Thich Nhat Hanh emphasizes the ideas that all things—including the self—are continually changing, and mutually dependent. Nothing exists in a fixed, finite state. And it is our attachment, our desire for things to remain unchanged, that causes us pain. Those of us grieving a changing climate can certainly relate to this. I feel pain when I see coastal communities lost to the sea. When I see heat-stressed cedars, declining salmon runs, starving orca. I sorrow amidst wildfire smoke, homes lost to the flames, or flood, wind, or rain. I grieve declining water tables, and rising sea levels. Realizing and accepting the impermanent nature of reality helps us cope with the pain of loss, and empowers us to work for a future we want to see. As he explains: "Our suffering is impermanent, and that is why we can transform it. And because happiness is impermanent, that is why we have to nourish it."

Dwelling in the present—with a spirit of awe and gratitude—is at the heart of much contemplative practice. When we arrive in the present moment, when we stop spending energy on regretting the past or worrying about the future, we are able, if only for the span of one breath at a time, to simply be *here, now*. And that is liberating. As Thich Nhat Hanh writes:

> Breathing mindfully, you simply
> Enjoy your in-breath and out-breath.
> You bring the mind home to the body, and you realize
> That you are alive, still alive, and this is a wonder.
> To be alive is the greatest of all miracles.

When climate anxiety or eco-grief threaten to overwhelm, contemplative practices ground us in the present, empower us to accept the changing nature of reality, and offer a deeper awareness of our interdependency. They offer pathways for cultivating emotional resilience, and a means to metabolize our grief, transforming it into compassionate action.

Contemplative ecology

Some contemplative practices help us gain spiritual insight through close attention to the natural world, what religious studies scholars call contemplative ecology. Theologian Douglas Christie explains that such practices "can help to ground sustained care for the environment in a deep feeling for the living world." Here, contemplative practice and scientific studies of ecology mutually inform each other, offering new means of understanding kinship and interdependence. While informed by religious traditions,

> the distinctively contemplative dimension of this renewal transcends religion (at least in narrow terms) and touches on

> a wider and more fundamental human concern: to truly know ourselves as part of the rich web of life. Contemplative ecology addresses anyone who wishes to think more deeply and carefully about what it is to be alive and attentive to the natural world, and to respond with care and affection.[10]

One example of this can be found in the work of Buddhist Studies scholar Stephanie Kaza, who grounds her discussion of Buddhist contemplation of the natural world in the notion of *intimacy*, which she defines as "a quality of mind—a willingness to be present with what is going on with full physical, mental, and emotional attention," and as much as possible to do so "free of interrupting barriers of self."[11] Kaza writes about being patiently present with a spider in her study, or learning to converse with trees, as moments when mindful attentiveness opens awareness to our interdependence with the natural world. But Kaza also cautions against the dangers inherent in our tendencies to romanticize nature, our anthropocentrism (not everything is about us!), and our inclination to commodify and consume experiences, seeking the exotic and the far-off, when insight and intimacy are in the here and now.

Historian Samuel Torvend provides another example, when he shows how Benedictine rules for monastic living simultaneously provided frameworks for day-to-day ecological contemplation and ways to resist imperial Christianity. Torvend describes St. Benedict's *ora* (communal prayer) and *labora* (labor such as gardening) as a daily contemplative practice grounded in ecological wisdom. While both were guided by the natural rhythms of the day and the seasons of the year, the *ora* created a contemplative space, while the *labora* linked that practice with one's seasonal labors and obligations to steward land and water. Benedict's teachings evoked "a sacramental imagination that recognizes the presence of God everywhere," and called Benedictines to be "faithful stewards rather than wasteful owners."[12]

Other helpful examples of contemplative practices exist within Celtic spirituality, a tradition emerging in fifth-century Ireland, Scotland, and Wales, when Christian monastics encountered pre-Christian Celtic traditions. These mothers and fathers of medieval Celtic spirituality sought sanctuary in out-of-the-way places—in sharp contrast to the Roman church that centered around seats of political and economic power. Here, nature served as a primary means of divine revelation. In the *Carmina Gadelica* (a collection of folklore and prayers gathered from the Scottish Highlands), creation is described as not just *good*, but also a manifestation of God's guidance, protection, and revelation.

> There is no plant in the ground
> But is full of His virtue,
> There is no form in the strand
> But is full of His blessings.[13]

And, of course, Indigenous traditions around the world emphasize attending to and learning from the natural world, so as to maintain harmonious relationships with it. Such practices include solitary reflection as well as the collective contemplation that occurs in ceremony, embodying and affirming relationships with more-than-human relatives. Reflecting on the spiritual traditions of his Hanis Coos culture, Don "Doc" Slyter puts it this way, "They say the Creator hid things out in plain sight. You're not going to see them unless you use that alertness. Ceremony to give thanks for what you receive is a really important thing to do. It makes you a part of what is around you."[14]

These examples may help us understand what contemplation *is*, but the question then arises: how does one *do* it? As might be expected, contemplative practices differ widely across traditions, reflecting different histories, cultures, and philosophical orientations to the world. In the rest of this chapter, I take a theoretical leap, to suggest four trail markers that may be helpful in discovering your own form of climate contemplation: breathe, center, create, and wonder.

#1: Breathe

Neuroscientists tell us that even ten mindful breaths can change our brain chemistry. And contemplative practices suggest that a focus on our breath can lead to insight, new ways of seeing that change how we relate to and live in the world. In many different traditions, attention to our breath helps to focus the mind, and to realize the interconnected nature of the cosmos. Some schools of thought describe an animated energy, sentient spirit, or sacred breath that animates all things. Daoist meditation includes the concept of *chi*. The Hindu Vedas introduce the concept of *ṛta*—the animating force or "beingness" upon which all things depend. The notion of the breath of life is deeply rooted in the Christian tradition, and often identified with the Holy Spirit, which animates the living world. Judaism teaches that at creation God breathed life into the first living things; a belief reflected in the Hebrew words *ruach* (breath/spirit) and *n'shamah* (soul/breath). In the Talmud, Jews are advised to pray upon waking *Elohai neshamah shenatata bi tehorah*. "My God, the breath/soul that you have placed within me is pure." For Rabbi Diane Elliot, this prayer guides her toward developing her own mindful breathing practice. "Reminding myself that each soul-breath I inhale from Source is *tehorah*, pure, becomes a touchstone for my day. Whatever challenges greet me, whatever missteps I take, I can return again and again to the gift of pure breath, soul, that remains unsullied, unshaken by the vicissitudes of the moment—refreshed, awakened, fully alive."[15]

Indigenous cultures of North America abound with philosophical traditions that emphasize a holy breath or wind that animates all of creation, and that also connects us with past and future generations. In Diné (Navajo) tradition, *nił'chi* or sacred wind is a sentient force, animating living things (which include mountains, rivers, and precious minerals). In Halkomelem Coast Salish culture, *shxwelí* is a fundamental animating spirit or breath that sustains human beings, ancestors, plants, animals, mountains, and waterways. All things are connected, because all things share this same spirit or breath. The Inuit term *sila* and the Yupiaq term *ella* can be translated as breath, consciousness, spirit, sky, wind, or weather, and are likewise used to refer to the fundamental unity within creation, while the Paiute term *puha* describes the sentient life force that sustains all things—from ceremonial regalia to the natural landscape. *Puha* transcends time, existing simultaneously in and uniting ancestors and future generations. I share all this to emphasize that breath as a site of revelation is not unique to any one tradition. Rather, this fundamental expression of life is widely recognized as both a tool of contemplative practice and source of insight. A first step in climate contemplation, then, may simply be finding moments to connect with our breath, and in those moments, remember how we are bound together.

As geneticist and environmentalist David Suzuki puts it, "we are embedded in air, all of us caught together in the same matrix .... Every breath is a sacrament, an affirmation of our connection with all other living things, a renewal of our link with our ancestors and a contribution to generations yet to come."[16]

#2: Center

Taking that deep breath can help us find the next step along this path: getting centered. And throughout human history, we've turned to different forms of prayer and meditation to do just that. We might think about *prayer* as the act of speaking with or appealing to a spirit or a deity, in contrast to *meditation*, which suggests attentive quiet, perhaps arrived at once one has run out of words. But prayer is also a contemplative practice, or at least it is when it facilitates transcendence of individual ego and realization of something greater than ourselves.

One example of this is Christian centering prayer, a practice grounded in the mysticism of Desert Fathers, St. Teresa of Avila, St. John of the Cross, Benedictine monasticism, and the writings of Thomas Merton. Here, the individual is advised to sit comfortably, choose a centering word, phrase, or short prayer that supports their intention, center on that word/phrase, and return to this word whenever distractions arise. The goal is not simply quieting the mind, but active consent to the presence of God within and experience of that Presence. The effects of such a discipline can be profound: neuroscientist Andrew Newberg at Philadelphia's Jefferson Myrna Brind Center of Integrative Medicine, found that nuns engaging in centering prayer had increased blood flow to the prefrontal cortex, improved focus, and improved memory.[17]

Ritual, ceremony, and movement can expand prayer's contemplative potential. When Jews don a prayer shawl, put on their *tefillin*, and *daven* (recitation of text with rhythmic motion), they are creating the conditions for contemplative insight. Five times a day, Muslims prepare to pray by performing ritual ablutions, removing their shoes, and stating their intentions. And then, orienting themselves toward Mecca, they engage their whole body in prayer through standing, bowing, kneeling, and prostration, while reciting from the Quran. Prayer provides the opportunity to quiet the mental chatter, attend mindfully to the present moment, and commune with the divine. Of course, not every prayer becomes a contemplative moment. But one might argue it is the purpose for which prayer began—to call attention, to quiet the voice that tells us to run ahead. And, instead, to be here now. And that stillness can inspire a third invitation for climate contemplation: a turn toward the creative, the intuitive, and the imaginary.

#3: Create

Contemplative practices can also be spaces of generative creativity. Ogunnaike suggests that poetry can be a form of "dynamic contemplation," and introduces us to the Sufi ceremony of *Samā'*, "which literally means listening," but refers to a gathering of poetry and recitation. These are expressive, collective spaces, where "most participants experience a profound introversion—a focus on one's own heart and inner reality, and ultimately the Divine Reality. Some people go into ecstatic states (*aḥwāl*) or experience 'openings' (*futūḥāt*) or undergo enlightenment. This recitation of poetry takes people to different states that would be difficult to access otherwise." Ogunnaike explains that the goal of contemplative practice is not a mind emptied, but a mind *dwelling*, richly and completely in *attentive presence*. Literal-minded language can never grasp such an experience, and so we must turn to the poetic.

> The Sufi tradition understands the world as a world of metaphor. Everything is a metaphor for the one true reality, the one consciousness, the Real—that is to say, God. And one important metaphor used for creation is speech. God speaks everything into being, and creation is ordered, and ordered speech is poetry, so the entire cosmos is essentially a poem. Poetry is thus an echo of the continuous creative act and can work to take us back to "who we were before we were".

In his poem "The Waterwheel," the Sufi poet Rumi invites us to enter into those crystalline moments of pure attention and mindful presence

> Our friendship is made
> of being awake …
> Stay here, quivering with each moment like a drop of mercury.[18]

#4: Wonder

I love contemplative practices, and have found solace in various practices when I needed it most. But I will also admit that the thought of bringing contemplation into my life isn't always inspiring. Sometimes it just makes me feel exhausted. My days are booked tight. I don't have hours for meditation, nor do I have the time or money for those gorgeous yoga-meditation retreats I read about online. How does contemplation work for working parents, particularly when we're not part of an intact culture where ceremonies and spaces for reflection are baked into our communal life? *Contemplation* as wonderful as it sounds, seems out of reach. Or, to borrow Rev. Dr. Barbara Holmes's words, "Contemplation is a soft word in a hard world."

For many of us, the idea of meditation may prompt an image of a (probably male) practitioner, free of obligations, seated in reflection, somewhere safe and comfortable. He doesn't have bills piling up, or children demanding attention. There are no bombs falling outside. This is someone who has escaped the demands of daily life. Holmes reminds us that this kind of "contemplation requires the privilege of time to retreat from the frontlines of everyday life, if only for a little while," and that

> for most people of color/culture and communities under siege, such comforts are inconceivable. We dare not shift our gaze for even a moment to consider an alternative reality. Survival requires an alert spiritual and embodied stance. To contemplate (in the ordinary sense of the word) during a crisis might increase

> the possibility that we miss or misread signs of danger in our immediate environment.[19]

This is an observation that may resonate with many of us, particularly those in the midst of a climate crisis, or working hard to stave one off.

But Cole Arthur Riley provides an alternative to a contemplative practice that depends on retreat from the world. And here lies our fourth and final element of climate contemplation: rediscovering wonder within the collective, embodied, messiness of the day to day.

> I used to think that Christian contemplation was reserved for white men who leave copies of C.S. Lewis' letters strewn about and know a great deal about coffee and beard oils. If this is you, there is room for you here. But I am interested in reclaiming a contemplation that is not exclusive to whiteness, intellectualism, ableism, or mere hobby. And as a Black woman, I am disinterested in any call to spirituality that divorces my mind from my body, voice, or people. To suggest a form of faith that tells me to sit down alone and be quiet? It does not rest easy on the bones. It is a shadow of true contemplative life, and it would do violence to my Black-woman soul.

Riley's demand for a different contemplation is akin to Ogunnaike's reflection on the west African Ifa tradition. "A lot of the contemplation in Orisha traditions," he explains,

> takes place in dynamic settings. People are dancing to music. People are singing. Some people think of moving your body as antithetical to contemplation, instead of a tremendous aid. In Ifa and other Orisha traditions, dancing, moving, singing, drumming are things that help us contemplate. The dances and complex polyrhythms and rituals are at once objects of contemplation as well as means of opening oneself up to more profound states of contemplation, of attending to what's really real.

Embodied experience reveals the divine in all things, and contemplation wakes us up to wonder, to encountering "the holy in the ordinary." For Riley, this practice of wonder counters despair, because "it works nearly the same muscles as hope, in that you find yourself believing in goodness and beauty even when the evidence gives you every reason to believe that goodness and beauty are void. This can feel like a risk to those of us who have had our dreams colonized, who have known the devastation of hope unfulfilled." Wonder becomes "a force of liberation .... Every mundane glimpse is salve on a wound, instructions for how to set the bone right again. If you really want to get free, find God on the subway. Find God in the soap bubble."[20]

Holmes also reclaims the possibility of contemplative insight for working and struggling people, what she calls *everyday contemplation*. "My contemplative practices include writing, music and dancing, prayer, stillness, social justice activism, and teaching."[21] Everyday contemplation is the cultivation of wonder. It abides in moments when we become aware that life itself extends from an infinite, abundant Source.

Why we need *climate* contemplation

Some contemplative practices are indeed the product of privilege and leisure. But I am most drawn to those that erupt from conditions of urgency. Because these are true expressions of the need of the moment—when cultures collapse, when colonizers batter down the door, when illness upends our security, and loss sends us reeling. In these moments of personal or collective crisis, our stability is lost. We are not where we *were*, and we don't yet know where we're going. We are bewildered. This is terrifying, and the potential for harm is real. But Holmes's approach to crisis contemplation can help us here, challenging us to consider the ways in which disruption creates contemplative space, when we experience that "cracking open, the rupture and shattering of self, community, expectations, and presumptions .... We may not have a choice about experiencing the crisis, but in community we do have choices about how we will survive." The climate movement needs contemplation because it disrupts the illusions of a static and individualistic self. And when our communities are in crisis, we're experiencing that disruption in real time. "The place that I name contemplative is a place of breaking, relinquishment, and waiting. This is not occurring in peaceful repose on our meditation pillows, not during the shared experiences of village life, but in the midst of disorienting freefall." It is an experience of "freefall from what we thought we knew, to a new story that is being written by events and experiences that we cannot control." In her work, Holmes never takes us to that theological fallacy that "everything happens for a reason," but she does insist that *we can create reason in the happening.*[22] The climate crisis forces us to let go—of control and expectations and assumptions—and in doing so, there is the potential for something new.

When he considers this moment of global breakdown, Aboriginal scholar and author Tyson Yunkaporta asks us to turn our attention toward the creative potential of what he calls "deep time diligence." As he explains, while we are in a moment of turmoil and undoing, the cosmos

> will tend towards order again, but it won't be the same order. New systems will emerge, and you've gotta be excited about that, you know, if you're looking at the big story, big picture arc of the world. It's not coming back, what was there before. It's not gonna be able to be held onto, what we have now. We are in for a rocky ride. And I guess we look at what emerges, and then figure out how we come into right relation there in order to hopefully retain some kind of role in the next system that emerges globally.[23]

Navigating this liminal time, requires "deep time diligence," a collective catastrophic risk analysis that aims at gathering the stories and knowledge we need, so we can continue as part of a system in flux.[24]

As Joanna Macy and Chris Johnstone reminds us, contemplative practice helps us see that "you are part of a much larger story, a continuing stream of life on Earth that has flowed for more than three and a half billion years and that has survived five mass extinctions. When you sink into this deeper, stronger flow and experience yourself as part of it, a different set of possibilities emerges."[25] Contemplative practice can help us remember that the future is not yet decided. And within this liminal moment, it is possible to find the insight and creativity we need to build a world for future generations.

Key takeaways

1. Spiritual resilience means nurturing our inner meditator, artist, and warrior. Building mindfulness and contemplative practice into our lives sustains our inner meditator, energizes the creativity of our inner artist, and gives guidance and determination to our warrior.
2. Mindfulness and contemplative practice are good for our mental health, strengthening our parasympathetic nervous system and ensuring we respond better to challenges when they arise.
3. Contemplative ecology integrates close engagement with nature into mindfulness practices.
4. Contemplative practices quiet the mind and help us become conscious of our connection to something greater than ourselves, often through a focus on breath, prayer, creativity,

or attending to the holy in the everyday, helping us become aware of the miraculous and numinous, even in the most mundane aspects of daily life.

5 The climate movement needs contemplative practice, both as part of self-care, and as part of the transformative work of changing the way we understand the nature of the world, and our relationship to it.

Invitation for further reflection

1 What are the contemplative practices within your tradition or culture? How might you learn more about them?

2 Where do you find moments throughout your daily life to cultivate awe and wonder? Try keeping a journal for a day or a week, noting down the moments you see throughout the day where you find delight, inspiration, interdependence, or "God in the soap bubble."

3 How might you incorporate meditation, mindfulness, or deeper awareness into your personal resilience? In your community? Your activism?

Want to learn more?

Visit our website at https://bloomsbury.pub/climate-spirit where you'll find recommendations for further reading and resources for individuals, reading groups, and educators.

8

Climate kinship

When I met the guy who would eventually become my husband, I had a few misgivings. I had a type, and he was not it. I dated brooding intellectuals, spiritual seekers, off-the-grid artists. But here was an extrovert utterly at ease in his own skin. He loved sports (ack!), and would opt for a happy hour over philosophical ponderings any day of the week. When we started dating, it was clear we didn't *get* each other—but we very quickly realized we couldn't get along *without* each other, either.

Things really got serious when I met his extended family in West Cork, Ireland. I'll never forget that first visit, a whirlwind of meeting aunties, uncles, cousins. I'd already fallen for *him*. But then I fell for his family and the brilliant green hillsides and windswept seas of Bantry Bay. Years later, when he (finally) got around to proposing, we were surrounded by cousins. I'm pretty sure he asked if I'd marry him. But I have to admit, I only remember him asking if I wanted to join the family.

The previous chapter explored how mindfulness and contemplative practice can ground us in the midst of eco-grief and climate anxiety, offering tools to transmute our pain into wonder, compassion, and something like peace. More than techniques for stress management, they are intended to guide us into deeper insight and awareness. The question then arises: what kind of insight are we after? In this chapter, I propose that insight into the ways in which we are interconnected and mutually dependent upon each other must be at the heart of liberative contemplation. Spiritual resilience lies in *radical relationality*, in rediscovering the strength of kith and kin. You're probably aware of the term kin. But *kith* may be unfamiliar. The word comes from the Old English cȳth, and refers to an intimate knowledge of a deeply familiar country or landscape, a landscape that is *inhabited*, filled with relatives, and infused with meaning and soulful nourishment. It's that soulful nourishment that I hope to point us toward here. In the first half of this chapter, we'll consider why those of us concerned about climate should care about kin and kith. In the second half, we'll look at different ways these concepts are understood, and how those distinctions can help us build spiritual resilience to transform climate grief into purposeful action.

Why climate work needs kinship contemplation

"Behold! A spiritual principle!"

Having hitched up her backpack, my mother aims her walking stick toward the nurse log. We are enroute to our wilderness campsite, and my wise mother takes every opportunity to point out the wonders of the forest—along with the wonders of the chocolatey trail mix in her snack bag. "After the mother tree falls, she keeps on feeding her babies." My sister and I note the infant hemlock trees running the length of the decaying log, like a row of soldiers standing at attention. Among them are fern, moss, lichen, red huckleberries, fungi of varying shapes, sizes, and hues, all nourished by the same source. Many years later, I will learn about systems theory, a fancy term for thinking about the interconnected nature of natural and social systems. But to me, it will always be nurse-log theory. Forest theory.

An essential step in growing climate resilience is transforming our perception, to see that we are beautifully and intricately interdependent within a web of human and other-than-human beings. Rather than succumbing to the dualism handed down from Western philosophy, which teaches that there is an essential divide between me and you, my soul and my body, man and nature, male and female, we come to find that we are in fact profoundly interrelated. We need to return to this vision, if only because failing to see our interdependency is what got us into this mess to begin with. We abuse the natural world and each other because we've forgotten that we are intertwined, and our destinies shared.

But this approach is also important because *trauma disconnects*, and therefore healing must *re-connect*. In *Learning to Live with Climate Change*, Australian climate researcher Blanche Verlie describes the trauma of climate change as a series of broken relationships.[1] It disconnects us from ourselves when we lose our sense of place. It disconnects us from others when we compete over scarce resources or argue over the political divide. And it disconnects us from the Earth as we live increasingly urbanized lives, with less access to healthy ecosystems. Or, as Barbara Holmes put it: "Connections heal because trauma disconnects us from the vital force that flows through gathered minds, bodies, and hearts."[2] If climate change fractures relationships, then our task must be to mend those breaks.

Anishinaabe scholar Lawrence Gross has compared the trauma of colonialism wrought upon Native American communities with the effects of the Black Death in medieval Europe, and identified similar patterns of response. He calls this collective disruption Post Apocalyptic Stress Syndrome, and names its symptoms: abandoning productive employment; an increase in substance abuse, violence, suicide, and mental illness; the abandonment of traditional religions and the adoption of fanatical and reactionary ones; loss of hope; generalized despair; survivors' guilt; and the collapse or weakening of social structures including family, government, healthcare, and educational systems. At the heart of this collapse? The loss of relationships that bound communities and generations together. My point is, relational restoration isn't just *nice*, it's essential for building resilient individuals and communities. As environmental ethicist Kevin O'Brien argues in *Meeting the Enemy*, the heart of America's climate-change-denial is our cult of radical individualism, a loss of a sense of collective responsibility and care.[3] This is why kinship contemplation is so important. It's a path toward reclaiming those moral relationships that sustain us.

Evolutionary biologists Lynn Margulis and Dorian Sagan would agree. In their work, they challenge the "survival of the fittest" cliche to instead argue for an *endosymbiotic* theory of evolution, in which we evolve not through competition but rather through *cooperation*.[4] In this theory, the species that survive are those best suited for collaboration and symbiosis. It's not our independence, but our ability to work within cooperative webs of relationships that keeps us alive. It's a perspective that helps explain why one of the most powerful ways to combat eco-grief or climate anxiety is to *take action in community*—whether that action is marching in a mass protest, lobbying congress, volunteering to care for the vulnerable, or joining a writing workshop.

Another reason why reclaiming kinship and relationality is so important is because resilient minds need more than just sleep, food, and exercise. As Rick Hanson explains, responding productively to stress requires "safety, satisfaction, and connection." In fact, chronic loneliness is very bad for our health. Without meaningful connections with others, our stress responses can get stuck in the "on" position, creating a feedback loop that may make it increasingly difficult to venture out into community. New research also shows that chronic loneliness increases systemic inflammation, damaging brain neurons and the synapses that connect them, and is associated with higher risks of cardiovascular disease, cognitive decline, and neurodegenerative diseases like dementia, Alzheimer's, and Parkinson's.[5]

Reclaiming our kith and kin can also help us realize our agency. I often hear my students lamenting that they feel powerless—doubting if anything they do can possibly make any difference. But acknowledging the interconnected nature of the world makes it an incontrovertible truth: when you are part of a system, what you do has an impact on the whole. *Each of us matters.* If you've been raised within the Western cult of individualism, this is easy to forget, particularly in the face of massive wealth and power disparities. While large corporations and the extremely wealthy may hold a shameful amount of power over our fate, it is not true that the rest of us are powerless. As Britt Wray writes,

> the helplessness we feel is a sham. Every decision counts, and from every moment forward, each choice has the potential to contribute to the prevention of more suffering. We've learned to maintain our helplessness ... The myth of the separate self has ripped many of us away from nature's intelligence and fueled this deadly crisis. The idea that we are separate from and superior to our environment, and humanity as a whole, is a cunning and powerful lie. Deconstructing this lie, and changing the 'dominant' mindset, is critical to shifting away from the path of destruction.[6]

In 2002, I was hiking in the foothills above Santa Barbara when I encountered a rattlesnake. Stretched across the trail, she was sunning herself, and quite content to stay right where she was. I had just left a graduate seminar about the personhood of plants and animals in

Indigenous traditions, and while I didn't expect the snake to speak English (I mean, come on), I also wanted to continue my hike. So I greeted the snake as politely as I could. I acknowledged that this hillside was her home, and that I was a guest. And I asked, could I please continue my walk? It's been a hard week, I explained. And it would mean a lot to be able to walk in these hills. The snake lifted her head, gave me a look, and then slowly slithered off the path and into the brush. I watched her go, elated.

Realizing that we exist within a world of kith and kin is key to climate work because it sparks compassion for others, prompting us to find solutions that are both effective and *just*. Studies have shown that when we feel compassion for a stranger suffering on the other side of the world, the same part of our brain is activated as when we feel concern for our immediate family. Essentially, when we feel compassion, we temporarily include that person within our circle of kinship.[7] And, when contemplative practices help us expand our notion of kin to *kith*, that is, to include the whole of creation, it transforms the way we see the world and our obligations to it. The bizarre notion that "humanity" can somehow exist outside of "nature" has allowed us to do irreparable harm to the world. Recognizing that we are *in relation with* the natural world helps explain why we feel pain when it suffers. As Joanna Macy and Chris Johnstone explains, "When we experience pain for the world, the world is feeling through us." This notion "doesn't make sense if we view ourselves only as separate individuals," but when "we perceive our deeper identity as an ecological self that includes not just us but all of life on Earth, then acting for the sake of our world doesn't seem like a sacrifice. It seems like the natural thing to do."[8] Because here's the thing, when we are connected to others—when we are aware of our kith and kin—it means we have obligations of gratitude and care. We know that what we are doing unto others, we are also doing unto ourselves.

Finally, realizing our interconnectedness matters because it builds our capacity for living with ambiguity and engaging with complexity. As we learned in Chapter 3, our brains prefer simple problems with simple solutions and obvious bad guys. But surviving in an era of climate change requires that we learn how to engage with complex and multifaceted problems and find hope and joy amidst unknowing and ambiguity. This is to say, understanding our place within a complex, interconnected, and sentient world is essential if we're to wrap our heads around the systemic nature of the problem, and the contradictory truth that things can be getting better and worse, all at the same time.

Kinship, the family of creation, and interdependence

In Nuu-chah-nulth creation accounts, all creatures were originally similar in appearance, and all spoke the same language. But as the world was brought into order, each being was endowed with a specific purpose, a unique role to play in the greater social order of living beings. Hereditary chief and First Nations Studies professor Umeek (E. Richard Atleo) translates the phrase *hishuk ish tsawalk* as, "everything is alive, and everything is connected." Understanding the full implications of that phrase requires understanding a closely related concept in Nuu-chah-nulth philosophy: "unity within diversity." Nuu-chah-nulth philosophy emphasizes a world of unity and wholeness that is guided by an awareness of and deep respect for biodiversity and the distinct personhood of all living beings. Umeek explains that while western biology classifies plants, fish, and animals separately from human beings, Nuu-chah-nulth peoples know them to be *quaʔas*, people, like themselves, with whom they should be in good relationship. This is a social philosophy that balances the fundamental underlying unity of creation with recognition of difference and respect for personal integrity. "Raven, Deer, Wren, and the entire diverse community of beings cooperate and work together, recognize each other, and practice the democrative principles of mutual consent and consensus building without compromising personal integrity." The Nuu-chah-nulth term *qwaasasa iš* gets at this culturally specific understanding of consent. It suggests an "accord, an agreement, a kind of consensus that reality is characterized by purposeful diversity." For Nuu-chah-nulth people, this understanding shapes proper behavior between people, including between human and other-than-human people.

One of my favorite examples of this is the Nuu-chah-nulth understanding that a kind person is not just one who offers help, but also one who asks for it. This is because, "asking for help when one needs help is to affirm the unity of creation; not asking for help when one needs help is contrary to wholeness."[9]

Indigenous North American origin stories are rarely about cosmic creation: more often, they are the stories of relatives. Of young women who marry the stars, or salmon, or bears. Of people who emerge from clam shells, ears of corn, hollows in the Earth, or stones in the river—born from the foods, waters, or lands that sustain them. Rarámuri scholar Enrique Salmón coined the term *kincentric ecology* to describe this Indigenous view of the natural world as an extended ecological family. Salmón's discussion is grounded in his people's concept of *Iwí*, the Rarámuri understanding that "everything around us is a direct relative of ours. When we breathe out, our Iwí is inhaled by all of life. Conversely, we inhale the Iwí of everything around us. We are in a constant kinship with all life, and it with us."[10] It is this understanding of life as kin, that shapes Indigenous understandings of functioning ecosystems. While many environmental activists have concluded that Earth would better off without human beings, in Indigenous philosophies humanity is a necessary part of this ecosystem, and (when we live as good relatives) we actually *enhance* the landscape. It's an understanding that rests on the knowledge that no living entities thrive alone: all are mutually dependent upon each other.

Because of this, many Indigenous teachers explain, the natural world does not just tolerate human beings, it actually *wants* to be in relationship with us. Patricia Whereat Phillps (Coos, Lower Umpqua, and Siuslaw) explains,

> Plants also have a spirit, so they're not treated like inanimate objects. They are living things. A lot of tribes teach that the plants want to have a relationship with people, going back thousands of years, these relationships with people digging and aerating the soil, which helps the plants in the long run. We're all working together with plants to create a thriving community.[11]

In her essay, "A Family Reunion at the End of the World," Robin Wall Kimmerer tells a story in which the original family of creation was fractured, when one species—humankind—forgot their relatives, and began to imagine themselves at the pinnacle of creation. The terrible result was a new kind of loneliness—*species loneliness.* Deep within, Kimmerer argues, we miss our relatives—these plants and animals and winds and weathers that we lived amongst with such intimate proximity for so many thousands of years. How could we not feel bereft and forlorn without them? And the bittersweet truth is that they miss us too: "All this time we have fed you, provided every single thing you need, sung you awake in the morning, and sung you to sleep at night, tried to teach you. We have loved you in every way we know how. And you didn't even know."

A kincentric ecology depends upon an animated, ensouled world, full of persons, with agency, sentience, awareness, who have rules, protocols, and social organizations all their own. It calls us to engage with both our kith and our kin. The task of Indigenous spiritual practices is to listen to these relatives, so that we can learn how to best be in relation with them. As Kimmerer so beautifully makes clear, kinship grounds us in love, and guides how we are meant to be.

> Kinship makes us feel part of this collective "we," while many of the social—and certainly economic—institutions in which we are embedded depend on alienation. They depend on isolation. If we are alienated from the living world, then we can commodify the heck out of it. We can extract everything and make it all into property, make it into natural resources, not the gifts of our relatives. So kinning is a very real antidote to saying that the world is just stuff and all this stuff belongs to us. Kinning with Grandmother Moon, with salamanders, with lichens on our rooftop—all of those are acts of resistance to the objectification and commodification of the world. But I want to say that it also brings us joy. It brings us joy and happiness, and that too can be understood as a radical reclaiming of who we are as humans.[12]

Reclaiming relationality empowers us. Because, within a relationship, what we do matters. And we can shape relationships through ethical speech, and action, and ceremony. The late Vine Deloria Jr. (Standing Rock Sioux) went so far as to say we ought to *minister* to the land, to care for it as it cares for us. This is a call for real gratitude—not the self-centered *#blessed!* gratitude of social media, but an orientation expressed through relational responsibility. When we reclaim our *kithship* with an animated world, we also reclaim our place within it, and our ability to change it—including the climate. And Indigenous traditions remind us again and again that our ability to impact the world around us does not have to be a bad thing. Blackfeet weather workers can exert control over weather.[13] Yakama ceremonies summon rain. Pueblo kachina dances welcome returning ancestors in the form of nourishing thunderstorms. While climate scientists have helped us understand how deforestation and burning fossil fuels are changing weather systems for the worse, Indigenous weather workers bring another way of conceptualizing the human–climate relationship, one in which nature and (human) culture are not separated, but intimately intertwined, mutually informing the other, so that all may flourish.

At its heart, kincentric ecology argues that human beings are co-equal participants in relational systems. Kincentric worldviews are not unique to Native North America. They can be found within place-based cultures around the world and throughout history. Essayist and poet Freya Rohn shows us that "there was no word, and thus no concept, of 'nature' in medieval Old English," citing literary historian Hana Videen, who explains,

> in the world of Old English there is no "creature" and no "nature"; instead we have *sceaft* (creation). *Sceaft* includes everything in the world ... humans, animals, plants, rocks and the sun, even dragons, phoenixes and other fantastical creatures. All that has been and ever will be is *sceaft*—animal, tree, mountain, river, people. No separation of humans from "nature," no separate names to parcel into hierarchies of rank, sentience, consciousness, "personhood." And because people are part of *sceaft*, they looked around them to understand how to live, learning about themselves from the other inhabitants of *sceaft*.[14]

The family of creation

I was on my way to the Divinity School at Vanderbilt University when I found myself behind a pair of young women. They were beautiful, blonde, quaffed, and skirted, a picture of privileged youth, glowing with health and walking like they owned the world. One reached up, giving the branch of a nearby tree a sharp tug. A flowering limb came away in her hand. She considered it for a moment before tossing it aside. Her friend made a sound of protest, to which the first tossed her hair. "God made that tree for me. So I can do whatever I want with it."

I overheard this conversation *decades* ago. But I remember it like it was yesterday, because that brief exchange summed up so much of what I believed to be wrong with the dominant American form of Christianity. This was the Christianity of empire and settler colonialism, a worldview rooted in dualism—of the separation of matter (which is corrupt) and spirit (which is pure, heavenly, and eternal). Within this hierarchy, spirit is superior to flesh, and humanity sits at the pinnacle of creation. It's a worldview that depends on a transcendent theology—a God that is separate from creation.

But there are other schools of thought that have also thrived in the Christian tradition—if perhaps farther away from the halls of power and empire. In contrast to transcendent theologies, these are *immanent* theologies, and they make different assumptions about God. First, they share a belief that nothing exists apart from God, because God is the source of all Being. In fact, God is Being itself. The word for the name of God in the Hebrew Bible (often translated into English as LORD) is the present-causative form of the Hebrew verb to-be. Literally, "the one who causes things to be, and keeps them being." If you also believe that "God is love" (1 Jn 4:7), then love can be seen as the force that creates and sustains life.

Second, in immanent theologies creation occurs when God extends Godself, giving shape and spirit to the world. *Life itself* is an exhalation of the breath of God. Here, creation is ongoing, and described as a series of emanations—light emanating from a Source. Life and existence are expressions of God, and cannot exist without God. Because of this, God can be found within and sustains all of creation. Essentially, because creation depends on the *emanation* of God, God is *immanent* in creation. (Stick with me, here.) Finally, we are connected to the rest of the cosmos because we are connected to God, animated by the same Spirit. However, unlike Indigenous philosophies, in Christianity, Judaism, and Islam human beings hold an elevated place in the hierarchy of creation, bestowed with a distinct responsibility to steward and care for God's creation—even while it *belongs* to God.

Origin of Alexandria (185–254 CE), articulates these ideas in *The First Principles*, the first systematic Christian theology. Origin argued that God holds the universe together, and imparts Being from Himself in a series of emanations. The first emanation from this Source is Christ, also known as Logos, or Wisdom (*Sophia*). The second is the Holy Spirit. Third are angels and humanity, rational and creative souls meant to be companions and conversation partners with God. Further emanations include animals, plants, and the rest of creation. Unfortunately, the curiosity of those rational souls led them farther and farther astray, until they forgot their connection to the Source of all Being. For Origin, there is no great "fall of man," nor is there original sin (as Augustine would argue two centuries later). Rather, sin, suffering, and evil stem from forgetting. Ultimately, all things will remember the source from which they come. This is *apokatastasis*, the restoration of all things, because God is "all in all."

A similar sentiment is shared by the fourth-century theologian Pelagius, contemporary and fierce opponent of Augustine. A founding father of Celtic Christianity, Pelagius flatly rejected Augustine's notion of original sin, arguing that because the Creator is manifest and revealed within creation, the material world (including humanity) must incline toward God and the good. For Pelagius and the emerging Celtic Christian church, the heartbeat of God beats within the natural world.

St. Francis of Assisi (1181–1226), the patron saint of animals and ecology, held that all of creation is a theophany—a manifestation of the presence of God's love, and through which we can experience

God's love. In Francis's *Canticle of Creation*, God's love binds all of creation together as a family, with Mother Earth, Brother Sun, Sister Moon, Brother Air, and Sister Water. Daniel P. Horan, Franciscan friar and theologian, offers a brilliant critique of the contemporary commodification of St. Francis, reducing him to niceties while ignoring the more radical aspects of his teachings.

> Anytime we reduce the saint to a medieval petting-zoo mascot or state simply that he 'loved animals' without regard for the radical truth about God and creation he intended, we are contributing to and operating according to the logic of the 'birdbath industrial complex.' St. Francis called all creatures—and not merely those nonhuman animals we classify as sentient, but rocks and trees alike—his sisters and brothers because, in a real sense, *they are* .... As Christians, we believe that we are part of God's family of creation, but we rarely act like it .... We are witnessing the consequences of that hubris on display before us in the manifold crises of pollution, extinction and global climate change .... We are related to and dependent on this planet in a way analogous to a child in a mother's womb. That mother—Earth—and all her children are facing an impending ecological omnicide, from which no one will escape. Therefore, as long as we ridicule this clear danger, we perpetuate the lies of the 'birdbath industrial complex' and promote a culture of death.[15]

For Quakers, a Protestant sect founded in the seventeenth century by George Fox, this immanent, *emanational* theology inspires a commitment to social and ecological justice. Because God animates and sustains all of creation, Quaker worship aims to quiet the mind so as to hear the Inner Light—the voice of God within. In their book *Quakers, Ecology, and the Light*, Cherice Bock and Christy Randazzo draw on this theological tradition to reflect on renewable energy—and solar power in particular.

> Although we have tended to interpret the Inward Light fairly anthropocentrically (with a focus on people), light moves through the whole ecosystem and makes life possible on this planet. The energy that is light transforms into living plants and other life on Earth. Humanity could not exist here without light, and without the other species and Earth processes that transform light into usable nutrients, and then back into soil. Read this way, we are able to see how the community of all life participates in the new creation, and human beings get to be participants in that community. But we are not the only ones. We are interdependent with other species; we need a thriving Earth community.[16]

In her work, Feminist eco-theologian Sallie McFague draws on the concept of *oikos* (family/household) to better explain how creation can be seen as an organic unity and expression of the body of God. For her, as it was for Origin and St. Francis, the redemptive work of Jesus is not just for human beings, but for all of creation. She uses the term *oikonomene* to describe creation as a divine household, "where all of creation are part of God's family (*familia Dei*)."[17] Theologian Kwok Pui Lan makes the case that God is *both* immanent and transcendent, while Ada María Isasi-Díaz prefers the term *kindom* over kingdom, arguing that it better reflects "the liberating family of God working together for love and justice, and is a metaphor closer to what Jesus intended." For her part, Wati Longchar, Indigenous theologian from Nagaland in Northeast India, explains that, "Creation is the first act of God's revelation. God cannot be perceived without water, wind, trees, vegetation, sky, light, darkness, animals or humans … God is present in creation," and we are all part of God's Earth family.[18]

African American theologians have also emphasized the relational nature of creation. Martin Luther King Jr. famously wrote, "All mankind is tied together; all life is interrelated, and we are all caught in an inescapable network of mutuality, tied in a single garment of destiny. Whatever affects one directly, affects all indirectly." Womanist theologians Rachel Elizabeth Harding and Rosemarie Freeney Harding explain that a "healthy respect for the unseen," helps explain Black Christian understandings of the web of life, and the spirit that binds all beings to one another. It's a view of the world that "cultivated an appreciation for both interdependence and restraint. The world is full of all kinds of living beings—humans, animals, spirits, plants, earth, waters, and winds—and we are all related to each other, but there are both appropriate and inappropriate ways for each to interact."[19] And this view is apparent as well within the work of womanist and process theologian Monica Coleman, who considers a view of God that is radically relational, one which honors religious pluralism and a God that seeks to be in conversation with creation.[20]

An immanent theology of God exists within the Jewish tradition as well, exemplified in the Jewish notion of *Shekinah*—the indwelling presence of God within creation. It is the *Shekinah* that leads the Hebrews when they're lost in the desert (Exod. 13.21), surrounds the Ark of the Covenant, and accompanies the people when they are sent into exile. The notion of a God present within creation can also be seen in the Jewish tradition of *tikkun olam*, healing the world. Introduced within the teachings of Isaac Luria (1534–72) and affirmed by the Baal Shem Tov (Israel Ben Eliezar, ~1700–60), Luria's story of creation is that of a God who is both within and encompassing of the cosmos. In the act of creation, God contracts God-self to make room for creation, placing divine light within vessels. Those vessels shatter. While most of God's light returns to God, some remains hidden, trapped, or concealed under shards. The task of human beings is to restore God to wholeness through good works and acts of holiness that liberate and heal the divine. Because of that, every individual human action may have cosmic consequences.

Shoresh is a Jewish cooperative farm near Toronto, with a mission to address three challenges: environmental crisis, poverty and hunger, and disengagement from Jewish tradition. Their work is inspired by a tenth-century tale, *The Letter of the Animals*. In this story, the world's animals have brought a lawsuit against humanity, protesting their enslavement. The Queen Bee herself testifies against humans: "They excuse all the cruelty they do because they believe everything is for their benefit alone; because they are our masters and we their slaves. They often can't see beyond their own appetites, beyond their own greed, and the whole world suffers for it." That story prompted the Shoresh community to consider their obligation to bees and other pollinators, including bee-keeping and care for their local ecosystem. Today, the farm blends sustainable agriculture with Jewish ethics and "creative rituals based on ancient teachings that engage and include bees as partners in their religious community."[21]

Within Islam, the Qur'an teaches that Allah has put Nature into order, that Allah is revealed in and worshipped by Nature. As İbrahim Özdemir writes,

> The Qur'an employs the perfect order of the universe as the proof not only of God's existence, but also of His unity ... God is the very meaning of reality; a meaning manifested and clarified, and brought home by the universe, developed further by humans. God is the dimension that makes other dimensions possible: He gives meaning and life to everything. For example, the Qur'an sees in the humble bee a recipient of divine inspiration, and constantly calls upon the reader to observe the perpetual change of the winds.[22]

Muslims are called to contemplate nature to discern the presence of Allah for he is "all around and within us," living in such intimacy with our fleshly selves that He is "closer to us than our jugular vein." As in other monotheistic traditions, humans play an elevated role in Islamic cosmology, called to serve as stewards of the natural world. As such, they "are personally responsible for the care and preservation of their brethren communities, be they human, plant, or animal. In this context every life-form possesses intrinsic value independent of its resource worth to humanity."[23]

The Quran is clear on this point, emphasizing that the whole of creation has value in and of itself, refuting a utilitarian worldview that would reduce creation to simply resources for our exploitation. It's a view that can be found throughout monotheistic traditions—although it is one not often recognized by those in power. "There is no animal on land, nor a bird flying with its wings, but are communities like you."[24]

Interdependence

If Indigenous traditions emphasize kincentric ecology, and monotheistic traditions emphasize a family of creation within the household of God, Buddhist traditions describe an interdependent and co-arising cosmos, while Confucianism, Daoism, and Hinduism offer conceptions of an animating force or energy that unifies the cosmos within a harmonious whole. In the former, the goal of enlightenment is to realize non-duality and interdependence, while in the latter traditions a goal may be to realign oneself with that harmonious whole.

In the Advaita Vedanta tradition in Hinduism, *advaita* (non-dualism), suggests that the spirit or soul within each living thing is an expression of Atman-Brahman, the highest Self or reality that connects and exists in all living things. The notion of *ṛta* reflects the order of the cosmos, unified by a common active creative energy, or animating force. Within Chinese philosophical traditions, *chi*–matter on the verge of becoming energy, energy on the verge of becoming matter–pervades all life, linking plants, humans, animals, and the divine within a balanced and harmonious flow, and reflects the essential oneness of the cosmos. As Neo Confucian scholar Zhangzai (1022–77) writes, "Heaven is my father and Earth is my mother, and even such a small creature as I find an intimate place in their midst. Therefore, that which fills the universe I regard as my body and that which directs the universe I consider as my nature. All people are my brothers and sisters and all things are my companions."[25] The Dao is not the same as a monotheistic God, but rather a conceptualization of the action, energy, and co-creating life within creation, the "basis of the emergence and unity of everything that exists."[26] Daoist meditation, movement, and breathing techniques in turn aim to align oneself with that unity. As the Dao De Jing famously reads, "from the one came the two, came the three, came the 10,000 myriad things."

As discussed in the previous chapter, different schools of Buddhist meditative practice assist in the realization of mutually dependent co-arising. That is, the notion that nothing exists in an unchanging, independent state. But rather, that all things are continually changing within an interrelated world. Thich Nhat Hanh puts it this way:

> Suppose I hold a leaf in my hand. What do you see? A leaf is a leaf; it is not a flower. But in fact, when we look deeply into the leaf, we can see many things. We can see the plant, we can see the sunshine, we can see the clouds, we can see the earth. When

> we utter the word leaf, we have to be aware that a leaf is made of non-leaf elements. If we remove the non-leaf elements, such as the sunshine, the clouds and the soil, there will be no leaf left. So, it is with our bodies and ourselves. We're not the same as, nor are we separate from, other beings. We're connected to everything and everything is alive.[27]

Kith, kin, and climate change

I take the time to explore these ideas because I'm convinced that an experiential understanding of the nature of our interconnectedness—with other humans, with past and future generations, with the natural world, and with Spirit—is vital for building both individual and collective resilience. It's an awareness that can help us cope with ambiguity and understand complexity, and has the potential to guide us toward empathy and compassion.

Human beings understand our kith and kinship with our human and more-than-human relatives in many different ways. Those differences reflect Nuu-chah-nulth understandings of *hishuk ish tsawalk*—unity in diversity. Greater awareness of our interrelatedness can help to metabolize our climate grief by reminding us that we are not alone, and that while we are mortal and all things change, we always remain part of the whole. We are sustained by our kith and our kin. Contemplating these ideas nourishes us in our work to address the climate crisis when they inspire a vision of a different kind of future. What would it look like if we built cities, trade policies, conservation networks, or criminal justice systems grounded in worldviews of interdependence, reciprocity, kithship, and mutual respect? What if, instead of self-interest and radical individualism, we approached the climate crisis with an eye toward building interconnected and mutually sustaining systems? (*Hint*: It would probably look a lot less like a massive centralized power station, and a lot more like a distributed energy grid.)

Key takeaways

1. Both sudden climate-related disasters and slow-burning climate anxiety can cause trauma. And trauma makes us feel isolated, cut off from the sources of support that sustain us. But connectedness is essential for our mental health, our collective resilience, and our ability to cope with ambiguity.
2. Indigenous kincentric philosophies articulate humanity's place within a world full of relatives. Here, our obligation is to learn the protocol for proper, respectful engagement, so that we can live in good relationship.
3. Monotheistic religions such as Christianity, Judaism, and Islam all include imminent theologies, where God is present within creation, and is the sustaining source of being. Here, we are all part of the family of creation, within the household of God.
4. Eastern philosophies such as Hinduism, Taoism, and Buddhism emphasize the impermanent and interconnected nature of the cosmos, and conceptualizes that unity through ideas like chi, ṛta, or the Dao.
5. While philosophical traditions differ wildly across time and space, they all seek to understand how human beings are in relationship with the rest of the cosmos, and how those relationships ought to guide ethical behavior. When we are part of an interconnected whole what we do—even as individuals—matters.

Invitation for further reflection

1. What does your tradition have to teach about kinship, compassion, or our relationship to the natural world? Or what do you know of other traditions?
2. What are ways you might remind yourself of interdependence or our kinship with the natural world in your daily life, or in the way you acknowledge the changing seasons?
3. Explore contemplative practices and meditations for thinking about interdependence. Visit this book's website, linked below, for recommendations for further reading.

Want to learn more?

Visit our website at https://bloomsbury.pub/climate-spirit where you'll find recommendations for further reading and resources for individuals, reading groups, and educators.

9

Decolonizing climate work

My dad's fourth-grade teacher wouldn't let the Native kid sit with the rest of the class. "She *hated* Indians," dad told me. James and my dad went to the same church. They were friends. But his teacher was outraged at an integrated classroom, and so she sent James to the back of the room, where a counter would separate him from the rest of the students.

> That didn't seem right to me. So when she asked if anybody else was an Indian, I raised my hand. I knew my grandpa was Native American, and besides, I wasn't going to let him sit there alone. Man, that ticked her off. James and I were seated facing the class on each end of the counter. The first day the teacher required wearing the tall pointy dunce hat which indicates stupidity. She wanted us identified as Native American, and isolated from the rest of the class. The hat lasted one day. We stayed in our positions for the school year.

Portland, Oregon, of the 1950s may not have been part of the Jim Crow south, but it had its share of bigots.

Then there was dad's high school graduation. It was 1966, and another one of his classmates had gotten in trouble—this time for not staying in the closet. The young man was gay, he was out, and school administrators chose graduation day to lay down the law. "Get straight," or forget about participating in commencement. Well, acting straight wasn't an option, and so this young man was relegated to the bleachers. He wouldn't be crossing that stage. "Anybody else?" the outraged teacher demanded, glaring at the surrounding would-be-graduates. My dad wasn't gay, but that didn't matter. He just quietly crossed the floor, and sat himself down on the bleachers. Dad didn't participate in his high school graduation. And he didn't care what people thought about him. "We show up for people who are getting bullied," he quietly told me. "Because it's the right thing to do."

I was well into middle age when I first heard these stories. All those years, and he'd never even hinted at these experiences. My kind, unassuming father, the guy who hates confrontation, modeled a different way to show up. You do it with physical presence and moral solidarity—even when it costs you something. "I'm telling you this," he went on, "not because I want you to think I'm some great guy. I just want you to know, this work you do, this focus on justice. Well, you come by it naturally. It's who we are."

Why justice?

I would like to think that justice needs no justification. Alas, the state of global politics would suggest that we still need convincing as to *why* compassion, equity, and decolonization matter, and why we must center justice if we're serious about the climate crisis. Building a ceremony of hope means stepping into the world we want to live in, one where "justice flows like a mighty river" (Amos 5:24). To that end, I start this chapter with three good reasons folks who care about the environment also ought to care, and care deeply, about justice and decolonization.

First, we need to care about justice because the origins of our present crisis lie in injustice. More specifically, racial inequality, Indigenous displacement, and cultural genocide.[1] Any response to climate change that is not grounded in restorative justice will be doomed to re-create the exploitative systems that got us here to begin with. Solving the climate crisis requires addressing its root causes: colonialism, extractive capitalism, hierarchy, radical individualism, human exceptionalism. We've assumed the natural world is inert and exists solely to be exploited, that some species matter more than others. We've assumed that some human beings deserve wealth, privilege, and safety, while others do not. And we've used those assumptions to justify the enslavement, removal, and outright extermination of human beings, and the destruction of entire ecosystems in the cause of temporary gain. It's genocidal violence which perpetuates environmental racism. In the siting of toxic chemical plants, land mines, and nuclear waste dumps in poorer communities. In high rates of murdered and missing Indigenous women. In the violent suppression of Indigenous activists. As Cole Arthur Riley has written, "it is hard to talk about climate change with someone kneeling on your neck."

But the environmental movement shares the blame, participating in what Indigenous activists call "green colonialism." A 2018 report by the Rights and Resources Initiative found that a quarter of a million Indigenous people have been driven from their homelands to make way for industrialized carbon off-set schemes or the creation of wilderness preservation areas.[2] Large-scale wind and solar projects have disrupted traditional hunting, gathering, fishing, and ceremony, while mining for resources like lithium and copper destroy sacred sites. Our clean energy transition will come at a cost—but a *just* transition requires the benefits be equally shared, and the costs not placed on the shoulders of those who have already paid too high a price. A just clean energy transition means not simply reifying systems of endless exploitation and extraction, but also *drawing down*, finding ways to live more equitably and sustainably. Simply put: those of us who have benefited from colonial systems have a moral and spiritual obligation to participate in addressing the damage those systems have caused. As Indigenous Studies scholar Michelle Jacob (Yakama) argues: "All peoples who live, work, learn, and play on Indigenous homelands have inherited the legacy of colonialism. In order to heal the soul wounds of intergenerational historical trauma, all peoples have an important role to fulfill."[3]

Second, decolonizing our energy transition isn't just the moral thing to do—it's also the smart thing to do. When you're facing the end of a world, it's wise to listen to those communities who have already experienced an apocalypse, and learned how to build resilient, transformative, and sustainable ways of living. As journalist Mary Annaïse Heglar explains, Black communities have long faced existential threats to their very existence, in the forms of slavery, segregation, environmental racism, and police brutality. Nonetheless, they built coalitions, created communities, and organized for resistance. "I'll grant that we've never seen an existential threat to all of humankind before," she writes.

> It's true that the planet itself has never become hostile to our collective existence. But history is littered with targeted—but no less deadly—existential threats for specific populations. For 400 years and counting, the United States itself has been an existential threat for Black people .... So the next time you want to "educate" communities of color about climate change, remember that they have even more to teach you about building movements, about courage, about survival.[4]

Choctaw theologian and former Episcopal bishop Steven Charleston likewise insists that it's time we started listening to and learning from those cultures and communities who have already experienced the end of their world. "My ancestors are a case study in survival .... If you wanted to find an experiential example of an apocalypse, you would be hard pressed to find one more total than what North America's Indigenous civilization confronted for more than four hundred years. If apocalypse means cataclysmic destruction–in essence, an end of the world–my ancestors went through it."[5]

Research has shown that restoration, conservation, and energy transition efforts are far more successful when they follow the lead of Indigenous and local communities. In 2018, a comprehensive study of twenty-eight nations found that the best way to preserve biodiversity and sustain forests was to recognize Indigenous sovereignty over their territories,[6] while a 2021 study calculated that the cumulative impacts of US and Canadian Indigenous activists led to a 12 percent decrease in those countries' carbon emissions—despite their being less than 2 percent of the overall population.[7] Or consider a 2024 research review of 648 empirical studies of conservation projects around the globe, which found a direct correlation between success and the degree to which Indigenous and local communities led the project, and local knowledge and protocols were respected.[8] Conservation, climate, and community projects succeed when they attend to the hard-earned wisdom of Indigenous and local communities. We need to start listening to those voices that have, up to now, been systematically excluded from decision-making.

Third, climate change is a justice issue because those communities who contributed the least to climate change are impacted the most. As Mary Robinson, former president of Ireland and UN Special Envoy on Climate Change, has written, "This injustice—that those who had done the least to cause the problem were carrying the greatest burden—made clear that to advocate for the rights of the most vulnerable to food, safe water, health, education, and shelter would have no effect without our paying attention to our world's changing climate."[9] Emissions from the wealthiest 10 percent in the United States and China alone are responsible for a two- to threefold heat increase in vulnerable regions of the world. The world's wealthiest 1 percent contributes 1,000 times more carbon than the poorest 1 percent, and more than twice the emissions of the 3.1 billion people who make up the poorest 50 percent.[10] All this, while climate change disproportionately impacts the vulnerable, amplifying natural disasters, increasing risks of drought, food and water insecurity, causing economic and political instability. And when hurricanes, floods, or wildfires hit home, those most at risk are the young, the old, the poor, the disabled, the sick, and the socially marginalized. While the impacts of climate change are being felt everywhere, their impacts will be most severe in the global south and in areas already struggling with poverty—the very places that have contributed the least to the problem.

Justice teachings from the world's religious traditions, whether grounded in kinship, interdependence, or an understanding of the family of creation, demand a response. They also show us that equitable communities are resilient communities. When everyone has access to clean air, clean water, healthy food, medical care, safety, rest, and a means of being in relationship with the natural world, communities are stronger and better able to withstand crisis when it occurs. We all benefit from our neighbors' stability. But more than this: when we understand our kinship with creation, we long to see all children safe and free. Martin Luther King Jr. famously said, "injustice anywhere is a threat to justice everywhere," and James Baldwin explained, "We have yet to understand that if I am starving, you are in danger."[11] And Cole Arthur Riley reminds us, "Liberation recognizes that I won't get free by anyone else's bondage."[12]

Fourth, centering justice and decolonization in climate work is the right thing to do, but it's also simply *good for us*. Climate change is, at its core, a problem of relational disharmony. And, as I've argued throughout this book, real resilience is radically relational. It requires continually re-weaving the ties that bind us to other human beings, the natural world, our ancestors, and Spirit. Unjust systems sever those ties. Just systems sustain and strengthen them.

The term "moral injury" was first used to describe the trauma soldiers experienced when required to act in conflict with their conscience. Climate psychologists now use the term to explain the impact we feel when forced to participate in unjust systems that harm other persons or the Earth. We are all, directly or indirectly, experiencing the moral injury and trauma of climate change. But we also all have the opportunity to experience what psychologists call *post-traumatic growth*, to grow into the "beneficial psychological, emotional, or social changes," that can follow a traumatic experience or natural disaster.[13] This book is not about assuaging our climate grief, but metabolizing it, and to do that the only way *out* is *through*. Moving from denial, through sorrow, and into action requires turning toward what is difficult, and facing it with courageous compassion. To get there, we need what Blanche Verlie calls "affective transformation," to "bear the burden of complicity in ways that hold us accountable and generate radical change."[14] The point here is not to wallow in self-centered guilt—that's simply not helpful. Rather, I want us to acknowledge the role of restorative justice in psycho-spiritual wellbeing. Until we can name the harm that has been done to us and by us, we cannot move on. If we're to transform our climate grief and anxiety into purposeful action we need to learn from our trauma. And that requires acknowledging our pain, being courageous with our discomfort, and reawakening our curiosity.

What is justice, anyway?

"But that's communism!" A look of horror has filled my childhood friend's face.

It's the height of the Reagan Era, deep in the Cold War. I'm only ten years old, and my friend's reaction has taken me by surprise.

"No," I try to explain, startled by her reaction. "That's just Jesus."

It's easy to see where I went wrong: I'd been reading the Bible. (Always a dangerous thing to do.) Turns out it's full of admonitions to sell all you have and give to the poor, to not store up your wealth, to trust like lilies of the field, and how hard it is to squeeze rich men through eyes of needles. Problem was, I hadn't yet learned to skip over these (inconvenient) truths.

But those lessons matter. Because we're far more likely to work for justice—particularly when it's painful or even just inconvenient—when we have a clear sense of what justice *is*, and why we ought to care about it.

When I ask my students what comes to mind when they hear the word justice, they usually say something along the lines of "an eye for an eye," or "equal rights." But there are other ways of thinking about justice that may be more helpful when it comes to transforming our grief and anxiety into restorative, relational action. In the next section, I want to introduce three lessons found in different religious and Indigenous traditions that might help us reconsider what justice means, and how it can inform climate work. First, justice is not about equal rights. It actually challenges us to go further, to privilege the needs of the most vulnerable, to seek out those who most need assistance, and put them first. Second, justice is not about punishment but renewal; it's about reclaiming the people we are meant to be, and the world we're meant to have. And, third, justice must include decolonization, because it must be grounded in restorative action.

Do unto others

If there's one thing the world's religious traditions agree on, it is the so-called Golden Rule. From ancient Egypt and Sanskrit texts, to Judaism, Christianity, Islam, Sikhism, Buddhism, and Baha'i, we find some variation on a common theme: treat others as you would have them treat you. Indigenous North American trickster stories about Coyote and Raven take this lesson a step further, as they tell listeners again and again that when we act out of self-interest we fail, making an ass of ourselves in the process. But when we act out of concern for others, we succeed, and change the world for the better.

In monotheistic religions, the Biblical prophets provide the foundation for definitions of justice, loudly and provocatively demanding that God's people reject false idols, and offer support for the poor, the widow, and the orphan. In prose simmering with barely contained rage, they call out the powerful, and demand care for the sick, the exile, the prisoner. Jesus may have sometimes talked in riddles, but he was most direct when telling his followers to care for "the least of these," the child, the refugee, the hungry, the thirsty, the sick. As Riley writes: "To me, it is not an oversimplification to say the Christian story is the tension between the promise of justice and liberation and the unjust and oppressive patterns in our daily lived experiences. I simply cannot comprehend the Gospel outside of this."[15] That call to radical compassion was so disruptive, it threatened an empire, and led to the cross.

Episcopal bishop of South Africa Desmund Tutu reflected on the role this justice tradition played for those activists suffering under the brutality of South African apartheid:

> If it weren't for faith, I would have given up long ago. I am certain lots of us would have been hate-filled and bitter. For me the Scriptures have become more and more thoroughly relevant to

> our situation. They speak of a God who, when you worship him, turns you around to be concerned for your neighbor. He does not tolerate a relationship with himself that excludes your neighbor. It is the horizontal dimension that makes our faith so thoroughly subversive in a situation of oppression and injustice. It speaks of the infinite value of human persons. We count for God because he treated us lovingly. Each one of us is the object of divine love as if we were the only person around. We are created in God's image and, therefore, each one of us is held to be a representative, a viceroy of God.[16]

In his 2015 encyclical *Laudato Si*, Pope Francis builds on this tradition of justice as care for the vulnerable, when he makes a clear connection between the "cry of the poor" and the "cry of the earth." *Laudato Si* draws from Catholic social teachings that value human life, dignity, rights, and responsibilities, and emphasize God's concern for the poor, peacemaking, and creation, all of which rest in turn on the notion of *imago Dei*: that creation is a living revelation of God.[17] Liberation theologians like Gustavo Guitierrez have likewise emphasized God's "preferential option for the poor," while eco-theologians like Sallie McFague have argued that "nature can be seen as the new poor, "not the poor that crowds out the human poor, but the 'also' poor; and as such it demands our attention and care."[18]

For climate scientist Katharine Hayhoe, her Christian faith animates her work.

> I'm a Christian and I believe that if you are someone who takes the Bible seriously, then you already care about climate change .... Climate change disproportionately affects the poor, the hungry, and the sick, the very ones the Bible instructs us to care for and love .... In fact, if Christians truly believe we've been given responsibility–

'dominion'–over every living thing on this planet, as it says at the very beginning of Genesis, then we won't only objectively care about climate change. We will be at the front of the line demanding action because it's our God-given responsibility to do so.

> Failing to care about climate change is a failure to love. What is more Christian than to be good stewards of the planet and love our global neighbor as ourselves? .... As a Christian, I believe we're called to love others as we've been loved by God, and that means caring for those who are suffering–their physical needs and their well-being—which today are being exacerbated by climate impacts. How could I not want to do something about that? .... To care about a changing climate, we don't have to change anyone's values or try to transform them into anything other than who they already are. We just need to be people who want this planet to continue to be a safe, hospitable home for us all.[19]

Biblical and Christian notions of justice are thus not merely an admonition that everyone ought to have equal opportunity, but a much more radical call to put *first* the safety and wellbeing of those who are least able to protect themselves, heal themselves, or sustain themselves. It is a call to be "God's hands in the world" in caring for "the least of these." It's this insistence on the radical compassion of Christ that inspired African American theologian Christopher Carter's call for food justice, where the costs and benefits are shared equally, and where such care is extended to the human beings who grow, transport, prepare, and consume the food, but also other living beings as well. This is not a call to offer "thoughts and prayers," but a divine commandment to transform our systems for the safety and wellbeing of all.

Restorative justice

Buddhist conceptions of right action are rooted in the Buddha's teachings of mutual co-arising (that everything is interdependent and continually changing). Meditation upon and clear understanding of the nature of suffering inspires compassion and a desire to reduce suffering in the world. The contemporary activist stream of Buddhism, known as "Engaged Buddhism," is associated with peacebuilding, hospice care, and environmental activism, animated by deep understanding of the nature of suffering, and sustained by mindfulness, compassion, and contemplative practice.[20]

Buddhist notions of justice are most often associated with a popular understanding of karma, which certainly helps to illustrate interdependence in perhaps more pragmatic ways: if one's actions have consequences, then good actions lead to good outcomes, and bad actions to bad outcomes. But Buddhist studies scholar James Blumenthal cautions against simplistic interpretations of karma, which might imply that our future is predetermined. "If future experience is entirely determined by past karma, it would undermine any real agency, which in turn would undermine karma doctrine itself." For Blumenthal, karma is meant to emphasize our ability to take action and change our fate, rather than doom us to our destiny, and it is our ability to choose to change, our ability to restore ourselves to right relationship, that lies at the heart of Buddhist justice.[21] We can reclaim our agency and change our future, if we give up wallowing in guilt and turn instead toward transformative action.

Blumenthal's Buddhist philosophy of justice is *restorative justice.* If retributive models of justice demand retribution (an eye for an eye), restorative models of justice work toward "resolution and peace between the criminal and victim." Rather than punishment, they seek to "heal the root cause of the crime and the damage inflicted in its wake." Furthermore, punitive models that demand retribution fail to live up to Buddhist standards of justice, he argues, because they deny the dignity of both the offender and the offended, and the possibility of restored relationality. Truly restorative models seek to reclaim the wellbeing of all those involved—both human and other-than-human. When it comes to environmental justice, truly restorative models would not simply pay off those who have been harmed (though that may also happen) but would go on to address the *root cause* of that harm, to consider how such harm was caused in the first place, and to restore us all to better relationship with the Earth, other creatures, and each other.

Cole Arthur Riley reflects this perspective when she frames true justice as the restoration of dignity. As she argues, real justice "does not demean the offender's dignity; it affirms it. It communicates that what has been done is not what the offender was made for. They, too, were made for beauty. In justice, everyone becomes more human, everyone bears the image of the divine."[22] It is this struggle—between the world as it may be and the world as it is meant to be, between *us* as we are, and *us* as we ought to be—that grounds the work of justice.

A wonderful example of the restorative potential of justice shows up in Anishinaabe territories. A verb-based language, in Anishinaabe, you do not say, "there is a river." Rather, you would say, "it is rivering." It's a language that acknowledges both a sentient, living world and the continually transformative potential within all beings. When Anishinaabe epistemology was reintroduced in tribal courts, it opened the door to restorative justice, reorienting the nature of victim and offender. For while you may have done wrong, you are not defined by that act. You are not a thief, but one who thieved. Not an abuser, but one who abused. Not a victim, but one who was victimized. Restoration, and transformation, remains possible.

Justice is not simply a matter of equal rights. It's more than that. It's about actively seeking out the least of these, and putting them *first*, before the wealthy and the powerful. It's not simply retribution, it's restoration.

Decolonize the work

Whether we understand our call to justice to be rooted in divine command, in a call to emulate the compassion of Christ, our essential interdependence with the rest of the cosmos, or the kinship obligation we have to care for our relatives, religious and Indigenous traditions around the world call us to be our better selves, to do unto others as we would have them to do unto us, to acknowledge that we are siblings within the broader circle of creation. This means that whatever solutions we seek, whatever work we do, *must begin* with a commitment to care for those who are the most vulnerable, to heed those who have been silenced, and to actively repair the injuries that have been caused. One way we can do that is by attending to a particular form of restorative justice: decolonization.

If you want to know what decolonization looks like, you might start by asking the Indigenous people of the Klamath River. Cutcha Risling Baldy (Hupa/Karuk/Yurok) sums it up: "It's not that hard to understand. In fact, it's really simple. Take. Down. The. Dams."

Decolonization is first and foremost about *giving the land back*. At minimum, settler colonial society can begin by simply honoring the legally binding treaties that our governments signed with Native nations, and never fulfilled. But at its heart, as Indigenous scholars Lyla June Johnson (Dine/Cheyenne), Patty Krawec (Anishinaabe), and Yuria Celidwen (Nahua/Maya) make clear, decolonization is about restoring Indigenous people's ability to be in relationship with and care for their lands and waters, foods and medicines.

The #LandBack movement is not about kicking people out of their homes (that's a colonial move, after all), it's about honoring Native sovereignty, and empowering them to protect and restore their homelands. If Euroamerican understandings of land ownership imply the *right* to do whatever you want with your piece of property, Indigenous notions are grounded in *responsibility*—to care for one's land, and ensure its wellbeing for future generations. Diane Teeman (Burns Paiute) puts it this way: "Everything has a right to be, and so we need to try and make sure that they're treated fairly."[23] Despite this straightforward guidance, climate activists may still be wondering how to proceed. So in the rest of this chapter, I want to offer three steps for decolonizing climate work: name the hurt that's been done, heed traditional ecological knowledge, and learn how to listen.

Name the hurt

My doctoral dissertation research took me to the Shoalwater Bay Indian Reservation in southwest Washington, where I was hoping to learn from the community's response to devastating rates of pregnancy loss that threatened their future as a people. These are the descendants of survivors. Their ancestors fled apocalypse, leaving behind their village sites on the Columbia River whose populations had been nearly wiped out by measles and smallpox, their homelands overrun by white settlers. Those ancestors had taken refuge on Willapa Bay. Then, in the late 1990s, they experienced a new threat to their survival. While their coastline looked pristine, the reservation was on the receiving end of a slew of toxic runoff from agribusiness, industrial forestry, and an old munitions dump. They were also hours away from the nearest Indian Health Service clinic. Tribal leaders fought back, securing funds to staff their own environmental assessment lab and build a wellness center integrating biomedicine with Native healing traditions.

In the midst of this crisis, they also welcomed a spiritual leader from a neighboring tribe, who brought traditional medicines and held a naming ceremony. In that ceremony, he bestowed upon contemporary tribal members the names held by ancestors who had been lost to disease. It was a powerful move, one that ensured those names—and the memories of those ancestors—survived. Names are a powerful thing in Coast Salish and Chinook culture. The word for receiving a name suggests that you are *wrapped* in it, like being wrapped in a blanket—another ritual that symbolizes honor, gratitude, and care. If you receive an ancestral name, you're obliged to wear it well, to keep it clean, so that it can be passed on to the next generation. Carrying a name is a responsibility. And that ceremony is a powerful example of what it means to remember the pain of the past—to literally name it—and draw from that painful past a means of healing for the future.

Trauma therapists and climate psychologists agree that personal and collective healing begins by recovering stories, documenting history, by naming what has been lost and the hurt that's been done. This feels particularly poignant in an era when state and national governments may be censoring our history, trying to erase from the record any acknowledgment of the violence of slavery, racism, segregation, or colonialism. The only way forward is to reckon, honestly, with our past. And that means insisting on histories that tell true stories, even those we might prefer to forget, and demanding that our own institutions—including our churches, universities, and businesses—reckon with the ways in which we have participated in and benefitted from unjust systems.

Heed traditional ecological knowledge

Some of the best guidelines for decolonizing climate work can be found in the growing field of Traditional Ecological Knowledge (TEK). TEK is a term coined by Indigenous philosophers to represent the collective knowledge that Indigenous people have derived from their relational engagement with a living landscape. It employs many of the same methodologies of Western science (observation, hypothesis, analysis) but also includes spirituality, philosophy, arts, and social and political organization. While Western science reveres objectivity (seeking to minimize human interaction with a test subject, for instance), TEK is all about those relationships. It asks, "how can we be in better relationship with the world around us?" And while Western science tries to identify universally true laws, TEK seeks deep local knowledge, grounded in relationship with place.

In his book *Sand Talk: How Indigenous Thinking Can Save the World*, Tyson Yunkaporta (Apalech Clan) draws from Australian Aboriginal teachings to identify four steps for doing good work with Native communities. Respect: align your work with local Indigenous values and cultural protocols. Connect: establish strong relationships of equal or equitable exchange. Reflect: as a group, collectively consider how the knowledge that has been shared with you should inform how you move ahead. Direct: act on that shared knowledge in ways agreed upon by all. Unfortunately, Yunkaporta notes, policy makers and business leaders tend to do these things in reverse order. They act, only to then realize they've caused deep offence to a local Indigenous community. They try to retroactively fix their mess, to build relationships where trust has already been damaged, only after the fact learning about the local values and protocols they should have known to begin with.

Q'um Q'um Xiiem Joanna Archibald (Sto:lo) identifies a similar set of principles to guide collaborative work with Indigenous communities, what she calls "the four R's": respect, responsibility, reverence, and reciprocity. First, show respect for Indigenous people, traditions, practices, and protocols. Then, acknowledge that you are responsible to that community, the Earth, and your ancestors. Be prepared to answer to them when your work is done. Show reverence for the knowledge you are given, for the spiritual relationships that that knowledge represents, and the history of harm that may be part of it. Finally, give back to the community and the Earth, as an expression of gratitude and a recognition of your obligation.[24]

But we should also listen to Indigenous people because we'll be better off if we do. Indigenous people are 6.2 percent of the global population, but steward 80 percent of the planet's biodiversity. When Native people's rights to their lands and waters are protected and restored, we all benefit, with healthier rivers, restored keystone species, and intact ecosystems. While settler colonizers thought they were discovering and subduing an untouched wilderness, they were in fact invading Native lands and waters that had been carefully managed. Indigenous people were planting gardens, clearing forests with controlled burns, managing species populations, and practicing aquaculture. And they were doing so using techniques they had learned over countless generations of listening to the sentient beings around them, and discerning how they could be in better relationship with them. As Native Hawaiian scientist Rosie Alegado puts it: "When I talk about Indigenous seascapes, what I really mean is that these are coastal and marine spaces that have been occupied and managed by peoples for millennia .... Like an aquatic forest garden."[25]

Learn how to listen

Indigenous people are profoundly concerned about the effects of climate change on their lands and waters: they stand to be impacted more severely and more existentially than other populations. They have also, on the whole, contributed the least to the problem. They overwhelmingly support a clean energy transition and the end of a fossil fuel economy. But they are also raising the alarm when confronted by settler colonial solutions that grow from the same toxic roots: extractive consumer economies, radical individualism, and hierarchical thinking that reduces Earth to resource, and sentient beings to "consumers" or obstacles to be removed. A justice model informed by radical compassion, restorative justice, and traditional ecological knowledge demands that we do not simply continue with business as usual, merely shifting from one form of extraction and exploitation to another. Instead, we have to learn how to listen to those who have historically been excluded from the conversation, to engage in real partnership, and real collaboration.

What may be clear by now, is that grounding climate work in justice and decolonization requires radical relationality. Environmental scientist and psychologist Bob Doppelt argues that resilient communities are defined by networks of support, grounded in healthy relationships. And you don't get good relationships or effective collaboration without first learning how to listen.[26] But there are two big challenges here. First, for those of us who have experienced trauma, engaging in difficult conversations can be painful, prompting defensiveness, or anger. It can be burdensome to speak up if you've been beaten down for doing so in the past, and it can be hard to listen, if you're hearing something that hurts. Second, we need to remember that listening is a skill more often demanded of the vulnerable. When you lack physical, social, or political power, you get very good at reading the room, heeding social cues, listening for the unspoken or implied threat. But for those of us who haven't had to rely on paying attention as a means of survival, listening doesn't often come naturally. So, when I say we need to learn how to listen, I also acknowledge that this is a tough skill to practice.

But learning to listen is so vital that Christiana Figueres, former Executive Secretary of the United Nations Framework Convention on Climate Change, described "listening deeply and sincerely" as the most underrated but impactful skill she brought to her work on climate engagement.[27] Thich Nhat Hanh and Sister True Devotion agree, centering compassionate listening in their book *Zen and the Art of Saving the Planet.* As they teach, listening begins by using mindfulness techniques to ensure that one is fully present, and attentive. Second, they advise listening not to find solutions, but to understand, "to give the other person a chance to speak out and suffer less." This is not palliative listening. The end goal is authentic connection and collaboration, because without that genuine understanding, "we cannot do anything; we cannot save our planet. Technical solutions have to be supported by togetherness, understanding, and compassion."[28]

If we want to achieve a *just* transition to a clean energy economy, climate activists must listen to and build relationships with those communities who have been marginalized and silenced, those who have borne the brunt of extractive economies. And this includes building unlikely alliances. Purity politics won't save the world (if nothing else, religious history makes *that* very clear), but cultivating community, tending relationships, and building coalitions just might. As Sarah Jaquette Ray argues in *A Field Guide to Climate Anxiety*, unlikely coalitions can be discovered through our shared values and our common care for future generations. Focusing on our disagreements runs counter to the cause of climate justice. "If we feel we're constantly battling some 'evil other' our anger and fear will deplete us. [But] knowing that a lot of people are with us, and that the rest are not as malicious as the media would have us think, we are much less likely to give up."[29]

Learning how to listen is a big part of the work of climate scientist Katharine Hayhoe, who points out that nearly three-quarters of Americans are concerned about climate change, but only a third of us are actually talking about it. Because of this, Hayhoe argues that one of the most powerful things we can do to address the climate crisis is *talk about it*. But she also advises we begin by listening. More specifically, listen for the values you share. Then consider how a warming climate might threaten those shared values. Finally, celebrate creative solutions, emphasizing the positive steps that we can take to make the world a better place.

Why do we need radical compassion based on an understanding of our interdependence? Why ought we expand that compassion to include the natural world? And why is this essential for spiritual resilience? Because if you believe you have an obligation to the Earth's most vulnerable, you simply cannot hide in your bunker. It means facing difficult histories—the wounds we've received and the ones we have caused. It means attending to those communities who have been silenced, learning the lessons of relational and restorative justice. It also means learning how to be still, to listen to those whose voices may be harder to hear. And it means being open to thinking differently, to changing the way we plan our cities, use our water, grow our food, generate energy, mine our minerals, or produce our clothing. When we know we have a moral obligation to look out for each other, the choices we make will begin to look very different indeed. Some of us may be motivated by divine commandment, others by a sense of our interdependence, our *kithship*, or the deep love that comes from being a creature on this precious Earth. But when we find that common ceremonial space of care, one grounded in relationship, respect, reverence, and reciprocity, we'll also find a well of resilience that keeps us going, even when all seems lost.

Key takeaways

1 We need to center justice in climate work because the unjust treatment of other humans and other species is what got us into this mess to begin with. Climate is a social justice issue: those who contributed least to the problem will be impacted

the most, and these are the most vulnerable among us. And it's also true that just systems are simply *better* for all of us. Just and equitable communities are more resilient—we all benefit when our neighbors are well. And conservation efforts are far more successful when they are led by local and Indigenous communities.

2 The world's wisdom traditions help us better understand what justice is. First, it is grounded in the golden rule—to treat others as we would want to be treated. Second, justice is not about treating everyone *equally*, but about actively seeking out ways to help those who are the most vulnerable: the poor, the young, the old, the refugee, the sick, the imprisoned. And, finally, we see that true justice is restorative, not punitive. It is not about vengeance, but restoring dignity and healing relationships.

3 Because colonial histories of extraction and abuse lie at the heart of our climate crisis, our solutions must be rooted decolonization. That means honoring Indigenous sovereignty over their traditional territories and restoring their right to care for their lands, waters, foods, and medicines. Decolonization also requires naming and facing our painful histories, being guided by traditional ecological knowledge, and learning to listen to those whose voices have traditionally been silenced.

Invitation for further reflection

1 What might it look like when we apply justice and decolonial values to our decision-making? How might that change your personal decisions? What might that look like on a systems-wide level?

2 Are there climate organizations in your area that include a focus on social justice? How so? What do they do? Are there ways you might be involved?
3 Do you live on colonized land? Do you know whose land you're on? How might you get to know more about this group? (See the link below for suggestions for further learning!)
4 Consider trying a compassionate listening exercise. Working in pairs or groups of three, choose one of these questions to answer. Take turns speaking and listening. Don't interrupt, just listen to understand. *What feelings arise when you think about climate change? What worries you, what places, people, or possibilities are you concerned about? What kind of activities, ideas, or initiatives energize you and get you thinking creatively? What kinds of activities, ideas, or initiatives deplete you and leave you feeling low?* Practice listening. Don't try and solve the issues they raise, simply hear the needs and feelings behind their story. If your mind wanders, pay attention to your breath, and remind yourself that you are listening, so that you can help reduce their suffering.

Want to learn more?

Visit our website at https://bloomsbury.pub/climate-spirit where you'll find recommendations for further reading and resources for individuals, reading groups, and educators.

10

Learn to listen

A tribal leader in Washington state is woken in the middle of the night by a phone call from an elder. She is inconsolable. Earlier that evening she tried to gather medicines in her family's traditional lands, a place they have stewarded for millennia. The road was blocked, the land fenced off, construction underway for a privately owned solar farm.

A Sami activist links arms with her fellow protestors, demanding the government of Norway recognize that its wind farms are a violation of human rights, disrupting the migration patterns of reindeer herds her people have cared for since time began.

Paiute activists write letters, stage protests, and struggle mightily against a proposed lithium mine that would devastate their traditional territories, and eradicate sacred sites. The international mining conglomerate is unmoved: they've already pre-sold the lithium to a major electric vehicle (EV) car manufacturer, and they plan to move ahead with the mine, no matter what.

A climate activist is seeking spiritual renewal. After surveying the religious marketplace, they decide to reenact an Indigenous ceremony in their backyard. They don't know much about it, but find instructions on the internet. When they come across a statement made by the tribe in question, asking spiritual seekers to respect their cultural autonomy and not copy their ceremonies, they decide to ignore their concerns. Don't spiritual traditions belong to everyone?

These are four very different situations, but all are examples of "green colonialism." Green colonialism is a term used to describe moments when Indigenous and marginalized people disproportionately carry the burden of meeting the energy and resource needs of the dominant culture. It happens when clean energy projects violate Indigenous sovereignty, threatening sacred places, species, and ecosystems. And it happens when Indigenous knowledge or sacred traditions are appropriated without consent.

These conflicts are often presented as a zero-sum game: honor Indigenous sovereignty and protect biodiversity *or* make the necessary large-scale changes to save us from climate chaos. I emphatically disagree. More than any other demographic, Indigenous people are deeply concerned about and fighting to address climate change. They are on the front lines of climate activism, and have done more (per capita) to combat the growth of fossil fuels, pipelines, coal terminals, and extractive economies than anyone. They stand to lose the most, should the worst of climate change come to pass. And, they've also contributed least to the problem. But Indigenous and other marginalized communities are often asked (or forced) to bear the cost of wealthy nations' transition to clean energy.

In the previous chapter I made the case that if we want to combat climate change, if we want to build a just and sustainable future, we would be foolish to rely on solutions that repeat the same colonial, extractive approaches that got us here in the first place. Because if we do, we are only responding to the symptoms of climate change—not its root causes. Before we rush forward to solutions (and we do need to rush), we need to make sure we're building from the right foundation, that our values and deepest wisdom undergird the decisions we make. Recall what Umeek and Kyle Whyte had to say in chapter one, real resilience has to first reckon with our relational disharmony, and building that resilience begins when we place real value on moral relationships.

In this chapter, I want to consider what it looks like when we apply justice and decolonization to cultivating spiritual resilience. How do we learn from other religious and spiritual traditions in ways that reflect those values? Umeek advises us to begin with recognition, respect, and reciprocity. Relational harmony requires *recognition* of a people's personhood and sovereignty. When we recognize another being's personhood, we also acknowledge their right to consent—over their territories, their bodies, and their intellectual property. Moral relationships are built on *respect*, particularly for those who have been denied a voice in the past—Indigenous peoples, marginalized communities, and our plant and animal relatives. Moral relationships also require *reciprocity*, an agreement of equal give and take. Indigenous communities have already paid more than their fair share toward our environmental debt—it's time for those who have benefitted the most from our carbon economy to pay the price for our transition away from fossil fuels. We have to move quickly, yes, but we also have to move in the right direction, and in the right way. When our work is grounded in recognition, respect, and reciprocity we ensure that we are not simply continuing to participate in the colonial and extractive systems that got us here in the first place.

The dangers of religious appropriation

The 1491s are the Native American comedy troupe behind my favorite TV series of all time—*Reservation Dogs*. Their classic YouTube sketch, "The Indian Store," begins with Dallas Goldtooth (Shakopee-Mdewakanton Sioux) and Bobby Wilson (Sisseton-Wahpeton Dakota) "indianning up" to sell "authentic" artifacts to their primarily white clientele. On offer are turquoise, spirit masks, and even dream catchers that will also boost your Wi-Fi signal if you hang them near your router. But when an Indigenous patron asks for books on the history of colonization, they draw a blank. They have books on vision quests, but politics? Treaty rights? Not so much.

Psychologists, cultural teachers, and climate scientists have all described this moment in human history as one of existential distress. Climate change presents us with a struggle of the soul, because more than a mere technological challenge, this is an ethical, moral, and spiritual dilemma. Rediscovering our proper place within the web of relationships on which we all depend will require a profound philosophical and spiritual shift in consciousness. This is a spiritual crisis, and so it makes sense to consider what the world's sacred traditions may have to say about how to survive it. Indeed, it's the premise of this book. But it is also a *colonial* crisis, one that has arisen from a particular way of being in the world, one deeply grounded in an ethos of utilitarianism, extraction, and exploitation. And so, we must pay particular attention to what those cultures who have survived colonialism have to say about it. As filmmaker Julian Brave Noisecat (Secwepemc) says: "Those who know what it means to lose our world and live might have something to lend to a broader humanity that now faces its own existential crisis in the form of disease and climate change."[1] In this chapter, I want to talk about *how* to seek answers to those questions, so that in our search we are not merely repeating the mistakes that got us here in the first place.

As a scholar of religious studies, I was trained to write and think about other people's sacred traditions with what my former professor Ninian Smart called "critical empathy." *Empathy* requires respect and humility, taking other traditions on their own terms, and doing one's best to understand them as they are experienced from within. The "critical" element isn't meant to imply being condescending or judgmental, but rather awareness of how those traditions are shaped by their historical, political, social, economic, and ecological contexts. It's not about reducing a spiritual tradition *to* those things, but it is about understanding how our very deepest questions are shaped by the context in which we live. That "critical" part of this approach acknowledges that religious traditions are internally diverse (there are many ways of being Buddhist, for instance), and that religious traditions change over time (the Christianity of fourth-century Egyptian monks has little in common with a twenty-first-century Texas megachurch). This approach may feel like a tricky balance, but it's essential. Because climate change brings an existential threat greater than any our species has faced before, and it's a threat that requires global engagement, deep interpersonal and intercultural communication, and a profound reexamination of our relationships to other living beings. And critical, empathetic understanding of religious and spiritual worldviews is at the very heart of it.

And, as an Indigenous Studies scholar, I was also trained to center respect, reverence, recognition, and reciprocity in my work, to listen to and learn from spiritual leaders without engaging in cultural appropriation.

If you're not sure how exactly to define cultural appropriation, you're in good company. There are obvious examples (the Pocahontas Halloween costume, the Cleveland Indians mascot, the faux Plains Indian headdress in the mosh pit at Coachella), but there are also a host of grey areas, and a wealth of online debates to accompany them. I find it most helpful to begin by thinking about *power*, and who has (or historically had) more of it. *Appropriation* happens when a more powerful group takes up the culture of a less powerful group and uses it to serve its own agenda, often for profit, entertainment, or self-fulfillment. When a *less powerful* group takes up the trappings of the dominant culture, that's *assimilation*, *accommodation*, or *code switching*. The distinctions matter, because there's a real difference in outcome, impact, and meaning. In the first instance, the already disempowered group is losing one of the few resources that remain solely in their control—their culture. The power imbalance tips even further into the favor of those who already have more than their fair share. In the second instance, the disempowered utilize an element of the dominant culture as a counterbalance, to try and move toward a (perhaps just slightly) more equal position. This distinction is most important when we're thinking about a group that has been subjected to the violence of colonialism and cultural genocide.

Religious appropriation most often takes the form of leveraging a practice or sacred symbol for personal benefit, extracting it from the community from which it comes, and separating it from the broader worldview that gives it meaning. It is a perfect expression of Western consumerism: we shop the spiritual marketplace, picking and choosing the style that suits us today, and which we may discard tomorrow, without consideration for the processes that produced it, or the possible harm in purchasing it.[2] Religious mimicry can be deeply offensive when it takes a profoundly sacred object or practice out of its appropriate context, in a way that compromises its original meaning, or that profanes what is sacred. More often than not, appropriation deals in superficialities, reinforces harmful stereotypes, and obscures a tradition's internal diversity.

Being warned away from religious appropriation can be a tough pill to swallow for some folks. The dominant Western ethos venerates individualism, free market capitalism, and personal rights, all orientations that justify the appropriation of any culture or religion that strikes your fancy. The argument goes: if it speaks to my soul, then it should be mine for the taking. But there are strong critiques within Indigenous communities against "wannabes" who appropriate Native spirituality. Exemplified most visibly in non-native reenactments of vision quests or sweat lodges, such incursions are seen as a form of colonial exploitation, where spirituality becomes another resource to be extracted from Native communities for the benefit of settler society. Culture bearers also point out that such examples of appropriation are dangerous: people have been injured and even died while participating in activities without the proper guidance or supervision.

In her excellent book *Stealing My Religion: Not Just Any Cultural Appropriation*, ethicist Liz Bucar wrestles with the distinctions between what she calls "religious appropriation," which causes harm, and "religious borrowing," which she argues may not cause harm.[3] The key, she explains, is whether or not we are cognizant of the ways in which appropriation interacts with oppression. Appropriation "relies on, and contributes to existing forms of structural injustice." To avoid appropriation and to ethically engage with other traditions, she advises that we become more aware of systems of inequality, that we ask: what is the historical relationship between my culture and the community in question? She reminds us to respect boundaries, to acknowledge that my individual freedom or intellectual curiosity should never come at the expense of another's well-being, that consent matters, and basic decency demands we respect a "no" when we hear it. The TLDR?[4] Done right, cultural exchange should advance justice, rather than reinforcing existing systems of oppression.

But here's where Bucar's conclusion may surprise you. Rather than do *less*, she argues, we should do *more*. Her rationale is this: problematic and damaging instances of appropriation, especially those that cause deep offense, are nearly always superficial, committed by people without a genuine connection with the communities in question, or real understanding of the webs of meaning that surround that particular practice or image. Bucar suggests that the solution is *deeper* engagement with and understanding of other religious and cultural worldviews. Take the time to learn their histories, discover their internal complexity and diversity, and gain an understanding of their philosophical, theological, and moral frameworks. Such a deeper engagement, she hopes, will inspire a shift from simple individual self-interest and toward genuine community connection. Real cultural exchange should challenge our assumptions, and illuminate new values and new ways of living, ensuring more of us are safe, and have what we need to thrive. Bucar's critique is particularly salient for this book, because while I'm arguing that religious and Indigenous traditions have lessons we all need to learn, I'm not suggesting we participate in religious appropriation for self-fulfillment. Rather, like Bucar, I would challenge us to move beyond *self*-help and *self*-care, and toward a consideration of how we can more fully realize our interrelatedness with all of creation, and from that realization mobilize for environmental justice and decolonization.

A decolonial approach to religious exchange requires that we get to know the political and historical context of religious and Indigenous traditions—including the difficult histories of colonialism. Spiritual theft is especially grievous for communities who have been targets of religious suppression. In the case of Native North America, Indigenous people have experienced centuries of overt physical and cultural genocide, including residential schools that did terrible harm to vulnerable children, suppressing Indigenous languages and cultures, severing community and familial bonds, and damaging the relationship between Indigenous people and their lands. The practicing of Indigenous religious traditions was outlawed in the United States from 1883 to 1978. To engage with Indigenous spirituality without first reckoning with that history is to perpetuate it. And besides, claims of allyship and solidarity ring hollow when absent of any real relationship with the community in question.

These are complicated ideas, but they matter, because the stakes are high, and the potential for harm is real. That's because sacred work is, well, *sacred*. In ritual and ceremony, we create our most valued communities, and we find ways of holding them together. It's where we define who we are, and find meaning in our collective identity. Within contemplative practices we gain a glimpse into the ultimate meaning of our life, and gingerly feel our way toward healing and hope. And that's why religious appropriation can cause real harm.

Treating the most precious and revered elements of someone's life as a costume, a theme for a party, or a stop on a tour, can cause profound offense. Taking up the very tools they rely on to preserve their identity and community—without invitation—becomes yet another colonizing or culturally genocidal move, regardless of however good one's intentions may be.

Rules for ceremonial engagement

So what's the alternative? How should we proceed? If we're going to be (theoretically at least) visiting the ceremonial space of others, how ought one to behave? Before we move into the final chapters of this book and consider the concrete steps each of us might take to be part of building a more just and sustainable world, I want to pause one moment to consider how we might best be guided in that work. What are best practices for listening to and learning from other cultures—particularly those who have been the target of colonialism or other forms of cultural genocide? As we gather wisdom and insight from different traditions, what are the rules of the road?

First, do your homework. Get to know the landscape, including the history of marginalization or settler colonial erasure that this community may have experienced. Second, center values of respect and reciprocity. Go only where you have permission. But show up when you are invited. Look for events open to the public or for activist opportunities led by community groups. Be alert for ways to give back. This might be financially, or it may be offering your support when communities are vulnerable or rallying for the issues that matter to them. Third, remember the distinction between borrowing practices or sacred symbols, and listening to and learning from the teachings of Indigenous or religious communities. It is problematic at best to performatively copy a spiritual practice. But it's an *obligation* to consider the teachings that practice is meant to convey. For instance, I would not advise my Christian students to go home and mimic a traditional Jewish Passover seder, but I *do* want them to think about the power of gathering over symbolic foods, and reflecting on shared histories and deeply held values. I would strongly discourage my non-native students from building a Lakota-style sweat lodge in their backyard. But I *would* encourage them to think about the importance of ritual cleansing and purification, and I hope they will let themselves be challenged by the concept of Earth as mother, rather than simply the third rock from the sun. I might remind them that Native Americans don't have a patent on heat and steam—and suggest they consider culturally appropriate ways of integrating physical experience and spiritual presence, finding safe spaces where we can speak from the heart with those we trust, and consider how we relate to Earth as beloved parent.

The spiritual practice of smudging is one good example of why this matters. In its most common form, smudging involves burning sage and wafting the smoke over and around people or spaces. It's considered spiritually cleansing and renewing. It clarifies, and dispels negativity. For many Native people, it's a meaningful part of ceremony. But smudging has also become commonplace among those who feel an affinity with Indigenous traditions. And this is problematic, in part because of its potentially performative nature (look how spiritual I am!), and in part because of its superficiality—especially when detached from any real engagement with Indigenous spirituality or community. But the biggest reason for concern is that the commodification of white sage has led to unregulated overharvesting and habitat destruction. As a result, white sage is now considered a threatened species, with different Indigenous groups calling for a ban on its sale. It's a vivid example of the unintended harm that cultural appropriation can bring. But here's the thing: the call for non-native folks to stop smudging with white sage doesn't mean that burning cleansing aromatics is somehow forbidden. Some Indigenous cultural advocates instead advise that spiritual seekers explore the medicinal plants one's own ancestors would have used for similar purposes, or use plants that are abundantly available, like rosemary, lavender, pine, thyme, cedar, or clove.

Let me say this again: this is not a zero-sum game. We do not have to choose between cultural isolation and appropriation, or between green colonialism and climate chaos. There's a middle path, and it requires that we do the work of building moral relationships. Recognize personhood and sovereignty. Show respect. Secure consent. Demonstrate gratitude and reciprocity. Insist that the benefits, and the costs, of the transition to a clean and sustainable economy are equally shared. Do everything we possibly can to minimize harm and protect cultural and biodiversity.

My point here is that all of us *should* be listening to and learning from other cultures and traditions—particularly those who have been historically silenced. Doing so requires care, respect, reverence, and reciprocity. It requires humility and restraint. Because it is also true that many of these spiritual leaders and teachers have been trying to get our attention for a long time. Those of us who are inheritors of settler colonialism have an obligation to listen, to be challenged, and to apply the teachings of culture bearers and knowledge keepers in ways that are informed, respectful, and responsible.

Key takeaways

1 Real solutions to the climate crisis must avoid repeating the mistakes of the past. This includes "green colonialism," in which Indigenous and marginalized people disproportionately

carry the burden of our transition to clean energy, and when Indigenous resources or knowledge are used without their consent.

2 The difference between cultural appropriation and cultural exchange lies in power imbalance. Cultural appropriation serves to reinforce inequality. Cultural exchange, done right, should advance justice, rather than reinforcing existing systems of oppression.
3 If you want to avoid religious appropriation, go deeper! Go beyond superficial stereotypes, and get to know the history, complexity, and internal diversity of a tradition. This book introduces many different traditions and practices—don't stop there! Check the link at the end of each chapter to find lists of additional resources for further learning.
4 Center values of respect, reverence, and reciprocity. Do your homework, honor boundaries, look for ways to give back.

Invitation for further reflection

1 If the climate crisis is a spiritual crisis, it will require spiritual, ethical, and profoundly relational solutions. Where do you look for spiritual support?
2 We can avoid religious essentialism by remembering that all religions and cultures are internally diverse, change over time as they adapt and respond to different needs, and are shaped by their broader social and historical context. Can you think of how a tradition you're familiar with has changed over time?
3 If we want to listen to and learn from other traditions and communities—particularly those who have been historically

marginalized or subject to genocidal policies—we've got to do it with reverence and care. What are some tools you take from this chapter for respectful learning?

Want to learn more?

Visit our website at https://bloomsbury.pub/climate-spirit where you'll find recommendations for further reading and resources for individuals, reading groups, and educators.

11

Climate calling

My grandpa Homer was one of the smartest people I've ever known. He had an instinctive, self-taught grasp of geometry, physics, botany, and fine carpentry, and he was also incredibly perceptive, seeing what people needed, and figuring out a way to make sure they got it. A bout of malaria derailed his trajectory for high school valedictorian, and the Great Depression stymied any chance he might have had of going to college, so over the course of his life, my grandfather had a lot of different jobs. He drove a truck. He worked on a farm. He upholstered furniture. He delivered the mail. Lots of jobs. But his vocation? That was loving people. He loved fiercely and generously, with the abundance of a rich man, even when he was pretty much broke. He was also one of the most contented people I've ever known.

If you've experienced burnout, struggled to find your path, or grown weary of career counseling, this chapter offers some good news. I teach at a Lutheran university. And Lutherans love talking about vocation. It's kind of our thing. Martin Luther revolutionized the concept, after all, insisting that nearly any profession could be a means of manifesting God's grace in the world, that it wasn't just reserved for the clergy. I'll be taking this a bit further, considering different ways religious and cultural traditions have for thinking about our calling, and how we're meant to live with purpose and meaning—particularly in troubled times. Here are four key ideas that those of us seeking a calling in a time of climate crisis need to know.

First, vocation is more than a job, or even your personal goals. Rather it's all about the values or qualities of being that you are meant to bring to whatever you do. At the end of the day, the question is not, did you do your job today? But instead, did you live into your values today? Steven Hayes, founder of Acceptance and Commitment Therapy, guides his clients through a process of identifying their core values, their "non-negotiables." As he emphasizes to his clients, *values* are not the same as goals. Because goals exist only in the past or the future. In fact, they lose significance almost as soon as we achieve them, leaving us forever looking for the Next Big Thing. In contrast, values are what we *always* have. We can get burned out trying to achieve goals, but we are enlivened by what we truly value. Goals hound us, but values draw us along, even when we're running out of steam. It's our values that make goals meaningful. Rather than trophies to win or objectives we *should do*, values are qualities of being that we cannot live without.[1]

Discerning what our values are is thus a key part of vocational reflection, and identifying those values that center and inspire one's life is essential to a life of purpose, particularly during this precarious moment of human history. We may never achieve the goal of a world of ecological harmony—certainly not in our lifetime. But we *can* spend every day joyfully living into our values of a just and sustainable world. Living into our values and purpose in the present moment ensures we don't miss out on our lives, single-mindedly focused on some distant goal. We can stop saying, "I'll enjoy my life once this project is done," when we insist that the project is not the purpose. Rather, the point is bringing our best, attentive self, enlivened by our core values, to whatever we happen to be doing.

A second piece of good news is that living into our values and taking action to combat climate change is good for us! As psychotherapist Sally Gillespie argues, "When non-engagement becomes the norm, it not only stymies action, but also stifles a liveliness that springs from consciously engaging with the world as it is, and ourselves as we are."[2] In a similar way, Sarah Jaquette Ray realized after years of working with environmental studies college students that "the holy grail of fulfillment is not 'happiness,' but finding our purpose." And the power of purpose lies in believing that we have a role to play in the events unfolding around us. Because "more than having marketable skills or being armed with information and arguments, *believing in your efficacy* will influence whether you try to fix the problems you see." Helplessness is toxic, stripping us of compassion, weakening our resolve, and increasing our anxiety. It leaves us in a state of paralysis. But the good news is, we do not need to save the world. Instead, we need only to find value and purpose in the actions we *can* take, right where we are. As Ray tells her students: "The work, not utopia, is the endgame."[3]

The third piece of good news is that every single one of us has a climate calling. If you've made it this far in this book, you care about climate change and you want to contribute to the cause of environmental justice. You may be a student wondering what career path to choose, a professional considering a shift into sustainability, a retiree wondering how you can contribute to the cause The reality is, every single thing we do relies on a healthy climate, and, for that reason, every activity we undertake has the opportunity to contribute to a more just and sustainable world. And while some areas have greater impacts than others—as have been ably documented by Project Drawdown—every piece of the puzzle matters.[4]

President Obama's science advisor John Holdren famously argued that climate change presents us with only three options: mitigation (reduce carbon emission), adaptation (figure out how to live on a changing planet), or suffering (care for those caught in the chaos of floods, drought, and famine). The more we do of the first two, he argued, the less we'll have to do of the third. In a similar vein, Joanna Macy illuminated the broad scope of climate-related work by presenting us with three large categories for action: Holding Actions, Sustaining Actions, and Shifting Actions. Holding actions hold back or slow down the impacts of a carbon-emitting economy. These include activism and policy work. Sustaining actions are those that innovate new systems, offering novel approaches to business, healthcare, education, energy, agriculture, and transportation that are both sustainable and restorative. Shifting Actions transform our collective consciousness, and include the work of thinkers and communicators, religious leaders, Indigenous culture bearers, philosophers, scientists, and artists, all of whom help to re-write the story our society tells about itself, the Earth, and obligations to our kith and kin. Climate callings are thus wide ranging and diverse: protesting, arguing, caring, sustaining, innovating, and creating.

And here is a final piece of good news: we're not in this alone. It turns out, vocation is radically relational! Most of the vocational reflection models you've probably seen—particularly in career counseling contexts—are fiercely individualistic. They ask, what do I want to do with my life? What will make me happy and fulfilled? What are my personal strengths? But religious and Indigenous traditions of calling are very different—they're grounded in reciprocity and community, where we are both supported by and called to care for others. We know that *taking action in community* is one of the best remedies for climate despair, an antidote to our feelings of powerlessness, and as the traditions we'll discuss in the second half of this chapter show, that potential community is bigger than we know. When we discover that we are situated within a web of human, ecological, and intergenerational kinship, our questions shift from "what do I want to do?" to instead: "who is supporting me? And whom can I support in return?"

Because here's what popular (secular) vocational reflection models almost always forget: If we are called, *someone is doing the calling.* There's someone on the other end of the line, and they're offering to help! That call may be coming from ancestors, community, the natural world, saints, spirits, or Creator. But always, there is something greater than ourselves, issuing an invitation, and waiting to see if we'll answer.

What sets sacred approaches to vocation apart from the secular is this: reciprocity and relationality. While the dominant culture emphasizes personal ambition, individual inclination, and financial success, sacred traditions center community, service to others, and an understanding that we are never alone, but rather drawing from a deep reserve of spiritual strength and guidance. Vocational discernment is not about trying to decide what *I as an individual* think I'd like to do. It's about heeding a voice calling us to act. In short, vocation is fundamentally relational, and based on an understanding that emerges in conversation with Spirit, ancestors, place, and community.

Christiana Figueres has written, "If you do not control the complex landscape of a challenge (and you rarely do), the most powerful thing you can do is change how you behave in that landscape, using yourself as a catalyst for overall change .... But all too often we move quickly to 'doing' without first reflecting on 'being,' what *we* personally bring to the task."[5] In the rest of this chapter, I invite you to step into that reflection on *being*: by whom are you called, and what is the unique contribution you are called to make in addressing the climate crisis?

Serving God in community

The Catholic Church adopted the term vocation from the Latin *vocari*: to be called. There's a pretty important assumption implicit in that phrase, the assumption that *someone is calling.* One's calling does not originate within the self. It may be mediated by saints or wise counsel, but it is ultimately from God, offering grace and strength to do what one is called to do. For most of Catholic history, having a vocation meant being called to a religious life as a cleric, monk, or nun. And, in the modern period, that one had also received a gift of divine grace enabling one to take up the difficulties of a religious life. The latter was an important distinction for women, who were previously denied access to the education and privilege necessary to rise in the church. Since the mid-twentieth century, Catholic notions of vocation have expanded to include other forms of ministerial service, including care for the poor or sick.

At their heart, Catholic understandings of vocation are not about individual ambition, but "calling in community, through community, for community." Individual gifts and inclinations are always brought to the service of others and for the cause of justice, taking seriously the notion that Jesus is incarnate in the poor and the powerless, that whenever one cares for the hungry, thirsty, naked, homeless, or imprisoned, one cares for Christ, and whenever one harms the vulnerable, one harms Christ (Mt. 25:40). The process of vocational discernment is likewise not individual but grounded in community. While traditions for private reflection certainly exist, insights are interpreted with the guidance of teachers and in light of historical tradition.

Sixteenth-century reformer Martin Luther challenged the Catholic assumptions of his day, including their interpretation of vocation. For Luther, God called all people, and all work could be sacred work. In this new tradition, God did not call Christians to withdraw from society, but rather to serve God through all "worldly" occupations, at home, in business, in politics, and in community. In this Protestant tradition, vocation was not tied to a specific role in the church, but rather to living out "the love of neighbor and God," wherever one happened to be.

The Lutheran tradition likewise argued for serving Christ through caring for the poor, because Christ is "incarnate in human need," and because every opportunity to engage in a loving relationship is an opportunity to serve God.[6] Lutherans centered this focus within their discernment process, asking first, what are the world's needs? Then, what are your particular gifts, and spheres of influence? What opportunities or limitations lie before you?

In the twenty-first century, many Christian communities have intentionally expanded this notion of vocational service to include care not only for humanity, but also the natural world. At my university, we define vocation as "being called with others to promote human and ecological flourishing," a definition that relies on this notion of vocation as a practice of community, in community, and in service to a community that includes all of creation. For his part, African American theologian Christopher Carter emphasizes this as well, writing that "the function of human life is a sacred vocation, namely to preserve and promote the life of the community," which includes "the more-than-human world."[7]

This sense of purposeful life grounded in relationality and care can be found in Islam as well, although the Muslim term *al-islam* "the submission," may be more apt than "calling." To be a Muslim is to be one who submits to Allah, who responds to God's call that has been "written on the hearts of human beings." As John Kelsay explains, God's will can be discerned through meditation upon the natural world, history, or sacred texts, and while Allah can communicate through signs, and while all Muslims are called to follow Islamic law and live lives of piety, an Islamic understanding of vocation has far less to do with what job one ought to have, and far more with how one ought to live. "Right conduct, heartfelt trust, and excellence in character are all important in answering God's call." Such ethical behavior is possible within many kinds of work, when done with intention, and with a heart of service to God and other living beings. The important distinction is whether or not such work is out of selfish motivations, or out of a desire to serve God and others. When done out of self-interest, "worldly vocations may constitute an obstacle to responding to the divine summons."[8]

Judaism likewise offers a rich intellectual tradition of guidance as to how one ought to live in the world. At the heart of those teachings are one's obligations to community and care for others.[9] Rabbi Amy Eilberg argues that Judaism's notion of purposeful living is radically relational, disrupting the individualism of modern society. For Eilberg, if the idea of a "calling" exists in the Jewish tradition it is reserved for the community as a whole—God called them to be God's people. As individuals, Jews honor God by observing Jewish law, which offers a means of sanctifying everyday life, "through prayer, blessing, and observance of the mitzvot (commandments), regular study of sacred text, and a life of service, all grounded in sacred community." However, when Eilberg reflects on teachings within the Biblical and textual tradition, she observes a clear pattern. A project

> born of arrogance and hyper-certainty more likely derives from personal ambition or impulsiveness than from the voice of the holy … self-aggrandizement easily crowds out the still small voice of the divine … A sense of calling arises from our deep-rooted understanding of the needs of our community or our world, and the way in which our own gifts and experiences may allow us to meet those needs. Finally, the process requires humility, including willingness to set aside more self-centered preferences in order to accept a call to serve.[10]

Reciprocity, relationality, and interdependence

Two terms within Hinduism (and the Bhagavad Gita in particular) help to provide another example of a tradition of purposeful living that is both relational and reciprocal. The first is *svabhava*, which "speaks of and commends works that flow out of one's nature," and implies that "one should not relinquish work that is in harmony with one's innate character." *Svabhava* suggests that one can honor God by aligning one's outward actions with one's inner disposition. Taken alone, *svabhava* could suggest a rather individualistic notion of divine calling. However, Anantanand Rambachan emphasizes that "one's individual nature cannot be considered separately from the fact that one belongs to an interrelated family, social, and cosmic order. Life is not possible outside of this interdependent order."[11] This tension is held in the complementary term *sadharma*, which suggests that "all individual lives and work have a social and cosmic significance because each contributes to the harmony and well-being of all."[12] *Svadharma* unites these two ideas in a single ideal. A factory worker may make components of life-saving medical equipment, but without a sense of the end result—or the role it may play in saving a life—their work may seem to lack meaning. However, insight into the whole gives meaning to the work. In a similar way, "understanding work as *svadharma* adds meaning and value by situating its significance in relation to the universal community .... Work is not only the expression of our special individual nature. It is also the special contribution we make to the universe." Good work is that which contributes to the flourishing of the world, and supports the universal common good. Choosing otherwise "is morally deplorable," and akin to theft, because it implies taking from the world without giving back. Furthermore, any work done in service to the needy can be seen as service to God, because God "exists in the heart of all beings," and "he who sees Shiva in the poor, in the weak, and in the diseased, really worships Shiva."[13]

In Mahayana Buddhism, one is called to attain awakening so as to lead others to awakening, and to reduce the suffering of all beings. One is also called to undertake "right livelihood," which includes tasks that demonstrate care for other sentient beings, and that do not contribute to suffering, ignorance, or the taking of life. Given Buddhist teachings of no-self, any notion of a vocational calling that suggests some fixed or absolute self simply doesn't make sense. But we are called to do work that sustains others, alleviates their suffering, and supports the Buddha's call to live lives of compassion. And, because we are in a state of continual, relational transformation, the shape of that work will necessarily change over time, taking many forms.

I find particularly compelling Thich Nhat Hanh's notion of aimlessness, or businesslessness (remember that one next time you're playing Scrabble). Thich Nhat Hanh explains that "it is possible to work and serve without getting lost in our work." We do that by living "deeply each moment of our work." This is the meaning of aimlessness. Here, our concentration is not on a particular goal or outcome (though we may certainly have one), but on mindful attention to the present. As he explains,

> to practice aimlessness is to identify what it is you're looking for, waiting for, or running after, and let it go. By removing these objects of seeking that are pulling you away from the here and now, you will discover that everything you want is already right here in this present moment ... Live your life in such a way that every step in the right direction and every breath along the way becomes the realization of your dream.[14]

Here lies a helpful insight for anyone committed to the monumental task of justly transforming our global energy systems. While taking action and doing the work is essential, what is equally essential is *how* and *in what spirit* we do the work.

In a similar vein, Mark Berkson shows how Confucian and Daoist traditions hold each other in creative tension, with Confucianism emphasizing one's obligations within an ordered and interdependent human society, while Daoism emphasizes the need to bring one's inner self into harmony with the rhythms and cycles of the natural world. For Confucians, each individual is called to perfect their moral character, uphold their obligations to their family, and contribute to a just and ordered society. Here, calling has to do with self-cultivation, but for profoundly relational ends. Self-cultivation includes developing one's heart, mind, body, and character. And as such, calling is not toward a career or profession, but rather, "the lifelong task of becoming a cultivated human being in relation to others .... We cultivate ourselves with the guidance of, alongside, and for the sake of others." Each person exists within concentric circles of relationships–from family, to community, to nation, to cosmos, and each is "called to fulfill [their] responsibilities to, and to contribute to the well-being of, the others in each of those relationships."[15] *Li*, or proper etiquette, is an outward manifestation of that inward orientation.

Confucianism shares this fundamentally relational notion of self–one that exists at the nexus of relationships—with Daoism. Here too, there is no independent self, but rather a profoundly relational one. But Daoism differs in its emphasis on relationality with the natural world, rather than the human one. The Daoist concept of *tian*, or heaven, suggests a cosmos endowed with morality, and inclined toward harmony. We are called to nurture our heavenly-inclined heart, and fulfill the obligations we have to our relatives—both human and otherwise, living and dead.

Daoist teachings include meditative and physical practices to align mind and body with the cosmos, while also challenging the strictures of human culture. Daoists advise the joy of "uselessness."

For example, a living tree is better off than one cut down and "put to use." For Daoists, one is called to mindfully attend to the present moment. In transcending and forgetting the self, we get out of the way, so the Dao can move. And when we find a state of flow, when we are utterly absorbed in skillful activities, we are able to follow the Dao. In this ideal state, "the narrative-producing, self-constructing mind moves out of the way and a worker *becomes* the work." From a Daoist perspective, then, we might be called to maximize time spent in flow. It is not a loss of self, or union with a transcendent deity. Rather, it is experiencing one's unique manifestation within the larger whole, and "a recognition that there are no boundaries between ourselves and the Dao."[16] For Daoists, flow can be found anywhere we find equanimity, and participate in the give and take of relational wholeness.

Wrapped in a vision: Calling to care

Vi taqšeblu Hilbert was a leader in the revitalization of Coast Salish Lushootseed language and culture, and she described her work as a gift. In a statement that reflects a fascinating integration of Coast Salish and Christian sensibilities, Vi described her calling as "*switulis uyayus*: work that the Creator was wrapping around me. I was ordained to do this work. It was always there, waiting for me to do."[17] To understand what Vi meant, you need to know the ritual significance of formally gifting a blanket in Coast Salish culture. Blankets are a representation of wealth, and when wrapped around someone in ceremony they are expressions of respect, appreciation, affection, and care. Being wrapped in a blanket is more than a present; it is an acknowledgment of a relationship, and a visible expression of the obligations that that relationship entails. Blankets represent protection and transformation, and are given whenever someone is stepping into a new stage of life (coming of age, graduation, marriage) or taking on new spiritual responsibilities (receiving an ancestral name, song, etc.). Receiving a blanket means taking up that new calling, accepting the responsibilities it entails, while also acknowledging that one is cared for and will be supported in that work.[18] When Vi used the expression *switulis uyayus*, for "the work that the Creator was wrapping around me," it implied a view of sacred work that is honor and obligation, but also a beautiful expression of care and protection, passed on from ancestors, woven by community, and empowered by Spirit.

Traditional Coast Salish notions of calling or vocation are also informed by a practice of seeking out spirit helpers within the natural world, who, through dreams and visions, will guide and empower the individual through life. Spirit powers are often inherited from one's ancestors, and manifest in the form of spirit songs and particular gifts or skills, such as public speaking, healing, carving, teaching, leading, fishing, hunting, or navigation. Each person is unique, and their relationship with their spirit power is private—but they share a common purpose: to care for community. These are not quests of individualistic self-discovery but expressions of radical relationality, manifestations of living relationship with one's ancestors and one's homelands, with the purpose of empowering individuals to serve and care for others.

Climate calling: Relational resistance

There are three main ideas that I hope you take away from this brief chapter. First, the climate crisis is a relational crisis, and finding our climate calling requires that we move beyond individual self-interest. Vocation is radically relational. Second, the very word "calling" suggests that *we are being called* by something beyond ourselves. It may be the calling of ancestors, wrapped around our shoulders like a blanket. It may be the call of a child, who needs our care. It may be the call of our community, or of the rhythms and harmonies of the natural world. It may be the call to serve God—manifest in the poor, hungry, imprisoned, or stranger. The joyful truth of this is that it means we are not alone, but surrounded by a wealth of strength and guidance upon which we can rely. Third, these traditions challenge us to give up our attachment to a particular job, and instead to live into values, into ways of being, into mindful presence. Herein lies a solution to burn out and discouragement. As Leanne Betasamosake Simpson (Anishinaabe) writes, "*how* we live, *how* we organize, *how* we engage in the world, the process, not only frames the outcomes, it *is* the transformation. *How* molds and then gives birth to the present. The *how* changes us."[19] It means remembering that *values* are not the same as goals. Values are qualities of living that make goals meaningful. We may never achieve the goal of a world of ecological harmony. But we can live into the values that will help to build that just and sustainable world. Living into our values and purpose in the present moment ensures we don't miss out on our precious life, distracted by a single-minded focus on a distant goal.

It's also true that having a clear sense of what you are called to do and what values you must prioritize is profoundly liberating. It empowers you to say yes, and it also frees you to say no. As a prayer quoted by Pope Francis says, "We cannot do everything, and there is a sense of liberation in realizing that. This enables us to do something, and to do it very well."[20] Or, as Kaitlin Curtice (Citizen Potawatomi) explains,

> An important part of the lifelong work of resistance is to understand both what we are responsible for and what we are not responsible for. It is not our responsibility to take on every single thing all the time. It takes courage to stop and ask what work is ours to do? What healing is for us to embody along the way? It means having the courage to say no to what isn't ours, so that we can say yes to everything that is, and say yes without fear.[21]

Coping with climate change will be a multi-generational effort that will come with both joyful achievements and devastating losses. To sustain the work, our focus must be trained on the task at hand, on the life in front of us, on this moment. We must grieve the lost coastline, name the lost species, weep over lost lives, but we will maintain hope by attending to the soil at our fingertips.

We may tremble here, standing as we do in this awful moment of human history. But what an amazing reckoning to know that each of us has a particular gift to offer, an utterly unique and distinct note to play in this symphony. In an era of climate crisis and social upheaval, we must all discern what role we are to play, what contribution we can make toward building a better world. It may not always be about making a living, but it will definitely be about making a life.

Key takeaways

1 The climate crisis is a relational crisis, and finding our climate calling requires that we move beyond individual self-interest, to consider by whom and for whom are we called.

2 Sacred traditions call us to care for God within "the least of these," affirming that we serve the Creator when we serve the most vulnerable. Other traditions challenge us to realize our true nature, to live into values of compassion, alleviating the suffering of others, or to find our place within a network of social and natural relations.

3 Vocation has less to do with being called to a specific job, and more to do with living into core values and ways of being. By focusing on the questions of *how* and *for what purpose*, we may find we can live into our calling in any number of ways. Wisdom traditions emphasize the importance of living

mindfully in the present moment, living fully into one's values with care, compassion, and relationality.

Invitation for further reflection

1. Complete this sentence: "When I think about the climate crisis, I feel X, and that is a reminder that I care about Z."
2. What people, places, activities, qualities of life, or moral virtues do you care about most? What are your non-negotiables?
3. At what times in your life have these values been important to you? How have you seen others manifest those values? What might you do to manifest these values more in your life? When have you avoided these values? Has that avoidance been costly for you? What keeps you from living into these values?
4. What people or places have supported and cared for you? What or whom do you feel called to care for?
5. What kind of work or quality of being would you most like to live into for the healing of our world? What action can you take in the next week, no matter how small—making a phone call, sending an email, or scheduling in some reflection time—that will help you live into these values?

Want to learn more?

Visit our website at https://bloomsbury.pub/climate-spirit where you'll find recommendations for further reading and resources for individuals, reading groups, and educators.

12

Hope is a ceremony

I confess: I love spoilers. I skip to the end of most books, and jump ahead in a dramatic series. If I'm going to enjoy a story, I need to know that everything is going to end up alright, that true love will prevail, that I'm going to be left with a satisfying, (mostly) happy ending. Frankly, I hate suspense, and only once I know how things will turn out can I settle into a story. It's probably why I read books I love over, and over, and over. (Hello, *Jane Eyre*, nice to see you again.) My spouse and I have reached a détente on this issue: he won't give me a hard time about it, and I'm sworn to silence. I like to think I've perfected a pretty good poker face, letting him keep his edge-of-his-seat adrenaline, if that's what he wants.

In much the same way, when I started learning more about climate change, I *really* wanted to know how the story will end. I wanted assurance. I wanted hope. And if I found it, I was going to stick an Airtag on it, so I could track that puppy down if it ever wandered off again.

And then I realized something.

Hope isn't a *thing*. It's not an object that can be lost, or found, or packaged for easy consumption. It's not an icon to hang on an altar.

Hope is a ceremony. It's a sacred practice. It's a seed that we plant when we take a clear-eyed view of the situation, that germinates when we speak aloud the future we want, and emerges from the soil when we take our first steps in the right direction.

Joanna Macy and Chris Johnstone use the term *active hope* to describe this, and write that it begins when we wake up "to the beauty of life on whose behalf we act."[1] Christiana Figueres prefers *stubborn optimism*, "envisioning our desired future, and then actively pulling it closer." Former president of the Czech Republic Vaclav Havel says it "is not the conviction that something will turn out well, but the certainty that something makes sense, regardless of how it turns out."[2] Per Espen Stoknes gets more nuanced, giving us four kinds of hope: Passive Hope (trusting that someone else will save us), Active Hope (a belief that if I do my part, everything will be just fine), Stoic Hope (outcomes are uncertain, but I'll do my part anyway), and Transformational Hope (envisioning systemic change and committing to work toward a new way of being in the world). I've always been intrigued by Archbishop Desmund Tutu's description of optimism as an over-caffeinated marketing executive trying to sell you something. But hope, he said, is a sailor caught in a storm who has no choice but to keep rowing, to reach shore or die trying. The point is, hope has never been a talisman we could grab hold of. It is the act of doing what is right, regardless of the likelihood of our success. Because to do otherwise is simply not an option.

When asked how he stayed hopeful, Thich Nhat Hanh advised his students to cultivate their inner artist, meditator, and warrior, "to find a way to cultivate compassion, calm, and clarity. If these can be kept alive, then there is hope. The worst enemy is despair, [but] calming and looking deeply nourishes our hope," because "if the meditator and the artist are alive in us, then the warrior will know exactly in what direction to go."[3]

Hope resides at the fulcrum of creativity, contemplation, and action.

It is the neighbor of joy. And joy is an expression of relational harmony.

We mustn't mistake joy for happiness. Happiness is the fleeting, dopamine-driven giddy pleasure of a good day, or some good luck. Joy runs deeper. It's grounded in loving connection, and because of that, joy is also intertwined with sorrow. Poet Ross Gay explains, "Joy is an emanation from our practicing of our entanglement, our belonging to one another, our reliance upon one another ... like mycelium running through our soil .... Joy is the evidence of our reaching across to one another in the midst of or as a way of caring for one another's sorrows .... Without sorrow, it's something else."[4]

Perhaps you're asking yourself, how can we possibly talk about hope or joy in the midst of so much that is so wrong? Aren't we beyond saving? I like Britt Wray's response:

> Stories such as 'we're doomed' or 'we're out of time' are often rooted in emotional reactivity and not evidence based .... How on Earth can you *know* what is going to happen, *regardless* of what actions are taken now and into the future? Such terrible outcomes are possible if we do nothing, but it will only get as bad–and as hot–as we let it .... Those of us who are alive right now have real power over how much future suffering and loss there will be, so we don't get to give up like that–not on the wider natural world and the plethora of living species, not on young people, not on future people who aren't yet born, and not on the billions of people already living in circumstances that resemble the collapse many of us are imagining.[5]

Time to make friends with ambiguity

When it comes to climate change, many of us want to skip to the end of the book, to be assured that everything is going to work out alright. It's a very human response, and part of the reason so many of us love genre fiction. Grab a book from the Romance section, and you're guaranteed a happily ever after. The Mystery will be solved, the Thriller resolved—with just the right amount of carnage. There's comfort in knowing the future. It's also why divination is one of the oldest forms of religious practice. We've been casting shells, spilling entrails, studying the stars, reading tea leaves, communing with spirits, and rallying around oracles for thousands of years.

I've known many Christians who close their eyes and open a Bible at random, hoping the Holy Spirit will guide them to a verse chosen just for them, or who write down their dreams, seeking signs and portents. While the Quran technically forbids divination, Muslims around the world still interpret dreams, observe footprints, read genealogies, palms, and star charts, invoke celestial bodies, offer recitations, and interpret omens. We humans cast die, palm nuts, cowrie shells, or coconut pieces. We chant poems, read cards, dreams, or visions, and craft complex interpretive systems in the hope of knowing what's to come. But, in practice, divination rarely if ever predicts the future. More often, it offers guidance. And when divination *works*, that is, when it builds spiritual resilience and personal growth, it reminds us that we are part of a greater whole, that we are not alone, but connected to Spirit and part of a wider community. It admonishes us, recalling us to relationships, to obligations we should fulfill, and to the abundant resources on which we can draw for help. Divination more often shows us that "hope" has a lot less to do with knowing the future, and a lot more to do with finding the will to do right in the midst of uncertainty, expanding our scope of vision beyond the limits of our own individual, material lives.

Hope is the voice of prophetic action. And despite what we think, prophets rarely predict the future. More often, they call for justice. They remind us of our duty to care for the poor, the widows, the refugees. The biblical prophet Amos castigated "those who trample on the needy and ruin those who are oppressed." Martin Luther

King Jr. and Congressman John Lewis called out racism as America's "original sin," and for a movement to "redeem the soul of America." Indigenous prophets call us back to the wisdom of ancestors, and warn of catastrophic danger when we worship wealth, harm our other-than-human relatives, or forget our obligations to past and future generations. They offer the promise of renewal, the chance to change course, to start over. As Desmond Tutu says, "In the middle of our faith is death and resurrection. Nothing could have been more hopeless than Good Friday—but then Easter happened, and forever we have to become prisoners of hope."[6]

Former Episcopal bishop Steven Charleston (Choctaw) calls our attention to four Native American prophets—Ganiaodaiio, Tenskwatawa, Smohalla, and Wovoka—teachers who faced apocalyptic destruction in their own time, and draws wisdom from their stories to guide us in an era of ecological collapse. He finds lessons about the folly of individualism, the need to remember our place within the family of creation, a sacred teaching that the Earth is our mother, loves us, and longs to be loved in return, and the wisdom that we must reject fear, in favor of renewal and reconciliation. God does not doom us to destruction, Charleston writes. We do that to ourselves. These prophets don't predict the future, they participate in the outraged, sorrowing, joyful practice of hope and lament, pulling us back from the brink, reminding us that we are part of an interconnected whole, that we have the power to choose between life and death, that we are not alone, and that we have been here before.[7]

Prophets are also master storytellers, guiding individuals (in the case of divination) and communities (in the case of prophecy) to a truer story, one that acknowledges the challenges we face, how we have failed, and the ancestors and Spirit(s) who stand ready to help. They situate us at the crisis point, and challenge us to write the next chapter.

Our story isn't written yet

At the conclusion of her novel *Ceremony*, Leslie Marmon Silko's lead character Tayo has found renewal. He has also found heartbreak: his path has taken him to a realization that his own trauma is part of a larger story, a terrible story that includes colonialism, displacement, uranium mining, atomic weaponry, and the devastation of ecosystems both at home and across the world. But he also realizes that he has a role to play within that story. And he comes to know that he is not alone—that the land loves him back:

> Yet at this moment in the sunrise, it was all so beautiful, everything, from all directions, evenly, perfectly, balancing day with night, summer months with winter. The valley was enclosing this totality, like the mind holding all thoughts together in a single moment. The strength came from here, from this feeling. It had always been there. He stood there with the sun on his face, and he thought maybe he might make it after all.

Silko doesn't shirk from the terrible destruction we have wrought on the planet and each other, but she also insists on the healing possible when we recover our relationship with a living, sacred, Earth.

The rising popularity of dystopian, post-apocalyptic novels and films has prompted many climate writers to wonder: where are the stories that envision a world in which we got it right? The possible futures where we *don't* drive ourselves to ruin? It isn't a minor point. Stories have power to shape who we are, and who we will become. For Barbara Holmes, moving from crisis to healing requires taking control of the story. And that means recovering memory, reviving the lessons of our ancestors, and "interpreting our trauma through the lens of our joy." We must demand stories that faithfully represent the dangers ahead, she tells us, without letting go of the future we want.

As folklorist Martin Shaw explains, "stories worth their salt don't tell us to get cranked up with either naive hope or vinegar-tinged despair. Stories tell us to keep attending to the grace. Keep an eye on the miraculous. It is not for us to blow the candle out; only the gods can do that."[8] So I offer this clarion call to all our storytellers: write us stories of a livable future, stories that inspire and enliven us, that will get us out of bed in the morning. And I offer this call to our readers: once in a while, put down that post-apocalyptic nightmare, and remember that stories have the power to make the world.[9]

Joanna Macy and Chris Johnstone have famously described this moment in time as a choice between three stories: Business as Usual, the Great Unraveling, or the Great Turning. In the first story, we ignore the problem and continue on just as we are, and in doing so doom ourselves to the horrors of climate-catastrophe and ecosystem collapse. The second story is the Great Unraveling, a tale of civilizational and ecological ruin. In this tale, we are already doomed. It's too late. All we can do is retreat to our private islands, hoard our resources, and await the end. This story dooms us just as much as the first, with its self-fulfilling apocalypticism and implicit permission to succumb. As Bill McKibben has said, "the trouble with obsessing over collapse … is that it keeps you from considering other possibilities. Either you've got your fingers stuck firmly in your ears, or you're down in the basement oiling your guns. There's no real room for creative thinking."[10]

Instead, we have to reclaim the original meaning of the word *apokalypsis*: revelation. It meant a tearing away of the veil, a chance to see the world as it really is. Because there's a third story to choose from: the Great Turning. This is a radically different story, one in which humanity lays claim to this pivotal moment, turning away from colonial, extractive economies, and toward building a just, sustainable world. This is a story grounded in respect, reverence, and reciprocity for all our relations. It's a story where we learn to listen—to each other, to the natural world, and to the Spirit. And we discover new, *better*, ways of being. If you choose the third story, then there is only one question to ask: what role will you play in that Great Turning?

Jewish philosopher and holocaust survivor Victor Frankl argued that human beings are wired to seek "healing through meaning," a process he calls *logotherapy*. But he also notes that transformative stories require generative spaces of uncertainty: because those are the moments when we discover who we are, and what we truly value. We are in one of those generative times, one of those periods of profound liminality. And liminality is scary. It's malleable, and unpredictable. It's why we surround those moments of the life cycle with such protective measures: rites of passage, ceremony, the guidance of elders. But the good news is that liminal spaces aren't just scary—they're filled with creative potential. They're moments when the old ways of doing things are left behind, and we discover new possibilities, new ways of being in the world. The terrifying, thrilling, and incredible opportunity of living in a time of profound change is that we have power to shape the world moving forward. And to do that, we need to begin to tell bold stories. To dare to imagine the world we want to live in. This isn't mere playful invention—it's how we survive.

Psychologist Sally Gillespie shows us that traumatic events and existential crises prompt the loss of orienting stories, myths that we have carried with us and cherished like holy gospel. Many of us will fight tooth and nail to hold on to those old mythologies, our myths of infinite economic growth, manifest destiny, human exceptionalism, radical individualism. But letting go of old stories frees us to write better ones.[11] And we simply cannot afford to cede the ground of storytelling to those who have already given up, who have pulled up the gangplank, and blasted off for Mars. We must resist the lure of stories that offer a predetermined conclusion, and reclaim stories still emerging, unfixed, and full of potential, where prophets point to the fork in the road.

Joining that story means surrendering the illusion of control, even as it also means reclaiming our agency, taking up the essential and irreplaceable role each one of us has to play in this new story.

As Katharine Hayhoe reminds us,

> One of the biggest reasons our actions matter is that what we do changes us. And the other big reason is that what we do and say changes others ... Yes, solar panels cut my carbon emissions, but they also make me feel empowered, as if what I do matters. They give me a sense of efficacy .... It's a true positive feedback cycle. When we feel empowered to act, individually and communally, that makes us not only more likely to act, but to support others to do so .... It inoculates us against despair.[12]

We need to unlearn our helplessness, giving sacred attention to every opportunity to effect change in our world. We need to reclaim the power of individual action, even as we work for systemic change.

adrienne marie brown's book *Emergent Strategy* helps us understand what that might look like.[13] Picture a kettle, set to boil. At first it looks like nothing is happening. (Tap the pot: is it even getting warm?) Then we see one small bubble. Followed by another, then another. Each is miniscule, separate, and alone. Inconsequential. But as more bubbles form, they coalesce, then, seconds later, as though from nowhere, a full rolling boil erupts. Emergent thinking requires that we back away from the notion that only singular, heroic, grand gestures matter. Instead, we're reminded that change happens when each of us do our part within a larger emergent movement of transformative action.

This kind of narrative requires setting aside some main-character-energy. It means grounding in the present moment, finding purpose in the process, and not putting off joy until the work is done. It requires knowing the power of small steps, and taking comfort that we are not alone in the work. As Macy and Johnstone explain,

> everything we do has ripples of influence extending far beyond what we can see .... We can't know how things will unfold. What we can do is make a choice about what we'd like to have happen, and then put ourselves fully behind that possibility. An inspiring wave of change is spreading through our world. The Great Turning is happening in our time, and we may already be participating in many ways.[14]

How do we build a ceremony of hope? We begin by creating a safe arena in which to work, sacred time and space to hold our fear and pain. Then we gather together our relatives, our kith and kin, the humans and the more-than-humans, ancestors and future generations, the spirits and the Spirit. And altogether, we start to tell a story of the world we want to see. But we don't just *tell* the story, we perform it. In ceremony, we *enter into* the story, and in so doing, we take up the power to change it, each of us, with our irreplaceable role in that greater tale we're telling together. In acts of everyday contemplation that story keeps going, energized by each bite of sacramental salmon, each dream we share over morning coffee, each relay we run for climate justice.

We were bewildered in our grief, lost in the wilds of it. But in that ceremony of hope, we recovered our *kithship*, our communion with a landscape intimately known. We do not know where we are going, but we know who we are with—all our relations.

Notes

Preface

1 Leslie Marmon Silko, *Ceremony* (New York: Penguin, 2006).

2 Lawrence Gross, *Anishinaabe Ways of Being and Knowing* (Routledge, 2016): 40.

Chapter 1

1 Peter Andre, Teodara Boneva, Felix Chopra, and Armin Falk, "Globally Representative Evidence on the Actual and Perceived Support for Climate Action," *Nature Climate Change* Vol. 14 (2024): 253–9.

2 Yale Program on Climate Change Communication, "Global Climate Opinion Factsheets." https://climatecommunication.yale.edu/visualizations-data/global-factsheets/. Julia Fine, Joshua Ettinger, Emily Goddard, John Kotcher, Hilyatuz Zakiyyah, Yuan Yue, Jennifer Carman, Seth Rosenthal, Kathryn Thier, Teresa Myers, Marija Verner, Jennifer Marlon, Emily Richards, Matthew Goldberg, Anthony Leiserowitz and Edward Maibach, "Climate Change in the American Mind: Public Perceptions of the Health Harms of Global Warming, Fall 2024," Yale Program of Climate Change Communication. https://climatecommunication.yale.edu/publications/climate-change-in-the-american-mind-public-perceptions-of-the-health-harms-of-global-warming-fall-2024/toc/3/.

3 Magdalena Gawrych, "Climate Change and Mental Health: A Review of Current Literature," *Psychiatric Policy* Vol. 56 No. 4 (2022): 903–15. Susan

Clayton and Tara Crandon, "Climate Change and Mental Health," *Annual Review of Clinical Psychology* (2024): 3.1–3.23. https://www.carbonbrief.org/mapped-how-climate-change-disproportionately-affects-womens-health/.

4 WHO Regional Office for the Americas, "Depression and Other Common Mental Health Disorders: Global Health Estimates" (October 17, 2017). Licence: CC BY-NC-SA 3.0 IGO.

5 Nick Higginbotham, Linda Connor, Glenn Albrecht, Sonia Freeman, and Kingsley Agho, "Validation of an Environmental Distress Scale," *EcoHealth* Vol. 3 (2006): 245–54. https://www.nature.com/articles/s44168-024-00172-8.

6 Ashlee Cunsolo and Neville Ellis, "Ecological Grief as a Mental Health Response to Climate Change-Related Loss," *Nature* Vol. 8 (2018): 275–81.

7 *All We Can Save: Truth, Courage, and Solutions for the Climate Crisis*, edited by Ayana Elizabeth Johnson and Katharine Wilkinson (One World, 2020): 237.

8 Rachel Maretin, "Her Antidote to 'Climate Grief' and a Shrinking Great Salt Lake? Don't Look Away," National Public Radio (October 8, 2023). https://www.npr.org/2023/10/08/1204141095/climate-grief-great-salt-lake-utah-terry-tempest-williams.

9 Rebecca Berru Davis, "Picturing Paradise: Peruvian Women's Art and a 'New Creation,'" *Valuing Lives, Healing Earth, Religion, Gender, and Life on Earth*, edited by Theresa Yugar, Sarah E. Robinson, Lilian Dube, and Teresia Mbari Hinga (Leuven: Peeters, 2021): 86.

10 Evan Berry, "Religion and Climate Geopolitics," *Current History* November 2024. *Climate Politics and the Power of Religion*, edited by Evan Berry (Bloomington: Indiana University Press, 2022): 283–9.

11 Willis Jenkins, Evan Berry, and Luke Beck Kreider, "Religion and Climate Change," *Annual Review of Environment and Resources* Vol. 43 (2018): 85–108.

12 Darren Dochuk, *Anointed with Oil: How Christianity and Crude Made Modern America* (New York: Basic Books, 2019). And, Kevin O'Brien, *Meeting the Enemy: The Power of Christian Climate Resistance* (Minneapolis: Fortress Press, 2025).

13 Carey Funk and Alec Tyson, "Millennial and Gen Z Republicans Stand Out from Their Elders on Climate and Energy Issues." https://www.pewresearch.org/short-reads/2020/06/24/millennial-and-gen-z-republicans-stand-out-from-their-elders-on-climate-and-energy-issues/, and Michael Lipka,

Becka A. Alper and Justin Nortey, "Younger Evangelicals in the US Are More Concerned Than Their Elders About Climate Change." https://www.pewresearch.org/short-reads/2022/12/07/younger-evangelicals-in-the-u-s-are-more-concerned-than-their-elders-about-climate-change/.

14 Becky Alper et al., "Spirituality Among Americans," Pew Research Center (December 7, 2023). https://www.pewresearch.org/religion/2023/12/07/spirituality-among-americans/. Hannah Ritche, "More People Care About Climate Change Than You Think," Our World in Data (March 25, 2024). https://ourworldindata.org/climate-change-support.

15 Layli Maparyan, *The Womanist Idea* (Abingdon: Routledge, 2012): 5.

16 Umeek (E. Richard Atleo), *Principles of Tsawalk: An Indigenous Approach to Global Crisis* (Vancouver: UBC, 2011): 37.

17 Kyle Whyte, "Critical Investigations of Resilience: A Brief Introduction to Indigenous Environmental Studies & Sciences," *Daedalus* Vol. 147 No. 2 (2018): 136–47.

18 Kaitlin Curtice, *Living Resistance: An Indigenous Vision of Seeking Wholeness Every Day* (Ada: Baker, 2023): 23.

19 Tom Driver, *The Magic of Ritual: Our Need for Liberating Rites That Transform Our Lives and Our Communities* (San Francisco: Harper San Francisco, 1991): 179.

20 Heather McTeer Toney, "Collards Are Just as Good as Kale," *All We Can Save: Truth, Courage, and Solutions for the Climate Crisis*, edited by Ayana Elizabeth Johnson and Katharine Wilkinson (One World, 2020): 75.

Chapter 2

1 Lise Van Susteren and Stacey Colino, *Emotional Inflammation: Discover Your Triggers and Reclaim Your Equilibrium During Anxious Times* (New York: St. Martin's Essentials, 2020).

2 B. Verplanken and D. Roy, "'My Worries Are Rational, Climate Change Is Not': Habitual Ecological Worrying Is an Adaptive Response," *PLOS* Vol. 8 No. 9 (2013): 1. M. T. Ballew, S. S. Uppalapati, T. Myers, J. Carman, E. Campbell, S. A. Rosenthal, J. E. Kotcher, A. Leiserowitz, and E. Maibach, "Climate Change Psychological Distress Is Associated with Increased Collective Climate Action in the US," *Npj Climate Action* Vol. 3 No. 1 (2024): 88. https://doi.org/10.1038/s44168-024-00172-8.

3 Susan Clayton and Tara Crandon, "Climate Distress Among Young People, an Overview," *Climate Change and Youth Mental Health*, edited by Elizabeth Haase and Kelsey Hudson (Port Washington: Climate Psychology Alliance of North America, 2024): 3–20. Tara Crandon, James Scott, Fiona Charlson, and Hannah Thomas, "A Theoretical Model of Climate Anxiety and Coping," *Discover Psychology* Vol. 4 No. 10 (2024): 1007.

4 George Marshall, *Don't Even Think About It: Why Our Brains Are Wired to Ignore Climate Change* (London: Bloomsbury, 2015).

5 Hans Rosling, *Factfulness: Ten Reasons We're Wrong About the World—and Why Things Are Better Than You Think* (New York: Flatiron Books, 2018).

6 Katharine Hayhoe, *Saving Us: A Climate Scientist's Case for Hope and Healing in a Divided World* (Miami: Atria/One Signal Publishers, 2022).

7 Per Espen Stoknes, *What We Think About When We Try Not to Think About Global Warming* (White River Junction: Chelsea Green, 2015).

8 Susteren and Colino, *Emotional Inflammation:* 55

9 Bob Doppelt, *Transformational Resilience: How Building Human Resilience to Climate Disruption Can Safeguard Society and Increase Wellbeing* (Abingdon: Routledge, 2016).

10 Richard G. Tedeschi and Lawrence G. Calhoun, "Post-traumatic Growth: Conceptual Foundations and Empirical Evidence," *Psychological Inquiry* Vol. 15 No. 1 (2004): 1–18.

11 Barbara Holmes, *Crisis Contemplation: Healing the Wounded Village* (Albuquerque: CAC Publishing, 2021): 108.

12 Lisa Feldman Barrett, *How Emotions Are Made: The Secret Life of the Brain* (Hammon: Mariner Books, 2018).

13 Steven Hayes, *The Liberated Mind: How to Pivot Toward What Matters* (Glendale: Avery, 2020).

14 Britt Wray, *Generation Dread: Finding Purpose in an Age of Climate Anxiety* (New York: The Experiment, 2023): 33.

15 Daniel Siegel, *The Developing Mind: How Relationships and the Brain Interact to Shape Who We Are* (New York: Guilford Press, 2020).

16 Rick Hanson, *Resilient: How to Grow an Unshakable Core of Calm, Strength and Happiness* (Nevada City: Harmony Books, 2018): 43.

Chapter 3

1 "A Tribe Once Declared 'Extinct' Helps Reintroduce Salmon to the Columbia River," *Mongabay* (July 2024).

2 Ross Gay, *Inciting Joy: Essays* (New York: Algonquin, 2022).

3 Rebecca Solnit, *A Field Guide to Getting Lost* (New York: Penguin Books, 2006).

4 Ray Cashman, "Dying the Good Death: Wake and Funeral Customs in County Tyrone," *New Hibernia Review / Iris Éireannach Nua* Vol. 10 No. 2 (2006): 9–25.

5 Rebecca Dobkins, *The Art of Ceremony: Voices of Renewal from Indigenous Oregon* (Seattle: University of Washington Press, 2022).

6 Dobkins, *Art of Ceremony*: 210.

7 Rachel E. Harding and Rosemarie Freeney Harding, *Remnants: A Memoir of Spirit, Activism, and Mothering* (Duke University Press, 2015).

8 Britt Wray, *Generation Dread: Finding Purpose in an Age of Climate Anxiety* (New York: The Experiment, 2022), 213.

9 Anita Diamant, *Saying Kaddish: How to Comfort the Dying, Bury the Dead, and Mourn as a Jew* (New York: Schocken, 1999).

10 James Young, "When a Day Remembers: A Performative History of "Yom ha-Shoah," *History and Memory* Vol. 2 No. 2 (1990): 54–75.

11 Damien Gayle, "Huge 'Butchered' Artwork Installed on North Sea Gas Rig by Greenpeace Activists," *The Guardian* (August 14, 2025). https://www.theguardian.com/environment/2025/aug/14/greenpeace-activists-install-huge-artwork-by-anish-kapoor-on-north-sea-gas-rig.

12 Allan Hepburn, "The Irish Way of Dying: 'Ulysses' and Funeral Processions," *The Canadian Journal of Irish Studies* Vol. 38 No. 1/21 / (2014): 184–207.

13 Erica S. Lawson, "Bereaved Black Mothers and Maternal Activism in the Racia State," *Feminist Studies* Vol. 44 No. 3 (2018): 713–35.

14 William Blaine-Wallace, *When Tears Sing: The Art of Lament in Christian Community* (Maryknoll: Orbis, 2020).

15 W. E. B. DuBois, quoted in Simon Stow, "Agonistic Homegoing: Frederick Douglass, Joseph Lowery, and the Democratic Value of African American Public Mourning," *American Political Science Review* Vol. 104 No. 4 (2010): 681–97.

16 Cole Arthur Riley, *This Here Flesh: Spirituality, Liberation, and the Stories that Make Us* (Cincinnati: Convergent, 2022): 98, 101.

17 Patricia Lysaght, "'Caoineadh os Cionn Coirp': The Lament for the Dead in Ireland," *Folklore* Vol. 108 (1997): 66.

18 Lysaght, "'Caoineadh os Cionn Coirp'": 66.

19 Barbara Holmes, *Crisis Contemplation: Healing the Wounded Village* (Albuquerque: CAC Publishing, 2021).

Chapter 4

1 Robin Wall Kimmerer, *Braiding Sweetgrass: Indigenous Wisdom, Scientific Knowledge, and the Wisdom of Plants* (Minneapolis: Milkweed, 2015).

2 A. P. Shoubridge, J. M. Choo, A. M. Martin et al., "The Gut Microbiome and Mental Health: Advances in Research and Emerging Priorities," *Molecular Psychiatry* Vol. 27 (2022): 1908–19.

3 Jonathan Foley, Fixing Food's Big Climage Problem. https://drawdown.org/insights/fixing-foods-big-climate-problem, and IPCC, "IPCC Sixth Assessment ReportWorking Group III: Mitigation of Climate Change." https://www.ipcc.ch/report/ar6/wg3/.

4 Mariaelena Huambachano, *Recovering Our Ancestral Foodways: Indigenous Recipes for Living Well* (Berkeley: University of California Press, 2024).

5 Seafha C. Ramos, "Understanding Yurok Traditional Ecological Knowledge and Wildlife Management," *Journal of Wildlife Management* Vol. 86 No. 1 (January 2022): 1—21. https://doi.org/10.1002/jwmg.22140.

6 Sena Yücel and Ziya Erokay Metin, "The Interplay Between Mindful Eating, Climate Change Awareness, and Psychological Well-Being: A Cross-Sectional Analysis," *Food Science, and Nutrition* Vol. 13 No. 8 (August 2025): 3.

7 Sharon Suh, *Occupy This Body: A Buddhist Memoir* (Los Angeles: Sumeru Press, 1999).

8 Joseph Espe Brown, *No Recipe: Cooking as Spiritual Practice* (Louisville: St. Martins, 2018).

9 *Brown, No Recipe.*

10 Thich Nhat Hanh and Sister True Devotion, *Zen and the Art of Saving the Planet* (San Francisco: Harper One, 2021).

11 Daniel Levitin, *The Organized Mind: Thinking Straight in the Age of Information Overload* (New York: Penguin, 2015).

12 Jan Chozen Bays, *Mindful Eating: A Guide to Rediscovering a Healthy and Joyful Relationship with Food* (Boulder: Shambhala, 2017).

13 Albert Raboteau, *A Fire in the Bones: Reflections on African American Religious History* (Boston: Beacon Press, 1986).

14 Christopher Carter, *The Spirit Soul Food of Race, Faith, and Food Justice* (Champaign: University of Illinois, 2021).

Chapter 5

1 Barbara Holmes, *Crisis Contemplation: Healing the Wounded Village* (Albuquerque: CAC Publishing, 2021): 57.

2 Max Weber, *The Protestant Ethic and the Spirit of Capitalism* (Abingdon: Routledge, 1992).

3 Tricia Hersey, *Rest Is Resistance: A Manifesto* (Warnerville: Little Brown Spark, 2022).

4 Abraham Joshua Heschel, *The Sabbath: It's Meaning for Modern Man* (New York: Farrar Straus Giroux, 2005).

5 Jonathan Neril, "Ecology and Shabbat," *My Jewish Learning*. https://www.myjewishlearning.com/article/ecology-shabbat/.

6 Cole Arthur Riley, *This Here Flesh: Spirituality, Liberation, and the Stories That Make Us* (Cincinnati: Convergent Books, 2023): 148, 151.

7 Riley, *This Here Flesh*: 156

8 Kevin O'Brien, *SJ, The Ignatian Adventure: Experiencing the Spiritual Exercises of St. Ignatius in Daily Life* (Chicago: Loyola Press, 2011).

9 Karen Armstrong, *Sacred Nature, Restoring Our Ancient Bond with the Natural World* (New York: Knopf, 2023): 101.

10 Rosemary Freeney Harding with Rachael Elizabeth Harding, "Hospitality, Haints, and Healing: A Southern African American Meaning of Religion," *Deeper Shades of Purple: Womanism in Religion and Society*, edited by Stacey Floyd-Thomas (New York: New York University Press, 2006): 107.

11 Onukwube Anedo, "Dreaming Ancestors Among African Americans: A Challenge to the Modern Igbo People," *Journal of Religion and Human Relations* Vol 1 No 4 (2012): 43–56.

12 Adam McGee, "Dreaming in Haitian Vodou: Vouchsafe, Guide, and Source of Liturgical Novelty," *Dreaming* (2012).

13 Sally Gillespie, *Climate Consciousness: Re-imagining Our World and Ourselves* (Abingdon: Routledge, 2020): 143.

Chapter 6

1 Lise Van Sustern and Stacey Colino, *Emotional Inflammation* (Louisville: Sounds True, 2020): 161.

2 Thich Nhat Hanh, *Your True Home: The Everyday Wisdom of Thich Nhat Hanh* (Boulder: Shambhala, 2011): 124.

3 Kathryn Schertz and Mark Berman, "Understanding Nature and Its Cognitive Benefits," *Current Directions in Psychological Science* Vol. 28 No. 5 (2019): 496–502. Patricia Hasbach, *Prescribing Nature: A Clinician's Guide to Ecotherapy* (New York: W. W. Norton, 2025), and Marc Berman, *Nature and the Mind: The Science of How Nature Improves Cognitive, Physical, and Social Well-Being* (New York: Simon Element, 2025).

4 Thomas Buckley, *Standing Ground: Yurok Indian Spirituality from 1850–1990* (Berkeley: University of California Press, 2002).

5 Quoted in the film *Canoe Way the Sacred Journey*. Produced by Mark Celletti and Robert Satiacum. Tacoma, WA: Cedar Media, 2009.

6 Umeek (E. Richard Atleo), *Principles of Tsawalk: An Indigenous Approach to Global Crisis* (Vancouver: University of British Columbia Press, 2011).

7 Liz Bucar, *Stealing My Religion: Not Just Any Cultural Appropriation* (Cambridge: Harvard University Press, 2024).

8 Paul Bramadat, *Yogalands: In Search of Practice on the Mat and in the World* (Montreal: McGill Queens, 2025).

9 Cole Arthur Riley, *This Here Flesh: Spirituality, Liberation, and the Stories That Make Us* (Cincinnati: Convergent Books, 2023): 67, 68.

10 Juliet Grable, "Healing Through Whitewater: Indigenous Youth Paddle the Newly Free-Flowing Klamath River," Jefferson Public Radio (June 27, 2025).

11 Tom Driver, *The Magic of Ritual: Our Need for Liberating Rites That Tranform Our Lives and Our Communities* (New York: Harper, 1992).

Chapter 7

1 Thich Nhat Hanh, *The Art of Living* (New York: Harper One, 2017).

2 Thich Nhat Hanh, *Zen and the Art of Saving the Planet* (New York: Harper One, 2022): 84.

3 Jill Bolte Taylor, *My Stroke of Insight* (New York: Plume, 2009), quoted in Lise Van Sustern and Stacey Colino, *Emotional Inflammation* (New York: St. Martin's, 2020): 141.

4 Robin Ortiz and Erica Sibinga, "The Role of Mindfulness in Reducing the Adverse Effects of Childhood Stress and Trauma," *Children* Vol. 4 No 3 (2017): 16.

5 "What Is Contemplation? An Interview with Loriliai Biernacki," *Contemplative Currents* (February 23, 2024).

6 "What Is Contemplation? An Interview with Muhammad Faruque," *Contemplative Currents* (April 4, 2024).

7 Mary Virginia Rojas, "She Bathes in a Sacred Place: Rites of Reciprocity, Power, and Prestige in Alta California," *Wicazo Sa Review* Vol. 18 No. 1 (2003): 129.

8 "What Is Contemplation? An Interview with Oludamini Ogunnaike," *Contemplative Currents* (December 6, 2024).

9 Thich Nhat Hanh, *Zen and the Art of Saving the Planet* (New York: Harper One, 2021): 88.

10 "Douglas Christie on Contemplative Ecology," Oxford University Press Blog (2013). See also Contemplative Ecology: Contemplation for a World

in Crisis. http://www.naturalcontemplative.com/essays/crisis.html, and Douglas Christie, *The Blue Sapphire of the Mind: Notes for a Contemplative Ecology* (Oxford: Oxford University Press, 2013).

11 Stephanie Kaza, *Green Buddhism: Practice and Compassionate Action in Uncertain Times* (Boulder: Shambhala, 2019): 5.

12 Samuel Torvend, *Monastic Ecological Wisdom: A Living Tradition* (Collegeville: Liturgical Press, 2023).

13 J. Philip Newell, *Listening for the Heartbeat of God: A Celtic Spirituality* (Mahwah: Paulist Press, 1997): 42.

14 Rebecca Dobkins, *The Art of Ceremony* (Seattle: University of Washington Press, 2022): 52.

15 Rabbi Diane Elliot, "Elohai Nehama: Breathing the Soul Alive," *My Jewish Learning*. https://www.myjewishlearning.com/article/elohai-neshama-breathing-the-soul-alive/.

16 David Suzuki, *The Sacred Balance: Rediscovering Our Place in Nature* (Vancouver: Greystone, 2022): 55, 66.

17 Andrew Newberg, *The Principles of Neurotheology* (Farnham: Ashgate, 2010).

18 Coleman Barks, *The Essential Rumi* (New York: HarperOne, 1995): 247–8.

19 Barbara Holmes, *Healing the Wounded Village* (Albuquerque: CAC Press, 2021): 42.

20 Cole Arthur Riley, *This Here Flesh: Spirituality, Liberation, and the Stories that Make Us* (Cincinnati: Convergent, 2022).

21 Barbara Holmes, *Crisis Contemplation: Healing the Wounded Village* (Albuquerque: CAC Press, 2021): 42, 43.

22 Holmes, *Crisis Contemplation*: 43–6.

23 Emmanual Vaughn Lee, "Deep Time Diligence," *Emergence Magazine* (February 19, 2024). https://emergencemagazine.org/conversation/deep-time-diligence/.

24 Emmanual Vaughn Lee, "Deep Time Diligence," *Emergence Magazine* (February 2024).

25 Joanna Macy and Chris Johnstone, *Active Hope: How to Face the Mess We're in with Unexpected Resilience and Creative Power* (Half Moon Bay: New World, 2022): 41.

Chapter 8

1 Blanche Verlie, *Learning to Live with Climate Change: From Anxiety to Transformation* (Abingdon: Routledge, 2023).

2 Barbara Holmes, *Crisis Contemplation: Healing the Wounded Village* (Albuquerque: CAC Press, 2021): 115.

3 Kevin O'Brien, *Meeting the Enemy: The Fossil Fuel Industry and the Power of Christian Climate Resistance* (Minneapolis: Fortress Press 2025).

4 Lynn Margulis and Dorion Sagan, *Slanted Truths: Essays on Gaia, Symbiosis, and Evolution* (New York: Copernicus Books, 1997).

5 A. J. Finley and S. M. Schaefer, "Affective Neuroscience of Loneliness: Potential Mechanisms Underlying the Association Between Perceived Social Isolation, Health, and Well-Being," *Journal of Psychiatric Brain Science* Vol. 7 No. 6 (2022). https://doi.org/10.20900/jpbs.20220011.

6 Britt Wray, *Generation Dread: Finding Purpose in an Age of Climate Anxiety* (New York: The Experiment, 2023): 41, 232.

7 Barbora Kucerova, Nava Levit-Binnun, Ilanit Gordon, and Yulia Golland, "From Oxytocin to Compassion: The Saliency of Distress," *Biology* Vol. 12, No. 2 (2022): 183

8 Joanna Macy and Chris Johnstone, *Active Hope: How to Face the Mess We're in with Unexpected Resilience and Creative Power* (Novato: New World Library, 2022): 73, 75.

9 Umeek Richard Atleo, *Principles of Tsawalk: An Indigenous Approach to Global Crisis* (Vancouver: UBC Press, 2011).

10 Enrique Salmón, "Kincentric Ecology: Indigenous Perceptions of the Human–Nature Relationship," *Ecological Applications* Vol. 10 No. 5 (October 2000): 1327–32.

11 Rebecca Dobkins, *Art of Ceremony: Voices of Renewal from Indigenous Oregon* (Seattle: University of Washington Press, 2022).

12 Robin Kimmerer, "A Family Reunion at the End of the World," *Kinship* Vol. 1 (Libertyville: Center for Humans and Nature, 2021): 111–24. See also kincentricleadership.org.

13 Rosalyn LaPier, *Invisible Reality: Storytellers, Storytakers, and the Supernatural World of the Blackfeet* (Lincoln: University of Nebraska Press, 2017).

14 https://substack.com/@freyarohn/posts. Hana Videen, "Why I Hoard Words," *Princeton University Press Blog*. https://press.princeton.edu/ideas/why-i-hoard-words.

15 Daniel P. Horan, "Beyond the 'Birdbath Industrial Complex' Is the Radical St. Francis of Assisi," *National Catholic Reporter*. https://www.ncronline.org/news/faith-seeking-understanding/beyond-birdbath-industrial-complex-radical-st-francis-assisi.

16 Cherice Brock and Christy Randazzo, *Quakers, Ecology, and the Light* (Boston: Brill, 2023).

17 Jea Sophia Oh, "Salim, Women, and Oikos: A Planetary Expansion of Family," *Valuing Lives, Healing Earth: Religion, Gender, and Life on Earth*, edited by Theresa Yugar, Sarah E. Robinson, Lilian Dube, and Teresia Mbari Hinga (Leuven: Peeters, 2021): 50.

18 Aruna Gnanadason, "Indian Women: Nurturing Earth, Protecting Life," in *Valuing Lives*: 142.

19 Rosemary Freeney Harding with Rachael Elizabeth Harding, "Hospitality, Haints, and Healing: A Southern African American Meaning of Religion," *Deeper Shades of Purple: Womanism in Religion and Society*, edited by Stacey Floyd-Thomas (New York: New York University Press, 2006): 106–7.

20 Monica Coleman, *Making a Way Out of No Way: A Womanist Theology* (Minneapolis: Augsburg Press, 2008).

21 Adrienne Krone, "Humans and Honey Bees," in *Valuing Lives*: 189, 199.

22 Yugar et al., *Valuing Lives, Healing Earth*: 50.

23 Yugar, et al. (eds.), *Valuing Lives, Healing Earth*: 9, 12, 76. See also *Qur'an, Surah Al-Baqarah*, 2: 186 (Oxford University Press, 2008).

24 Quran 6.38.

25 Yugar et al., *Valuing Lives, Healing Earth*: 53

26 Wang Zhongjiang, "The Development and Varieties of 'Oneness' in Early Daoism," *Journal of Chinese Humanities* Vol. 10 (2024): 108–28.

27 Melvine McLeod (ed.), *Your True Home: Everyday Wisdom of Thich Nhat Hanh* (Boulder: Shambhala, 2011): 49.

Chapter 9

1 Status of Tribes and Climate Change Report, *Institute for Tribal Environmental Professionals* Vol. 2 (Flagstaff: Institute for Tribal Environmental Professionals, 2025). https://itep.nau.edu/resources/publications/.

2 Vicky Tauli-Corpuz, Janis Alcorn, Augusta Molnar, Christina Healy, and Edmund Barrow, "Cornered by PAs: Adopting Rights-based Approaches to Enable Cost-effective Conservation and Climate Action," *World Development* Vol. 130 (2020): 104923–35.

3 Michelle Jacob, *Yakama Rising: Indigenous Cultural Revitalization, Activism, and Healing* (Tucson: University of Arizona Press, 2014).

4 Mary Annaïse Heglar, "Climate Change Ain't the First Existential Threat," *Resilience* (March 6, 2019). https://www.resilience.org/stories/2019-03-06/climate-change-aint-the-first-existential-threat/.

5 Steven Charleston, *We Survived the End of the World* (Minneapolis: Broadleaf, 2023).

6 Pamela Brubaker, "Indigenous Women Act to Defend Mother Earthmpowerment and Solidarity," *Valuing Lives, Healing Earth–Religion, Gender, and Life on Earth*, edited by Theresa Yugar, Sarah Robinson, Lilian Dube, and Theresa Mbari Hinga (Leuven: Peeters, 2021): 182.

7 Indigenous Environmental Network, *Indigenous Resistance Against Carbon* (Washington: Oil Change International, 2021). https://www.ienearth.org/indigenous-resistance-against-carbon/. "Carbon Emissions of Richest 1 Percent More Than Double the Emissions of the Poorest Half of Humanity," Oxfam International (21 September, 2020). https://www.oxfam.org/en/press-releases/carbon-emissions-richest-1-percent-more-double-emissions-poorest-half-humanity.

8 Neil M. Dawson et al., "Is It Just Conservation? A Typology of Indigenous Peoples' and Local Communities' Roles in Conserving Biodiversity," *One Earth* Vol. 7 No. 6 (2024): 1007–21.

9 Mary Robinson, *Climate Justice: Hope, Resilience, and the Fight for a Sustainable Future* (London: Bloomsbury, 2018): 4.

10 Laura Cozzi, Olivia Chen, and Hyeji Kim, "The World's Top 1% of Emitters Produce over 1000 Times More CO2 than the Bottom 1%," (Paris: IEA). https://www.iea.org/commentaries/the-world-s-top-1-of-emitters-produce-over-1000-times-more-co2-than-the-bottom-1.

11 James Baldwin interview with Mavis Nicholson (BBC, February 12, 1987).

12 Cole Arthur Riley, *This Here Flesh: Spirituality, Liberation, and the Stories That Make Us* (Cincinnati: Convergent, 2022): 194.

13 Lise Vansustern and Stacey Colino, *Emotional Inflammation* (Louisville: Sounds True, 2020): 19.

14 Blanche Verlie, *Learning to Live with Climate Change: From Anxiety to Transformation* (Abingdon: Routledge, 2021): 8.

15 Riley, *This Here Flesh*: 129.

16 "Prisoner of Hope," *Sojourners Magazine* (February 1985). https://sojo.net/magazine/february-1985/interview/prisoner-hope.

17 Alyssa Moore, "'Solidarity Among Creatures,' Catholic Exegetical Grounds for Fellowship with Nonhuman Creation," *Valuing Lives, Healing Earth–Religion, Gender, and Life on Earth*, edited by Theresa Yugar, Sarah Robinson, Lilian Dube, and Theresa Mbari Hinga (Leuven: Peeters) 58.

18 Sallie McFague, *Super Natural Christians: How We Should Love Nature* (Minneapolis: Fortress Press, 1997): 6.

19 Katharine Hayhoe, *Saving Us: A Climate Scientist's Case for Hope and Healing in a Divided World* (New York: Simon and Schuster, 2021): 19, 23, 33.

20 Harvard Pluralism Project, "Buddhism and Engaged Social Action." https://pluralism.org/buddhism-and-social-action-engaged-buddhism.

21 James Blumenthal, "Towards a Buddhist Theory of Justice," *Journal of Global Buddhism* Vol. 10 (2009): 321–49.

22 Riley, *This Here Flesh*: 123.

23 Rebecca Dobkins, *Art of Ceremony: Voices of Renewal from Indigenous Oregon* (Seattle: University of Washington Press, 2022): 38.

24 Jo-Ann Archibald, *Indigenous Storywork: Educating the Heart, Mind, Body, and Spirit* (Vancouver: UBC Press, 2008).

25 Nina Dietz, "Grief, Hope, Joy: Faith in the Time of Climate Change," *Inside Climate News* (December 25, 2024). https://insideclimatenews.org/news/25122024/faith-in-the-time-of-climate-change/

26 Bob Doppelt, *Transformational Resilience* (Abingdon: Routledge, 2016).

27 Christiana Figueres and Tom Rivett-Carnac, *The Future We Choose: The Stubborn Optimist's Guide to the Climate Crisis* (New York: Vintage, 2021).

28 Thich Nhat Hanh, *Zen and the Art of Saving the Planet* (New York: Harper One, 2021): 213, 187, 192, 196.

29 Sarah Jaquette Ray, *A Field Guide to Climate Anxiety* (Berkeley: University of California Press, 2020): 112–13.

Chapter 10

1 Julian Brave NoiseCat, "How to Survive an Apocalypse and Keep Dreaming." https://www.thenation.com/article/society/native-american-postapocalypse/ (June 2, 2020).

2 Wade Clark Roof, *Spiritual Marketplace: Baby Boomers and the Remaking of American Religion* (Princeton, 2001).

3 Liz Bucar, *Stealing My Religion: Not Just Any Cultural Appropriation* (Cambridge: Harvard University Press, 2022).

4 For those of you who are unaware of this internet slang, TLDR is short for "Too Long; Didn't Read."

Chapter 11

1 Steven C. Hayes, "Buddhism and Acceptance and Commitment Therapy," *Behavioral Practice* Vol. 9 No. 1 (2002): 58–66.

2 Sally Gillespie, *Climate Consciousness: Re-imagining Our World and Ourselves* (Abingdon: Routledge, 2019): 3.

3 Sarah Jaqette Ray, *A Field Guide to Climate Anxiety* (Berkeley: University of California Press, 2020): 53, 75, 61.

4 Project Drawdown. https://drawdown.org/.

5 Christiana Figueres, *The Future We Choose: The Stubborn Optimist's Guide to the Climate Crisis* (New York: Vintage, 2021): 37.

6 John Kelsay, "Divine Summons, Human Submission: The Idea of Calling in Islam," *Calling in Today's World: Voices from Eight Faith Perspectives*, edited by Kathleen Cahalan and Douglas Schuurman (Grand Rapids: Eerdmans, 2016): 94.

7 Christopher Carter, *The Spirit of Soul Food: Race, Faith, and Food Justice* (Champaign: University of Illinois Press, 2021).

8 *Calling in Today's World*: 94.

9 As Rabbi Rami Shapiro has written in a commentary on Micah 6:8: "Do not be daunted by the enormity of the world's grief. Do justly, now. Walk humbly, now. You are not obligated to complete the work, but neither are you free to abandon it."

10 Amy Eilberg, "Hineini (Here I Am)," *Calling in Today's World: Voices from Eight Faith Perspectives*, edited by Kathleen Cahalan and Douglas Schuurman (Grand Rapids: Eerdmans, 2016): 3, 18.

11 Anantanand Rambachan, "Worship, The Public Good, and Self-fulfillment: Hindu Perspectives on Calling," *Calling in Today's World: Voices from Eight Faith Perspectives*, edited by Kathleen Cahalan and Douglas Schuurman (Grand Rapids: Eerdmans, 2016): 115.

12 Kathleen Cahalan and Douglas Schuurman, "Preface," *Calling in Today's World: Voices from Eight Faith Perspectives*, edited by Kathleen Cahalan and Douglas Schuurman (Grand Rapids: Eerdmans, 2016): xiv.

13 Rambachanm, "Worship": 117, 130.

14 Thich Nhat Hanh, *The Art of Living* (New York: Harper One, 2023).

15 Mark Berkson, "The Cultivation, Calling, and Loss of the Self: Confucian and Daoist Perspectives on Vocation," *Calling in Today's World: Voices from Eight Faith Perspectives*, edited by Kathleen Cahalan and Douglas Schuurman (Grand Rapids: Eerdmans, 2016): 189, 167–8.

16 Berkson, "The Cultivation Calling": 180–5.

17 Janet Yoder, "Vi Hilbert (1918–2008)," *History Link*. https://www.historylink.org/File/7130.

18 Leslie Tepper, Janice George, and Willard Joseph, *Salish Blankets: Robes of Protection and Transformation, Symbols of Wealth* (Lincoln: University of Nebraska Press, 2017).

19 Leanne Betasamosake Simpson, *As We Have Always Done: Indigenous Freedom Through Radical Resistance* (Minneapolis: University of Minnesota Press, 2020).

20 United States Conference of Catholic Bishops, "Prophets of a Future Not Our Own." https://www.usccb.org/prayer-and-worship/prayers-and-devotions/prayers/prophets-of-a-future-not-our-own.

21 Kaitlin Curtice, *Living Resistance: An Indigenous Vision for Seeking Wholeness Every Day* (Grand Rapids: Brazos, 2023): 189.

Chapter 12

1 Joanna Macy and Chris Johnstone, *Active Hope: How to Face the Mess We're in with Unexpected Resilience and Creative Power* (Novato: New World Library, 2022): 35.

2 Sarah Jaquette Ray, *A Field Guide to Climate Anxiety* (Berkeley: University of California Press, 2020): 121.

3 Thich Nhat Hanh, *Zen and the Art of Saving the Planet* (New York: Harper One, 2021): 159.

4 "Ross Gay on Inciting Joy While Dining with Sorrow," *NPR* (February 21, 2023). https://sojo.net/magazine/february-1985/interview/prisoner-hope.

5 Britt Wray, *Generation Dread: Finding Purpose in an Age of Climate Crisis* (Toronto: Knopf Canada, 2022): 155.

6 "Interview with Desmond Tutu," *Sojourners Magazine* (December 24, 1984). Tutu is referring to Zechariah 9:12 here, "return to your fortress, you prisoners of hope."

7 Steven Charleston, *We Survived the End of the World: Lessons from Native America on Apocalypse and Hope* (Minneapolis: Broadleaf Books, 2023).

8 Martin Shaw, "The Radical Power of Storytelling," *Yes!* (March 10, 2020). https://www.yesmagazine.org/health-happiness/2020/03/10/radical-power-storytelling.

9 Rebecca Solnit, "'If You Win the Popular Imagination, You Change the Game': Why We Need New Stories on Climate," *The Guardian* (January 12, 2023).

10 Bill McKibben, *Earth: Making a Life on a Tough New Planet* (Bramerton: Black Inc., 2010): 99.

11 Sally Gillespie, *Climate Crisis and Consciousness: Re-imagining Our World and Ourselves* (Abingdon: Routledge, 2019): 34–5.

12 Katharine Hayhoe, *Saving Us: A Climate Scientist's Case for Hope and Healing in a Divided World* (Los Altos: Atria/One Signal, 2022): 196, 199, 202.

13 adrienne marie brown, *Emergent Strategy: Shaping Change, Changing Worlds* (Chico: AK Press, 2017).

14 Macy and Johnstone, *Active Hope*: 113–14, 191.

Index